Evidence-Based Practice in Educating Deaf and Hard-of-Hearing Students

PROFESSIONAL PERSPECTIVES ON DEAFNESS: EVIDENCE AND APPLICATIONS

Patricia Elizabeth Spencer and Marc Marschark, Series Editors

Evidence-Based Practice in Educating Deaf and Hard-of-Hearing Students

Patricia Elizabeth Spencer and Marc Marschark

Evidence-Based Practice in Educating Deaf and Hard-of-Hearing Students

Patricia Elizabeth Spencer and
Marc Marschark

OXFORD
UNIVERSITY PRESS

2010

Oxford University Press, Inc., publishes works that further
Oxford University's objective of excellence
in research, scholarship, and education.

Oxford   New York
Auckland   Cape Town   Dar es Salaam   Hong Kong   Karachi
Kuala Lumpur   Madrid   Melbourne   Mexico City   Nairobi
New Delhi   Shanghai   Taipei   Toronto

With offices in
Argentina   Austria   Brazil   Chile   Czech Republic   France   Greece
Guatemala   Hungary   Italy   Japan   Poland   Portugal   Singapore
South Korea   Switzerland   Thailand   Turkey   Ukraine   Vietnam

Published by Oxford University Press, Inc.
198 Madison Avenue, New York, New York 10016

www.oup.com

Oxford is a registered trademark of Oxford University Press.

Library of Congress Cataloging-in-Publication Data

Spencer, Patricia Elizabeth.
  Evidence-based practice in educating deaf and hard-of-hearing students/
Patricia Elizabeth Spencer and Marc Marschark.
     p. cm.—(Professional perspectives on deafness)
  Includes bibliographical references and index.
  ISBN 978-0-19-973540-2
  1. Deaf children—Education. 2. Hearing impaired children—Education.
I. Marschark, Marc. II. Title.

  HV2430.S68 2010
  371.91'2—dc22

                                                        2009046440

Printed in the United States of America
on acid-free paper

PREFACE

Books are not written by accident, but sometimes they are not planned. This one certainly wasn't. It happened like this:

In 2008, the National Council for Special Education (NCSE) in the Republic of Ireland contracted with the Center for Education Research Partnerships at the National Technical Institute for the Deaf to provide them with "an international review of the literature of evidence of best practice models and outcomes in the education of deaf and hard of hearing children." As soon as the contract was signed, the authors set to work. The resulting report, completed about a year later and accepted by the NCSE following revisions, included recommendations and implications specific to the Irish context, given current services and educational programming provided for deaf and hard-of-hearing children in a variety of settings. We wish to extend our thanks to Jennifer Doran of the NCSE, Sean O'Murchu of the Department of Education and Science, Lorraine Leeson of the University of Dublin, Patricia Sapere from the National Technical Institute for the Deaf (NTID), and the many students, parents, and teachers in Ireland who provided us with information in preparing that report.

Obviously, however, that is not the end of the tale. By the time the report was finished, it was over twice as long as we had expected. More important, we discovered that a truly comprehensive review of the literature on educating deaf and hard-of-hearing children held a variety of surprises. Some of the assumptions that we had long held as researchers and teachers of deaf students turned out not to be grounded in empirical evidence, and others turned out to be just plain wrong. On the other hand, we discovered remarkable convergence across studies in several domains relevant to foundations and outcomes in deaf education—findings indicating that we actually know more than we think we do in at least some respects. Together with the fact that our reference list alone was almost as long as we expected the entire Irish report to be, these revelations led to an obvious conclusion: Somewhere in there was a book that needed to be written. With permission of the NCSE, the support of Catharine Carlin and Abby Gross at Oxford University Press, and the wisdom of three anonymous reviewers, the book before you is the result.

As we describe in chapter 3, in our efforts to produce an evidence-based summary of what we know, what we don't know, and what we thought we knew (but really don't) about educating deaf and hard-of-hearing children, this volume draws almost exclusively from peer-reviewed articles, government reports, and books that gave us confidence in the findings reported. Surely we missed some studies that would have been informative, and our emphasis on relatively recent research means that we do not discuss a vast quantity of excellent, earlier work in the field, even if we did benefit from familiarizing or refamiliarizing ourselves with it.

We also recognize that far more information on the topics considered in the following chapters is available from unpublished reports, conference presentations, and various websites. In the current social, political, and economic climate, however, it is only empirical findings—and, in particular, those that can be deemed trustworthy by virtue of having strong methodologies and having gone through the editorial review process—that can be expected to convince "the powers that be" of the necessity for educational change. For too long, support services and educational programming for children with significant hearing losses have been guided or at least heavily influenced by politics, preferences, and administrative expedience. Even while proponents of one perspective will castigate others for philosophical rather than fact-based decision making, they, too, may be caught up in the desire to do what they think is right for deaf children, even if they are lacking empirical support for anything different.

Given our experience in the field and, more recently, our efforts to find consistency in diversity and our obsession with reconciling contradiction, we are confident that most readers will find something to like and something to dislike in the following pages. Indeed, as we have begun to talk about our findings at professional meetings, some of the conclusions presented here already are having an impact. New studies have begun (in support or dispute of such conclusions), some information previously provided to parents and teachers has changed or been dropped, and at least two reports we cite as actually contradicting their authors' claims have been removed from websites. In the chapters that follow, therefore, the reader can expect that some beliefs long held dear will be shown to lack (at least empirical) merit, and things that perhaps one might wish were not the case indeed are. But we, too, have had to deal with surprises and with expectations that turned out to be unfounded.

Perhaps our most notable disappointment was that we were unable to find support for some kinds of programming we truly believe in. Take early intervention. We have known for over a decade that deaf and hard-of-hearing children who receive early intervention services do better than peers who do not receive such services in language and social development as well as in early academic achievement. So why do we not know anything about the long-term influences of early intervention on language fluency, social-emotional functioning, and especially academic achievement in the later school years? The earliest cohorts of deaf children who received early intervention programming are now at least university age. Did a greater proportion of them graduate from high school? Gain entrance to universities? Graduate and perhaps even earn a graduate degree? Why is nobody asking these questions?

Take bilingual-bicultural education. As much as we both believe in its potential, why is there no evidence to support existing bilingual programs—in either language or academic domains? Is no one conducting program evaluation? Or have they not been successful, but nobody wants to talk about it? And what about the *cultural* part of bilingual-bicultural education? Does learning about Deaf culture and Deaf heroes contribute to deaf children's identity or self-esteem? Is anyone making more than a token effort to teach Deaf heritage, and if so, where are such programs described?

For the sake of balance, and because we really do have some questions, consider also cochlear implants. Cochlear implantation, particularly when it occurs during the first year or two of life, contributes significantly to deaf children's academic achievement. Certainly, part of this benefit results from improved hearing and concomitant language acquisition, but children with implants still generally lag behind hearing peers in achievement. Why? Is it simply that they do not have complete access to the auditory signal (similar to the situation of children with minimal hearing losses)? If so, are the effects as specific to reading comprehension as they appear, or have we simply not looked into other domains of development and achievement?

These and many other questions surfaced even as we discovered exciting links we did not expect, studies we had previously overlooked, and points of convergence that suggested new possibilities for research and practice. We did look for answers to these "missing questions," and some of them we found. Others seemed more elusive, and other people were as surprised as we were that some questions simply had not been asked. In the original NCSE report, for example, we noted that several deaf students we spoke with in Ireland complained that teachers' expectations often were too low, and they needed to be challenged more. Some observers in the United States similarly lament that some teachers and parents frequently do not push deaf students hard enough, but frequently "let them slide" because they are deaf. A reviewer of the NCSE report asked, in all naïveté, "Why has no one investigated this issue?" Good question.

So, as lengthy as this "report" turned out to be, it raises many more questions than it answers about best practice in educating deaf and hard-of-hearing students. Maybe we should not have expected anything different. But, remember, we did not plan to write this book. Perhaps it was not an accident, but it just happened. We did not come into it with any agenda other than summarizing the available evidence, and we leave it wishing there was more. In between, we have come to appreciate all the more those parents and teachers who have been so successful in raising and educating bright, motivated, and talented deaf children and have helped them to succeed. If we could capture all that they know and all that they do, we would bottle it and give it away. For now, however, this book is where we are. Whether or not we are happy with all of our conclusions, we believe them to be sound even if, in most cases, we believe that more research is needed.

To the extent that the information provided here spurs further research or influences educational policy and practice, the effort that went into this volume will have been well worthwhile. If it contributes to enhanced educational opportunities for deaf and hard-of-hearing children and their academic outcomes, we will have succeeded beyond our dreams. We are nothing if we are not realistic.

Preparation of portions of this book was supported by the National Council for Special Education (Republic of Ireland). That information is reproduced here with permission of the NCSE, but responsibility for the research contained herein (including any errors or omissions) remains with the authors. The views and opinions contained in this report are those of the authors and do not necessarily reflect the views or opinions of the Council. Preparation of this report also was supported in part by grant REC-0633928 from the National Science Foundation. Any opinions, findings and conclusions, or recommendations expressed in this material similarly are those of the authors and do not necessarily reflect the views of the National Science Foundation.

PHOTOGRAPHY CREDITS

[Chapter One] p. 3 – Linda Burik, Courtesy Western Pennsylvania School for the Deaf

[Chapter Two] p. 10 – Linda Burik, Courtesy Western Pennsylvania School for the Deaf

[Chapter Three]   p. 25 – Courtesy Hong Kong Jockey Club Signed Bilingual and Co-Enrolment Programme

[Chapter Four] p. 38 – Courtesy Ron Outen

[Chapter Five] p. 49 – Courtesy Patricia Elizabeth Spencer

[Chapter Six] p. 81 – Courtesy Patricia Elizabeth Spencer

[Chapter Seven] p. 119 – Linda Burik, Courtesy Western Pennsylvania School for the Deaf

[Chapter Eight] p. 135 – Linda Burik, Courtesy Western Pennsylvania School for the Deaf

[Chapter Nine] p. 153 – Marc Benjamin, Courtesy National Technical Institute for the Deaf

[Chapter Ten] p. 171 – Linda Burik, Courtesy Western Pennsylvania School for the Deaf

[Chapter Eleven] p. 187 – Marc Benjamin, Courtesy National Technical Institute for the Deaf

CONTENTS

11.   **Issues and Trends in Best Practice 187**

References 195

Index 235

Evidence-Based Practice in Educating Deaf and Hard-of-Hearing Students

1 Introduction and Key Findings Index

This volume is about what we know and what we don't know about educating deaf and hard-of-hearing children. The latter category primarily consists of new questions yet to be answered (e.g., the long-term impact of early intervention on academic achievement). However, it also encompasses some long-standing assumptions that were never based on empirical evidence (e.g., sign language interferes with deaf children's learning to speak) and some newer beliefs that also lack research support (e.g., the academic benefits of bilingual education). Our finding of a lack of evidence to support such claims does not mean that they are wrong, only that there is not yet sufficient evidence to believe that they are of general (if any) utility in educating children with significant hearing losses. The problem is that around the United States and elsewhere parents, teachers, and administrators are making decisions about academic placement and teaching methods for those children on the basis of what is frequently incorrect or at least incomplete information.

It has long been acknowledged that individuals interested in deaf education usually can find a reference to support almost any position. Importantly, those references frequently consist of secondary sources (or worse, secondary sources that evidently did not read the primary source), theoretical or philosophical claims that have morphed into apparent "facts," and research of limited scope due to either small or non-comparable samples. At the same time, it is important to recognize that the deaf and hard-of-hearing children in school today are different from those we were educating only a decade ago. As we will describe in the following chapters, some findings and conclusions that might have been valid in the past therefore do not follow in the current environment of early intervention, improved hearing aids, and rapidly changing technology. This means that some conclusions that may have made sense 20 years ago are no longer helpful today, and vice versa. What has been lacking is a single comprehensive review of evidence-based practice approached from an objective position that seeks only to enhance academic opportunities and outcomes for deaf and hard-of-hearing children. When such a line of attack is taken, as we have done here, one discovers that we know less than we thought we did in some areas, but we also know more than we thought we did in others.

As a prelude to the following chapters, we offer the following key points, drawn from a detailed analysis of the evidence base in educational research related to deaf and hard-of-hearing children. But beware! These highlights are intended only as "teasers" of things to come. They should not be taken out of context as definitive statements of fact that do not require qualifications. With a population as heterogeneous as deaf and hard-of-hearing children there are always qualifications. To fully understand each of the highlights, therefore, we have provided page numbers that will allow readers to quickly find a more detailed and often more nuanced or qualified discussion about it.

Chapters that follow will describe the way in which we conducted the literature review that produced these key points. The goal of this introductory list, and of the book as a whole, is to raise questions and encourage readers to delve more deeply into what we know about deaf and hard-of-hearing children, their patterns of development, and their lifelong learning. In reconsidering what we know, what we don't know, and what we only thought we knew, readers will discover—as we did—why people hold some beliefs that are not supported by reliable or trustworthy evidence. In other cases, the opposite will be apparent, and we will discuss how numerous research studies and carefully documented observations actually converge to support a belief or attitude that is held by teachers, researchers, administrators, and other professionals.

Our hope is that by providing a comprehensive but concise record of the evidence base in deaf education, more effective interventions and services for deaf and hard-of-hearing students can be promoted and further research undertaken. At the outset, however, readers are warned that one consistent and well-documented conclusion across the literature on deaf education is that no one system, no one approach, will be optimal for all deaf and hard-of-hearing students. Individual needs, strengths, and experiences interact to produce a population of students that is even more diverse than the population of hearing students. Taken together, recent advances in knowledge, technology, and pedagogical practice offer professionals providing services to deaf and hard-of-hearing students great opportunities—if they are willing to accept change. We no longer need to be hampered by past expectations and assumptions. Instead, we have the facts we need to be able to move forward with all deliberate speed, to grasp the initiative, and to be able to promote optimal and "on time" development of deaf and hard-of-hearing children—academically, socially, linguistically. As Confucius noted, "To know what we know, and know what we do not know, that is understanding."

KEY FINDINGS INDEX

It recently has become clear that even minimal hearing loss (16–25 dB) can affect academic achievement, and thus there are likely to be many students who need extra educational services but are not receiving them. (p.10)

All indications are that the amount of time the hearing loss goes unidentified has significant effects on subsequent development. (p.12)

Understanding of the effects of hearing loss on development is complicated by what appears to be an increasingly high incidence of cognitive, motor, and other disabilities in the population of students with hearing loss. (p.14)

Early identification and intervention can greatly decrease barriers to language learning faced by deaf and hard-of-hearing children during the early years of life, although they have not been eliminated. (p.20)

It remains the responsibility of all who read research reports to do so with a critical eye and to be alert for the tendency to trust something one already believes rather than something that contrasts with pre-existing beliefs. (p.23)

Readers should recognize that deaf education is not alone in its frequent reliance on beliefs and inadequately investigated processes, policies, and procedures. This is a difficulty that characterizes education in general. (p.26)

If not all of the teachers implement their assigned curriculum accurately and follow the curricula as they are designed, no amount of elegant statistical analyses will produce a valid study. (p.29)

Given the limitations and complications of conducting research with the deaf and hard-of-hearing student population, it is necessary to look across studies and various study designs to identify convergent ideas as well as to shed light on assumptions that fail to be supported across various studies. (p.34)

In the absence of early services for deaf and hard-of-hearing children and their families, countries pay a much higher monetary price for rehabilitation and support services than they would pay for universal newborn hearing screening (UNHS) and early intervention. The price levied against children's futures cannot be estimated. (p.38)

Parents held expectations that early identification and intervention would be sufficient to make their child be like a hearing child, although that expectation is not supported by the data. (p.42)

Children who are identified early and receive early intervention have been found to demonstrate language development in the "low average" level compared to hearing children. (p.42)

There has been no indication of any negative effects from early identification and intervention on social-emotional functioning or any other aspect of development. (p.44)

If children with hearing loss are not provided rich visual language models that they can process or special programming and assistive listening devices that allow effective access to auditory-based language input, they can reach pre-school and even the primary school years with severely impoverished (if any) language skills. (p.49)

Some children have been found to make age-appropriate progress using oral approaches to language development (with no one particular approach favored); however, even proponents note that many if not most of these children have failed to keep pace with hearing peers. (p.54)

Even with early cochlear implantation, language abilities remain on average below those of hearing peers. (p.56)

Even when produced in a "relaxed" form in which not all English grammatical morphemes were represented, Total Communication and Simultaneous Communication were effective communication mediums and also provided effective bases for English language development. (p.68)

Sign/bilingual programming, in which a natural sign language serves as the first language and medium of communication in the classroom, has a strong theoretic basis but to date lacks sufficient evidence to allow evaluation of its language development outcomes. (p.80)

Perhaps the most long-term and vexing challenge in deaf education is the continuing difficulty experienced by students with regard to print literacy. (p.81)

There is a clear literacy-learning advantage for children who arrive at school with age- appropriate language skills. (p.83)

Shared reading is fruitful in early at-home intervention and early school years for supporting development of hearing children, with positive effects on developing vocabulary, building phonological knowledge, and increasing motivation for attention to books. (p.88)

Despite the fact that cochlear implants generally increase access to auditory-based language, findings to date have failed to demonstrate that they eliminate children's delays in literacy development. (p.91)

Parents and other adults also are likely to use restricted vocabularies in interactions with deaf and hard-of-hearing children, sometimes because of lowered expectations concerning a child's knowledge or hearing and sometimes due to the adults' own lack of skills in sign language or unambiguous oral communication. (p.96)

Skill in ASL does *not* interfere with development of English skills. (p.104)

Given available published data, it is not possible to ascertain whether attaining fluency in a first, natural sign language will provide a means of strengthening literacy skills in a second language for deaf and hard-of-hearing students. (p.107)

Deaf students have been reported to be less aware than hearing students when they do not comprehend what they are reading. (p.109)

Differences in the environments and experiences of deaf children and hearing children might lead to different approaches to learning. (p.120)

Deaf children's dependence upon visual communication makes the pace and timing of turn-taking exchanges different from that which most hearing adults expect. (p.122)

The opportunity to participate in rich conversational exchanges was the mechanism for advances in theory of mind abilities. (p.124)

Deaf individuals remember less from sequential memory span tasks involving both verbal and nonverbal materials compared to hearing individuals. (p.128)

Even at college age, deaf and hard-of-hearing students frequently do not spontaneously apply well-developed problem-solving strategies. (p.132)

Pre-school-aged deaf children have some of the basic knowledge necessary for mathematics learning, but they lag behind hearing peers in other areas. (p.136)

There are widespread indications that the mathematical and problem-solving experiences provided to most deaf and hard-of-hearing students are insufficient in frequency and structure to achieve the desired outcomes. (p.138)

Deaf and hard-of-hearing children are less likely than hearing children to bring previous knowledge and experience to the task of acquiring mathematical skills. (p.143)

Researchers have suggested that writing can be a supportive component of a strong science curriculum for deaf and hard-of-hearing students. (p.147)

Successful teachers tend to have both training in the subject matter being taught and knowledge about the learning styles and patterns of students who are deaf or hard of hearing. (p.151)

Despite the strong emotions associated with this difference of opinion, there is little empirical evidence that either mainstreaming or separate education generally is better for deaf and hard-of-hearing students. (p.153)

Practically, separate schools may be better equipped to handle the needs of children with multiple disabilities but, theoretically, comparisons of academic outcomes in the two settings are inherently invalid because the children who attend them are different. (p.155)

The shift toward educating more deaf and hard-of-hearing students in general educational classrooms early requires changes in teacher preparation for both general education teachers and those specializing in deaf education. (p.157)

Teachers supporting deaf and hard-of-hearing students need to be able to serve as advocates for their students and to facilitate the students' becoming advocates for themselves. (p.158)

Teachers in general education classrooms should not assume that deaf and hard-of-hearing students comprehend language as well as their hearing classmates, and teachers need to monitor students' understanding frequently. (p.165)

Neither sign language interpreting nor real-time text has any inherent, generalized advantage over the other in supporting deaf students in secondary or postsecondary settings. At the same time, both provide superior access relative to no communication support. (p.168)

Social benefits accrue from co-enrollment and integrated placements where a significant number of children with hearing loss become part of a class that involves two or more co-teachers, at least one of whom specializes in education of deaf and hard-of-hearing children. (p.169)

A least 35% and perhaps over 50% of deaf and hard-of-hearing students in the United States have an additional, educationally significant condition or disability. (p.171)

Programming for children with hearing loss and multiple disabilities should incorporate approaches that have shown evidence of success with various types of disabilities. At the same time, it is critical that interventions be sensitive to and provide appropriate accommodations for hearing loss. (p.172)

None of the investigators were able to identify specific predictors of outcomes of cochlear implantation for children with multiple disabilities, including mild cognitive delay and hearing loss. (p.176)

Placement decisions cannot validly be based on etiology or labeling of the disability associated with hearing loss. (p.184)

2 Demographics, Diversity, and Foundational Issues in Deaf Education

If we are to be able to evaluate the available evidence and determine best practices in educating deaf and hard-of-hearing students, it is essential that we first know the prevalence of hearing loss in student populations in different age groups. The answer to this question is not as straightforward as it might seem. Mitchell and Karchmer (2006) pointed out that there is no legal definition of "deaf," at least not in the United States, although the National Health Interview Survey defines a deaf person as "one who is unable to understand speech" and a hard-of-hearing person as "one who has difficulty understanding speech" (Ries, 1994). For educational purposes, the U.S. government refers to students as "hearing impaired" if they receive special services to support educational needs related to hearing loss. This is a bit of a circular definition, but it is a practical solution. However, it recently has become clear that even minimal hearing loss (16–25 dB) can affect academic achievement and thus there are likely to be many students who need extra educational services but are not receiving them (e.g., Goldberg & Richburg, 2004; Marschark, Lang, Albertini, 2002; Moeller, Tomblin, Yoshinaga-Itano, Connor, & Jerger, 2007). These students frequently are not included in counts of deaf or hard-of-hearing students, and teachers (and perhaps the students themselves) may not be aware of their special needs.

A "LOW INCIDENCE" DISABILITY

It is generally agreed that hearing loss in childhood is a relatively infrequent phenomenon, and it is referred to as a "low incidence" condition (Mitchell & Karchmer, 2006). Available statistics show similar levels of prevalence across what are referred to as countries with "developed" economies, generally ranging from slightly over 1 to about 2 children per thousand births (e.g., Fortnum, Summerfield, Marshall, Davis, & Bamford, 2001). In the United Kingdom, for example, a 1998 survey of children between 9 and 16 years old was conducted by the Medical Research Council of the Institute of Hearing Research in Nottingham and found that the incidence of hearing impairment greater than 40 dB (a level labeled "moderate" and historically considered to be of educational significance) was about 1.65 per 1,000 live births. When corrections were made in estimates to account for children who were missed in the survey, it was suggested that the incidence of educationally significant hearing loss could be as high as 2.05 per 1,000 (Fortnum et al., 2001). These estimates are similar to those reported from another group in the United Kingdom, the Wessex Universal Hearing Screening Trial Group (1998). When they included children with lesser degrees of hearing loss (unilateral [single-ear] and losses less than 40dB), hearing loss was estimated to occur in about 2.5 of every 1,000 children. Figures from the United States (Mehl & Thomson, 2002) and from Australia (Johnston, 2003) generally are within the same range as the UK studies.

Although relatively mild levels of hearing loss were historically considered to have little impact on a child's development, this attitude has changed over time and such a condition is thought to indicate higher-than-average risk of difficulties in language and academic development (see, for example, Bess, Dodd-Murphy, & Parker, 1998; Goldberg & Richburg, 2004; Moeller, Tomblin, et al., 2007); therefore, prevalence numbers that include children with lesser degrees of loss may be especially pertinent. The majority of deaf and hard-of-hearing children have hearing losses in the mild to moderate range, not the severe to profound range (Moeller, Tomblin et al., 2007). Children with lesser degrees of hearing loss typically can hear and express spoken language, but they may require amplification from hearing aids to do so effectively. The receptive language performance of children with mild to moderate or even unilateral hearing loss will be negatively affected in noisy environments, and learning in such settings may require more energy and attention focus than is required of hearing students (Marschark et al., 2002). In contrast with children with lesser hearing loss, those with severe-to-profound or profound hearing losses typically are unable to process spoken language signals effectively without the use of cochlear implants (see Spencer, Marschark, & Spencer, in press, for a review).

It should now be evident that the use of the broad term "deaf or hard-of-hearing" in referring to the population of interest in this book is intended to recognize both the heterogeneity of the population and the uncertainty with regard to the language input and educational environments most conducive to learning. Differences in the age at which hearing loss occurs also contribute to individual differences in needs and performance within the deaf and hard-of-hearing student population. That is, not all hearing loss occurs by birth; it can occur "progressively" over the first several years of life, even when the source of the hearing loss is hereditary (Arnos & Pandya, in press). Children who initially are hearing but who experienced losses either gradually (*progressive* losses) or suddenly (*acute* losses) during the first years of life often retain more attention and sensitivity to sound than their counterparts who are congenitally deaf (Marschark et al., 2002). Hearing loss in children also can also result from diseases such as meningitis and measles, which continue to cause hearing loss into adolescent years. Such diseases sometimes may cause other disabilities and developmental difficulties, further complicating students' needs.

There also remain many cases in which hearing loss is present but not identified at birth. Even in the best of health care systems, some children with hearing loss may be missed during hospital or early-life screenings. In other cases, parents do not return for further testing when an early hearing assessment shows questionable results. Where early screenings are not routinely provided, there are, of course, few ways for parents or physicians to know that a newborn has a hearing loss. Yet all indications are that the amount of time that the hearing loss goes unidentified has significant effects on subsequent development (Yoshinaga-Itano, 2003). Early identification thus is economically important for society as well as being developmentally and educationally important for children and their families.

The above issues related to the incidence of hearing loss, the timing of identification and intervention, and individual child characteristics all complicate the conducting of research and the evaluation of programming outcomes for deaf and hard-of-hearing children. The relatively small number of deaf and hard-of-hearing children has sometimes contributed to a lack of societal focus on the needs of this group and has made many traditionally respected research approaches and designs impossible. That is, without large groups of children to compare across different types of programming and interventions—especially given the diversity of this population—it is difficult to determine their effects on different children's development and academic achievement. As Mitchell and Karchmer (2006) pointed out, the increasing dispersion of deaf and hard-of-hearing children in local schools, as opposed to special schools or centers, has further complicated collection of data about effective practice and outcomes. Given the difficulties associated with locating and evaluating "representative samples" of deaf and hard-of-hearing students, it becomes necessary to look for convergence—or agreement—across a number of studies when talking about outcomes of research and educational efforts for this group. Rarely can a single study or small group of studies produce trustworthy and useful results when considered in isolation.

DEAF AND HARD-OF-HEARING CHILDREN IN COUNTRIES WITH DEVELOPING ECONOMIES

In countries considered to have "emerging or developing" economies, the proportion of children having hearing loss is estimated to be about twice that of developed countries, but accurate numbers are difficult to find. Four of every 1,000 children born in India are estimated to have severe to profound hearing loss (Ansari, 2004, cited in Leigh, Newall, & Newall, 2010), but a study of 284 6- to 10-year-old students in the southern state of Tamil Nadu found that 11.9% had a hearing loss when all levels of loss were considered (Jacob, Rupa, Job, & Joseph, 1997). Similarly, 7.9% of children in Pakistan are estimated to have some level of hearing loss (Elahi et al., 1998). Bu (2004, cited in Leigh et al.) estimated that approximately 3 of 1,000 children born in China have a permanent hearing loss. According to Leigh et al., this rate would indicate that approximately 60,000 children in China alone are born with hearing loss each year. Other researchers suggest that at least 6% of children across the developing world are deaf or hard of hearing (e.g., Olusanya & Newton, 2007). Unfortunately, there are few data regarding the developmental and educational histories of these children, many of whom live in countries where health issues of life or death have still not been effectively addressed. This situation continues despite the fact that as early as 1959 the United Nations Declaration of the Rights of the Child (http://www.unhchr.ch/html/menu3/b/25.htm) called for both special treatment for children with disabilities and support for their physical, mental, and social development.

With the dissemination of information indicating developmental benefits of identification of hearing loss early in life, the World Health Assembly has called for implementation of procedures to identify hearing loss during infancy and toddler years (World Health Organization, 2001). Currently at issue is the question of how and whether universal newborn or early testing for hearing loss is economically and practically feasible in many developing countries. Leigh et al. (2010) have analyzed various approaches to early identification in developing countries and concluded that screenings targeted toward children determined to be at high risk, while clearly not preferable when universal testing is possible, may be the best way to gradually introduce early testing (see, e.g., Madriz, 2000; Mung'ala-Odera et al., 2006; cf. Olusanya & Okolo, 2006, who call for universal screening). However, Leigh et al. pointed out that identification without the potential for follow-up support also can have negative effects, and many countries do not have the capability of setting up such support systems. Despite these concerns, positive outcomes of early screening have been reported (e.g., Olusanya, Luxon, & Wirz, 2005) regarding outcomes in Nigeria,with other countries encouraged to follow suit.

Given the general lack of information available about the development of children in economically less developed countries of the world, the review presented in this book concentrates on those who live in the "developed world," where economies are sufficiently advanced to provide the resources for developmental and educational support that many children need. This review of information of the outcomes of such support can provide guidance and ideas that when implemented through culturally sensitive practices may provide a basis for program development for children in currently less developed countries.

MULTIPLE DISABILITIES, OR CHILDREN WITH DUAL DIAGNOSES

Understanding of the effects of hearing loss on development is complicated by what appears to be an increasingly high incidence of cognitive, motor, and other disabilities in the population of students with hearing loss. Both Moores (2001) and Mitchell and Karchmer (2006), who used appropriately weighted estimates based on the Gallaudet Research Institute (GRI) Annual Survey of Deaf and Hard of Hearing Children and Youth, reported the presence of multiple disabilities in about 40% of the U.S. population of deaf and hard-of-hearing students. Shallop (2008) reported that 39% to 54% of children with cochlear implants have a disability in addition to hearing loss. These high percentages may be due in part to professionals' increasingly being able to identify developmental difficulties in younger and younger children, but they also reflect changing prevalence in the causes of hearing loss. Most notable in this regard are the increased survival rates of infants experiencing severe trauma or disease prenatally or early in life—events that can result in chronic problems across a number of developmental systems including hearing.

In short, any complicating factor that is known to occur in hearing children can also occur in the population of children who are deaf or hard of hearing. This includes conditions such as Autism Spectrum Disorder, behavior and attention disorders, learning disabilities, visual impairment, and motor disabilities typified by cerebral palsy. Edwards and Crocker (2008), for example, estimated that between 3% and 10% of children with hearing loss in Scotland have specific learning disabilities. This estimate is in agreement with that of Mitchell and Karchmer (2006) for the United States, reporting that about 8% of their large sample had learning disabilities despite having general intellectual functioning within the average or higher range.

Increasing interest in Autism and Autistic Spectrum Disorders also is now evident among both researchers and educators working with deaf and hard-of-hearing children. Vernon and Rhodes (2009) argued that the increased incidence of Autism Spectrum Disorders, also referred to as Pervasive Developmental Disorder (PDD), in the hearing population is paralleled by an increase in the population of children with hearing loss. A treatment called Applied Behavior Analysis (Lovaas, 1987), which uses using positive and negative reinforcement to shape behaviors, has been shown in controlled studies to have some effect on hearing autistic children, but it is labor intensive and expensive, and reports of its use with deaf children are limited (see Easterbrooks & Handley, 2005/2006). There is also a long history of specialized programming for students who have a combined hearing and vision loss, and very specific and intensive programming is required for children who are deafblind from birth or become so in their early years (Knoors & Vervloed, in press; van Dijk, Nelson, Postma, & van Dijk, 2010; see chapter 10).

It is generally concluded that the combined effects of multiple disabilities are multiplicative and not merely additive (Jones & Jones, 2003; Knoors & Vervloed, in press; van Dijk et al., 2010). This situation results in part because some approaches that would help a child compensate for a specific disability can be limited by the presence of a hearing loss. For example, children with visual impairment will have limited access to language input from signing or speech reading ("lipreading" or "speechreading"), and children with learning problems such as those referred to as "learning disabilities" may be further hampered if they experience attention or memory problems or have intrinsic difficulties acquiring a language regardless of modality. Children with serious chronic health conditions are likely to miss school and other intervention experiences, and those with motor impairments may be challenged in production of either sign or speech and require alternative communication methods.

Despite recognition of these complexities, teachers who are trained in programming for one or the other disability may not be adequately prepared to deal with a child who has more than one such condition. Children with multiple disabilities thus may sometimes be placed in educational environments that fail to account for their hearing loss or, alternatively, inadequately program for other disabilities. Unfortunately, due to the varied characteristics of children with multiple disabilities, there is little research base to guide educational approaches (see chapter 10 for further discussion).

DEVELOPMENTAL CHALLENGES

Childhood hearing loss, even when no other developmental challenges are present, typically puts a child at high risk for language, social, and academic difficulties regardless of whether significant resources are available. As a result, despite many advantages and strong efforts to provide supportive programming for deaf and hard-of-hearing students over the past century in developed countries such as the United States, the United Kingdom, and the Netherlands (Moores, 2001), average academic achievement levels of these children remain significantly below those of hearing children. Importantly, this pattern persists despite evidence that nonverbal cognitive levels as measured by tests of I.Q. or "intelligence" are similar for children with and without hearing loss (Braden, 1994; Maller & Braden, in press; Vernon, 2005; cf. Akamatsu et al., 2008; see chapter 7).

The fact that many, if not most, children who are deaf or hard-of-hearing face challenges in acquiring language skills is the primary explanation given for the high rate of academic delays and difficulties. When exposure to and experience with language is limited by inability to hear what is being spoken to and around them, and when alternatives such as sign language are not available, it is nearly impossible for children to develop language at a rate that will support "on time" academic skills. Some children who are deaf or hard-of-hearing have deaf parents who provide early and natural language experiences and who generally feel confident to raise their children without assistance. This is a very small group, however. In the United States, for example, it represents only about 5%–6% of all children with hearing loss (Mitchell & Karchmer, 2004). Thus, over 90% of children with hearing loss have hearing parents who are neither experienced with nor knowledgeable about development of deaf children or accommodations necessary to support their language needs. Accordingly, language delays have been common. And, as we shall see, although deaf children with deaf parents frequently show higher academic achievement than deaf children with hearing parents, even they typically do not perform at the same academic level as their hearing peers.

Academic Achievement

Given frequent delays in language development, it does not seem surprising that delays have also been commonly reported for deaf and hard-of-hearing children in print literacy skills—reading and writing. A major source of such data, as well as other demographic and academic achievement information concerning deaf and hard-of-hearing students in the United States, is the Gallaudet Research Institute Annual Survey of Deaf and Hard of Hearing Children and Youth. That survey is acknowledged to capture only about 60% to 70% of deaf and hard-of-hearing students in the United States, likely missing many children who have lesser hearing losses, are the only ones in their schools with hearing loss, and may be functioning well with cochlear implants or hearing aids. Although many of the highest performing deaf and hard-of-hearing students may be underrepresented in the survey, the information has been obtained about such a large section of the population that it has considerable validity and importance.

Ongoing publications and analyses from the GRI have reported on the data obtained through the survey and its associated collection of academic testing results. For example, Holt, Traxler, and Allen (1997) and Traxler (2000) reported analyses of performance of a national sample of deaf and hard-of-hearing students, aged 8 to 18 years, on the Stanford Achievement Test, 9th Edition. They found that the median (the point at which 50% of students score above and 50% below) of the deaf and hard-of-hearing students, many of whom were older than hearing students in the same grade, was at the "Below Basic" skill level. The median scores of 15- to 18-year-old deaf and hard-of-hearing students were similar to those of hearing students in third to fourth grade (8 to 9 years old). This finding, as jarring as it might be, is consistent with results from other researchers and other studies (e.g., Paul, 1998). Several additional factors need to be kept in mind, however. One is that the variability (i.e., individual differences in scores attained) within deaf/hard-of-hearing groups is consistently wider than that in the hearing groups, and it tends to increase with age. Another issue, as Mitchell and Karcher (in press) pointed out, is that it is likely that higher performing deaf and hard-of-hearing students will make make the same amount of annual growth in academic achievement as hearing students. Finally, factors associated with literacy achievement in the U.S. hearing population (such as ethnic status, home language, and parents' socioeconomic status or educational levels) also associate with the literacy achievement of deaf and hard-of-hearing students.

Mitchell (2004) concluded that the GRI survey is more heavily weighted toward non-White ethnic groups, toward students with lesser amounts of time in mainstreamed or ("regular") classrooms, toward students with more severe hearing loss, and toward schools in the southwestern area of the United States than is the case in the government's IDEA Child Count data. The GRI survey database also has a somewhat higher proportion of older students (age 18 years to 23 years) and lesser representation of younger students than is indicated in the government database. Given this difference and the lack of representation of children below the age of 6 years, the scores currently available for deaf and hard-of-hearing students on the Stanford Achievement Test appear more representative of students born before the early identification of hearing loss became common. The scores may not hold true when the population that is likely benefiting from earlier identification, earlier language development, and advanced audiological services reaches adolescence.

Although the focus in deaf education traditionally has been on students' needs in language and literacy areas, deaf and hard-of-hearing students of high school age continue to perform at only the 80th percentile of the average score of hearing students on standardized math tests (Holt et al., 1997; Traxler, 2000). That means that the average high school–age student with hearing loss in this database obtained mathematics test scores similar to those of an average hearing student in the fifth or sixth year of school (10–12 years old). This delay is not just with regard to "word" or story mathematics problems, although that is an area in which deaf and hard-of-hearing students appear to have the most difficulty. A variety of studies has demonstrated that those students also typically evidence significant difficulties in basic calculation skills such as multiplication and division, in dealing with fractions, and in general concepts about numbers (e.g., Kelly & Mousley, 2001; Qi & Mitchell, 2007; Traxler, 2000; Wood, Wood, & Howarth, 1983).

The high incidence of difficulties in both literacy and mathematics among deaf and hard-of-hearing students clearly will affect their abilities to acquire information and skills in other academic areas, and these two domains have been the most extensively studied aspects of deaf and hard-of-hearing students' academic achievement. However, lags of this sort are found across the curriculum. A number of studies, for example, have indicated that deaf and hard-of-hearing students enter mainstream college classrooms with less content knowledge than their hearing peers across a variety of subjects in natural science and social science as well as mathematics. This initial disadvantage explains at least in part why they leave the classroom with less information than hearing classmates (Marschark, Sapere, Convertino, & Seewagen, 2005; Marschark, Sapere, Convertino, Seewagen, & Maltzen, 2004).

The impact of such academic limitations among both younger and older deaf and hard-of-hearing students goes beyond that on the individuals and their families, extending to society at large, which may lose future contributions that would otherwise be made by these students. It is important to remember, however, that such delays are neither universal nor inevitable. Across varied educational settings and contexts, there are deaf and hard-of-hearing students who excel academically. The primary challenge facing deaf education is to discover what kinds of services and learning environments can best support development of those children who are *not* acquiring academic knowledge and skills at rates that match their potential. Better tools for assessing deaf and hard-of-hearing children's competencies and predicting their future achievement will greatly facilitate this effort. (See chapters 5 through 10.)

Social-Emotional Development

Difficulties associated with hearing loss can extend beyond the academic area and are not uncommon in children's social and emotional development. Edwards and Crocker (2008) summarized research indicating higher-than-average risk for behavioral problems and attention difficulties in deaf and hard-of-hearing children. Some of these difficulties may stem from the etiology of a child's hearing loss. Edwards and Crocker, however, along with earlier researchers such as Meadow (1980), attribute a significant portion of these problems to the overall incidence of language delays. Those delays can interfere with a child's acquiring words or signs needed to accurately communicate and understand various emotional states and, more generally, can interfere with general parent-child and sibling-child communication. This situation is most obvious when parents are hearing and children have sufficient hearing loss to preclude effective use of spoken language (Meadow-Orlans, Spencer, & Koester,2004).

Deaf individuals with deaf parents have been reported to score on average higher on measures of self-esteem than those with hearing parents (Crowe, 2003; Woolfe, 2001). Although this finding has not been limited to children whose deaf parents used sign language, parent use of sign language in general has been found by other researchers to support development of social-emotional strength—again perhaps because of enhanced early communication experiences (Bat-Chava, 1993). Wallis, Musselman, and MacKay (2004), for example, retrospectively compared small groups of deaf child–hearing mother dyads, finding that either early signing or beginning early and remaining in an aural/oral program (thus suggesting successful acquisition of spoken language) resulted in fewer mental health difficulties in adolescence. They concluded that a match between mother and child language mode supports social-emotional development. Further evidence of the importance of early communication experiences was provided by Greenberg and Kusché (1998). Their PATHS (Promoting Alternative Thinking Strategies) curriculum was designed to improve children's social-emotional communication and behavioral functioning. Convincing evidence points to success in improved outcomes.

Difficult social interactions beyond the family settings have often been reported when deaf and hard-of-hearing children did not have sufficient numbers of peers with whom they could identify and communicate easily. There are divergent reports concerning social status and interaction patterns between deaf and hard-of-hearing students and their hearing peers, however, with some researchers suggesting that children with hearing loss may be generally neglected or isolated but others showing no differences in social interaction patterns among children with and without hearing loss (see Antia, Kreimeyer, & Reed, 2010, for a review). For example, deaf individuals who identify as "bi-cultural" and thus indicate the ability to relate to both deaf and hearing persons have been reported to have the most positive sense of self-esteem (Bat-Chava, 1993, 2000; Silvestre, Ramspott, & Pareto, 2006). Yet, Israelite, Ower, and Goldstein (2002) found that hard-of-hearing students tended to identify themselves as different from those who are deaf, suggesting that education providers need to consider these students' special challenges in "fitting in" with either hearing or deaf students.

Both early family-related, and later peer-related challenges can result in deaf and hard-of-hearing children being at risk for social-emotional difficulties. Negative outcomes are neither inevitable nor unavoidable, however. There have always been many deaf and hard-of-hearing individuals who have overcome the challenges they faced, both individuals who attended schools for the deaf and those who were in the mainstream. Happy, well-educated, productive deaf and hard-of-hearing students and adults are certainly not hard to find! In addition, many recent and emerging practices—technological, educational, and cultural—are rapidly increasing the potential for positive developmental outcomes.

ADVANCES IN THE DEVELOPMENT OF DEAF AND HARD-OF-HEARING STUDENTS

Despite all of the complexities faced by researchers and educators, significant advances have occurred in the past few decades that hold promise for much improved rates and patterns of development for students who are deaf or hard of hearing. One of these is the practice of identifying hearing loss early in infancy and of providing immediate support to families. (See chapter 4.) Where effective early intervention is provided, average language and early literacy functioning of young children with hearing loss improves significantly, on average, compared to situations in which children's hearing losses are identified at later ages (e.g., Moeller, 2000; Yoshinaga-Itano, 2003). Early identification and intervention can greatly decrease barriers to language learning faced by deaf and hard-of-hearing children during the early years of life, although they have not been eliminated. Expectations are that increased language and communication experiences should support better academic progress and social-emotional functioning, and early evidence suggests that is the case. Research-based information is just now emerging, but as with language and academic difficulties, social-emotional difficulties among deaf and hard-of-hearing children and adolescents seem to stem from a lack of appropriately supportive experiences rather than decreased hearing sensitivity per se.

An experience that is known to be particularly supportive of development in deaf and hard-of-hearing children is exposure to and interaction with adults and other children who are fluent in a natural sign language (or, some report, a type of sign "system" that has been developed to supplement spoken language—see chapter 5). Immersion in a language-rich environment of a natural sign language (e.g., American Sign Language, Auslan, or British Sign Language) can promote "on time" language development, even though these children's first language will be signed and not spoken (e.g., Meadow-Orlans et al., 2004; Spencer & Harris, 2006). Natural sign languages have been recognized for some time to be as complex and flexible as spoken languages (e.g., Emmorey, 2002; Stokoe, 1960). Higher levels of sign language skills have been found to associate with higher literacy skills in signing children (e.g., Padden & Ramsey, 2000; Strong & Prinz, 2000), including those who have cochlear implants (e.g., L. Spencer, Gantz, & Knutson, 2004) and although there is considerable argument, some researchers have concluded that early signing actually supports the learning of spoken language (e.g., Connor, Hieber, Arts, & Zwolen, 2000).

The acquisition of spoken language also has become more attainable with advances in technology, including more sophisticated hearing aids and cochlear implants, especially in combination with early identification of hearing loss. These technologies allow many more deaf children access to information from spoken language than has been the case historically, and thus increases are reported in speech perception, speech production, and spoken language skills (e.g., Geers, 2006; Spencer, Marschark, & Spencer, in press).

Evidence is emerging that language gains supported by cochlear implants also provide support for early literacy development (e.g., Geers, 2006: L. Spencer & Oleson, 2008). Positive effects are not universally reported, however, and there continues to be active research concerning factors that either interfere with or promote effectiveness for individual children. Even those children who are considered "successful" users of cochlear implants, for example, typically evidence developmental delays relative to hearing peers. Thus while technological advances have created more opportunities for many deaf and hard-of-hearing students, they are not a panacea (e.g., Pisoni, Conway, Kronenberger, Henning, & Anaya, 2010). Advanced hearing aids and cochlear implants do not change a deaf child into a hearing child. In almost all cases, special educational and social supports are still needed.

It should be kept in mind that cochlear implants are available for most children with profound hearing loss (and occasionally those with severe hearing loss), but they are not appropriate for those with lesser degrees of hearing loss. Further, research indicates that a cochlear implant typically gives a profoundly deaf child access to auditory information that is similar to that received by a child with a hearing loss in the moderate range who uses a hearing aid, not the clear signal available to hearing children (e.g., Blamey & Sarant, in press). Because current research indicates that even lesser degrees of hearing loss place a child at risk for difficulties and delays in both language and literacy development (e.g., Goldberg & Richburg, 2004; Moeller, Tomblin et al., 2007), such challenges are not likely to be completely resolved by use of amplification devices or cochlear implants.

Despite some limitations, advanced technologies are clearly having positive impact on the developmental and educational achievements of deaf and hard-of-hearing children and are a major source of excitement and hopefulness regarding their potential for the future. At the same time, variability in the outcomes of use of these devices can cause even greater individual differences in the population than has been the case in the past. For this reason, and because many current teachers have not received training that allows them to work comfortably with the range of communication abilities and preferences of this population of students, providing appropriate communication and academic support has become even more complex.

Processes of Evaluation

As the preceding sections make clear, identifying and implementing approaches that take into account the high degree of diversity within the population of deaf and hard-of-hearing children remain major challenges facing deaf education. This diversity reflects not only language and learning experiences but also the specific profile of abilities that characterizes individual children. Recognition of this challenge, which differs in degree but not in kind from that faced by educators in general education who work with hearing children, is an important step toward developing more effective practice.

The determination of effective educational practices requires evaluation at a number of different levels. Most educators and other professionals are acutely aware of and highly experienced with the process of preparing and evaluating an individual student's progress for the purpose of individualized educational programs, or IEPs (in the United States) and similar plans in other countries. Knowing what to do—that is, knowing what options are available and potentially viable when growth is not proceeding as expected—however, requires access to an evidence base of effective practices. Such a base, in turn, requires both formalized research and careful clinical and educational observation/documentation concerning the progress of individuals and groups of students in varied programs. Outcomes then can be related to characteristics of learners, programs, and individual implementation.

As noted earlier, the relatively small population of children with hearing loss, the broad range of language and learning experiences, the frequent presence of additional disabilities, and the increasing dispersion of those students across a variety of educational settings make the creation of such a comprehensive evidence database difficult. Traditional group-based research and evaluation is particularly difficult with this population (Fortnum, Stacey, Barton, & Summerfield, 2007; Mitchell & Karchmer, 2006). As a result, despite a rapidly increasing number of research and evaluation publications that have addressed varied developmental and educational issues of deaf and hard-of-hearing students, it is rarely possible to draw firm conclusions on the basis of a single or even a small group of reports. Instead, it is necessary to survey the full range of information available and look for convergent findings across a number of investigations in which conditions or approaches differ.

When similar findings occur across carefully designed studies and across different research and teaching contexts, it becomes possible to trust that those findings are meaningful. Still, it remains the responsibility of all who read them to do so with a critical eye and to guard against the tendency to trust something one already believes rather than something that contrasts with preexisting beliefs. To provide readers with some guidance in this respect, the next chapter describes various approaches taken by investigators and government/educational agencies to produce research findings that can be as free of bias as possible and therefore to become part of a trustworthy and reliable evidence base to guide practice. Armed with that information and the background provided by these first two chapters, we can move on to the development and education of deaf and hard-of-hearing children.

SUMMARY: UNDERSTANDING AND EDUCATING CHILDREN WITH HEARING LOSS

Even though deaf and hard-of-hearing children make up only a small proportion of the world's children, their actual number is both impressive and compelling given the challenges they face. Work to further support their development and efforts to extend the reach of services found to be effective can have an overwhelming effect on the quality of life experienced by these children and can support their greater contributions to the societies in which they live. Information establishing an evidence base for effective practices is building rapidly, but both more and more targeted data are required. In this regard, we can identify five key issues that should guide this effort.

- Both research and careful documentation of the progress of individual children and groups of children are needed to determine the effectiveness of various programming and intervention approaches for children who are deaf and hard-of-hearing.
- Research findings need to be critically examined and should be held to high scientific standards; however, it needs to be recognized that research with low-incidence groups such as deaf and hard-of-hearing children is inherently more difficult and will require comparison of findings across studies and different subgroups of the population before valid conclusions can be drawn.
- Information is especially needed regarding options and outcomes for children who have multiple disabilities and for children in countries where support services are rare or only emerging. Both individual and

cultural needs must be considered when programming efforts are planned and implemented.

- Although the relative impact of various factors on the development of deaf and hard-of-hearing children is not clearly established, it is evident that they function academically, on average, at levels lower than their innate ability to learn would predict. Social and psychological functioning is influenced by a number of variables, including perhaps most importantly home and peer communication. These topics require ongoing research efforts.
- Many students who are deaf or hard of hearing function at high levels. Success is not only possible but it is often seen and reported. Research and programming efforts must account for the higher achieving portion of the population of students with hearing loss both in hopes of identifying factors that can accelerate development of other students and to assure that challenging programming and wider opportunities are made available.

Many researchers, educators, and clinicians have contributed to the information base about deaf and hard-of-hearing children, their families, and their developmental and academic progress. However, the quality and scope of the information is varied, and a critical overview is required to establish and interpret evidence on which to base future programming and intervention efforts. Implementing the review requires comparing and contrasting findings and documentation across a variety of studies and of contexts to identify what is known to be helpful—and what ideas may not have been proven to be effective. Our goal in the following chapters is not to criticize particular studies or downplay the significant progress that has been made. We can do better, however, and the remainder of this book is intended to both guide practitioners in providing services for deaf and hard-of-hearing children and to identify those areas in which more work is needed.

3 Evaluating the Evidence in Deaf Education: Methods for Obtaining Trustworthy and Useful Information

For too long, practice in education of deaf and hard-of-hearing students has been based more closely on beliefs and attitudes than on documented evidence from research or the outcomes of interventions. In this book, the focus moves toward "evidence" and away from "belief" as we provide a comprehensive and critical review of existing published reports about approaches to education and intervention—using periodicals, books, and other available resources. "Critical" in the way we are using the term does not necessarily mean "negative." Instead, it implies that we are evaluating the trustworthiness and the validity of research and practice reports based on the methods used and the conclusions reached—sometimes forming an opinion that they are worthy of implementation, sometimes concluding that they are seriously flawed, but most often identifying both positive contributions and limitations in the report or the way the study was conducted. The resources we have identified and addressed in this book consist primarily of peer-reviewed professional journal articles, governmental reports (i.e., from government agencies, educational entities, funding bodies, etc.), and books and book chapters that include verifiable outcome data.

Anecdotal, "personal stories," and non-reviewed reports are occasionally considered, but these are identified as such. It is important to recognize that the reliability and validity (or the trustworthiness) of conclusions and interpretations are generally considered to be stronger in peer-reviewed articles and reports than in those that are published without having received rigorous review from others in the field. Trustworthiness may be of special concern and may be less rigorously enforced and established in reports from issue-oriented agencies and individuals—whether in print on paper or on the Internet.

We expect that most if not all investigators in the field of deaf education would acknowledge that there is more literature in this field than in which one can put high confidence. For that reason, this review carefully distinguishes what we know, what we do not know, and what we think we know—but do not yet have sufficient empirical or trustworthy evidence to accept with confidence. Except where specific issues are raised or qualifications are made in the attached report, all of the material included herein is drawn from studies we believe to be credible, although their conclusions may be incomplete or require cautious interpretation. Readers will note that more detail is given about some reports and research studies than about others. This does not necessarily reflect our judgment about the quality or reliability of the study. In some cases, we have focused on a study because it presents ideas that appear to be particularly innovative, important, or useful. In other instances, a study is reviewed in detail to provide readers with a more in-depth and thus practical understanding about a research or intervention approach than could be given in just a few sentences.

Although this review clearly points out weaknesses in the database about development and education of deaf and hard-of-hearing children, readers should recognize that deaf education is not alone in its frequent reliance on beliefs and inadequately investigated processes, policies, and procedures. This is a difficulty that characterizes education in general (Mosteller & Boruch, 2002; Odom et al., 2005)—at least in the United States and likely in other countries as well. Continuing failure to identify and implement educational methods to optimize students' learning has prompted calls in general, and particularly in special education, for carefully evaluating what is known and for increasing the degree of scientific rigor and validity of studies that are conducted. Accordingly, the following section, addressing research and evaluation designs relevant to deaf education, is primarily drawn from sources aimed at general and special education. That discussion is included to orient the reader to differences in the ways that research is designed and conducted that influence the degree to which results can be interpreted with confidence and the degree to which they can be generalized—that is, whether they can be expected to hold true for students beyond those who participated in the study. Although the careful and appropriate use of statistics is required for such generalization, the way the study is designed (who and how many students participated, what was measured—how and when and by whom) is at least equally important. Some studies, in fact, are not designed to be interpreted through use of statistics. These studies, sometimes called "qualitative" and often based on interviews or on careful observation and recording of actions and behaviors, must also meet specific standards for quality if their results are to be considered reliable.

Subsequent chapters in this book address specific topics, looking for convergent or consistent findings across studies and content areas. Discovery of consistently positive findings can be taken as probable evidence that a practice or an idea has merit and can be of assistance in guiding practice; consistent failure to find positive outcomes suggests that, even if based on a widely accepted theory, the practice does not have merit. A lack of convergence—that is, a lack of consistent findings across studies—indicates that more study is needed, perhaps with a special focus on characteristics of the students and teachers who participated, the measures that were used, or the context in which the practice was implemented.

DESIGNS FOR RESEARCH AND EVALUATION ON EDUCATIONAL PRACTICE AND OUTCOMES

It is increasingly recognized that educational practice, both for general and for special populations, needs to be based on scientifically valid evidence of successful interventions. Yet, the Council for Exceptional Children (CEC), the preeminent advocacy group in the United States for children with disabilities, stated on its website: "While the [U.S.] law requires teachers to use evidence-based practices in their classrooms, the special education field has not yet determined criteria for evidence-based practice nor whether special education has a solid foundation of evidence-based practices. Also, those teaching strategies that have been researched are difficult for teachers to access" (http://www.sped.ced.org, accessed September 24, 2008). In fact, there remains considerable argument about what characterizes acceptable evidence with respect to best practices in education.

The CEC's Division of Research reminded researchers that more than one type of research method has usefulness and that they should choose research designs while keeping in mind the type of question being asked, the amount of information already known on the topic, and characteristics of the sample participants. A set of reports from the CEC focused on four different research and evaluation methodologies used in special education: (a) randomized experimental group designs (Campbell & Stanley, 1966; Gersten et al.,2005), (b) single-subject experimental designs (Horner et al., 2005; Tripodi, 1998), (c) correlational designs (Thompson, Diamond, McWilliam, Snyder, & Snyder, 2005), and

(d) qualitative designs (Bogdan & Biklen, 2003; Odom et al., 2005). Each of these designs can, when carefully implemented, provide evidence of the effectiveness of educational practices.

Randomized Clinical Trials, or Experimental Research

Some agencies—for example, the What Works Clearinghouse sponsored by the U.S. Department of Education's Institute of Education Sciences (http://ies.ed.gov, accessed 6 June 2008)—have taken a conservative approach, stressing randomized experimental group designs (or randomized clinical trials, RCTs) as the "gold standard" for evidence-based practice. RCTs are *quantitative* studies in that they are based on data or information that is numerical—scores, counts of the number of times something happened, number-based ratings of attitudes or feelings. Such trials are *experimental* because they compare the outcome of a curriculum or an intervention across two or more groups under carefully controlled conditions. In addition, such designs require that assignment of participants to the groups be done using a randomized approach—for example, pre-existing groups and classrooms of students should not all be assigned to one or the other experimental group in the research, but instead all students should have an equal chance of being selected to participate in one group or another. Randomizing in a research context, although using more sophisticated methods, is essentially like the process of drawing a lottery ticket from a hat. The group into which an individual is placed—either the "experimental" or the "control" group that does not receive the experimental treatment—is a matter of chance. Oddly enough, this random or chance placement is actually necessary if many available statistical analysis procedures are to be valid.

Inferential and descriptive statistics, often quite sophisticated ones, are used to evaluate the outcomes of RCT studies, but it is the initial design of the study that has most importance for its interpretation and trustworthiness. The strength and reliability of the measures used to collect data are critical. Do they measure what they say they measure (*validity*)? If the measure is given to a child more than once, will each administration to that child produce reasonably similar scores (*reliability*)? Are the measures (whether standardized tests, counts of child behaviors, number-based ratings of attitudes or feelings, etc.) appropriate for use with the participants in this particular study? Are the randomly selected groups similar a priori on the characteristics that matter?

Most important, when outcomes of a curriculum, an intervention, or an educational approach are being measured and compared, have the lessons or interventions actually been implemented as planned? This is referred to as "fidelity of implementation" and it is critical that this be clearly established before study results are analyzed. For example, suppose a research group is comparing the outcomes of a new math-skills curriculum with those of an existing curriculum.

If not all of the teachers implement their assigned curriculum accurately and follow the curricula as they are designed, no amount of elegant statistical analyses will produce a valid study. Similarly, if researchers study the effects of an approach, such as comparing the results of varied "free reading" time across groups of students, the outcome can be invalidated if they determine that the students do not actually engage in reading during the time allowed. Or a comparison of outcomes of deaf children in "oral" versus "signing" programs is not valid if, in fact, the parents and teachers in the sign program do not all use signs fluently. Therefore, even the use of RCT designs for research and evaluation can be flawed and can fail to produce the kind of information expected if there are errors in the design and the execution of the study. On the other hand, RCT studies are among the few types of studies that when properly conducted can actually give evidence that a cause (the intervention applied) is directly responsible for an outcome or effect.

Quasi-Experimental Research

Quasi-experimental research is a more frequently used approach in education than is RCT. Researchers using this approach include existing groups or attempt to match participants in the groups on factors thought to be important (for example, socioeconomic status or, in many developmental studies, mothers' education levels) or to statistically control for those factors. The groups may be given different interventions, with outcomes compared, or sometimes the outcomes of "naturally occurring" interventions can be measured. For example, Meadow-Orlans (Meadow-Orlans et al., 2004) conducted a series of studies investigating the quality of mother-child interaction in groups of deaf children with signing deaf mothers compared to those with hearing mothers. She referred to this as a "natural" experiment, in which the "intervention" was the mothers' behaviors with their children. She hypothesized that deaf mothers' easier communication with and positive attitudes about their deaf children would result in better developmental outcomes. She repeatedly found this to be the case (e.g., Meadow-Orlans, 1997; Meadow-Orlans et al.). Findings from such studies must, of course, be interpreted with caution, and studies with quasi-experimental designs are especially vulnerable to the possibility that intervening variables or factors of which the researcher is unaware are actually responsible for group differences in outcomes. For example, groups that were compared may have different pre-study histories of experiences and skills that could have affected the outcome (some of these might be irrelevant or "wash out" with larger random samples but not with small or self-selected ones). Or the groups may differ on some factor that, unknown to the researcher, is actually the cause of an effect being tested. Thus, there might be some pre-existing difference between deaf and hard-of-hearing students in mainstream schools versus schools for the deaf that can affect outcomes and that the researchers failed to think about when setting up the study. Some pre-existing differences can be handled through use of additional statistical methods, but only within limits.

Donovan and Cross (2002) pointed out that establishing equivalent groups in samples comparing interventions with special education populations can also be complicated by the differing degrees of disability in specified groups and by overrepresentation of minority groups in some special education populations. However, repeated quasi-experimental studies, using different groups of participants and conducted in different environments or by different research groups, can build confidence in cause and effect findings if they converge or are consistent.

Single-Subject Research

Another experimental approach to quantitative research on the outcomes of a specific intervention or activity is referred to as single-subject or single-case research. As the name implies, this approach involves a single participant or case (although a "case" can be a group considered as a whole, such as a classroom or a school). Some researchers use the approach on a number of cases individually and then look across the data to draw conclusions about the usefulness of an approach across cases. There are several ways to set up this kind of study, but all include measuring the target or goal behavior before, during, and after a specific approach or intervention is implemented (see, for example, Horner et al., 2005, for a more in-depth discussion, and books such as that by Tripodi, 1998, in which clinical applications are discussed). Quantitative outcome measures are recorded for the individual over time according to a carefully planned schedule. The researcher, clinician, or teacher typically makes a chart that shows how the outcome measure changes (or in some cases fails to change) over time as steps in the intervention are implemented. In this way, each person or case serves as its own "control" or "comparison group." Measurements are usually continued for some time after the specific intervention has stopped in order for researchers to see whether behavior or performance changes are maintained.

As with RCTs or quasi-experimental research designs, the selection and measurement of the behaviors in a single-subject study must be shown to be valid, that is, appropriately representing the goal behavior or attitude being measured, and careful and reliable measurements must be made. Of course, it also is critical that the intervention or curriculum is being implemented as it was meant to be. The single-subject approach would be especially appropriate for use in answering questions such as whether a particular type of intervention would reduce an individual student's number of behavior disruptions or perhaps increase time on task.

Single-subject studies have only infrequently been reported in the research literature about deaf and hard-of-hearing students, but a philosophically similar technique called response to intervention (RTI) has emerged in which an intervention or type of service is systematically intensified for an individual student over time to determine what level is required to promote appropriate progress (National Center on Response to Intervention, http://www.rti4success.org, retrieved August 5, 2009). This approach has promise for making decisions about the kinds and intensity of services needed by individuals from special populations and others who need highly individualized programming. It remains an approach that is aimed at meeting the needs of individual students, however, and is not typically used in research.

Correlational Research

Another form of quantitative research uses measures of correlation or association to look for relations between two or more characteristics in groups of participants, their programming experiences, or other aspects of development and education. This kind of research design does not produce results that can be definitely interpreted as showing cause and effect. Thompson et al. (2005) proposed that it nevertheless can provide important information for evidence-based practice when conducted using sophisticated statistical or logical methods to exclude alternative interpretation of results. Many available studies forming the evidence base in deaf and hard-of-hearing–related research have used this kind of approach, along with other statistical methods for analyzing the data that were collected. Many of these studies have investigated multiple outcome measures at the same time, and statistics such as multiple regression have been used for the analysis. Regression analyses estimate the relative strength of the association between factors, some of which can be the outcome or outcomes being measured. Spencer (1996), for example, investigated the associations among child language levels, mother and child hearing status, and children's amount and level of play behaviors. She found that language levels were strongly associated with (or "explained significant variance in") the sophistication of the children's play. It was not possible to conclude on the basis of this one study, however, that language "caused" the children's play to progress.

A statistical approach called structural equation modeling (SEM) can be used in correlational studies and can more readily be interpreted as indicating cause and effect between participant characteristics or interventions and child outcomes. SEM analyzes several rival "hypotheses" or best-informed predictions of the associations between various factors and the outcomes being measured. These predictions or "models" are typically based on competing theories about how a phenomenon or outcome arises. Thus, when a particular model or prediction is affirmed, it also has theoretical or logical support, and cautious interpretations can be made about the impact of the various factors included in the model on the outcome measures. This approach requires relatively large numbers of participants to be effective, and it has rarely been used in studies involving deaf or hard-of-hearing children. However, Connor and Zwolan (2004) used SEM in an investigation of sources of reading comprehension of 91 prelingually, profoundly deaf children who used cochlear implants. They found evidence confirming their hypotheses that age of implantation and both pre- and post-implant vocabulary size influenced reading comprehension, but a negligible effect was found for communication mode/method used prior to implantation. Their analysis was limited to some degree because of what was considered to be a relatively small number of participants.

Qualitative Research

Not all useful research and evaluation projects depend upon the collection of quantitative or numerical data. Qualitative research designs can provide detailed descriptive knowledge, especially related to *processes* of learning—how or why change is occurring. Information produced by qualitative research (e.g., observational studies, informal interview studies, extensive and systematic personal reports, or life histories) is not expected to be generalizable—that is, the same patterns of outcomes may not be expected to occur for other groups of students. However, consumers of that research can be provided with enough information to judge the extent to which it is applicable to their own specific situations (Brantlinger, Jimenez, Klingner, Pugach, & Richardson, 2005). Qualitative studies can also serve as sources of hypotheses or predictions to be investigated in follow-up experimental or correlational studies.

Lang and Albertini (2001) pointed out that qualitative designs can be especially useful with small populations, including classes of deaf and hard-of-hearing students, where it is difficult to set up controlled experimental studies. However, qualitative research requires specialized skills, and such studies should not be attempted by persons who are not fully aware of best approaches to the collection and analysis of qualitative data (see Bogdan & Biklen, 2003, for a useful guide to qualitative research in education).

Qualitative studies are typically considered to have stronger validity (or trustworthiness) if data are collected in several different ways from different participants and across fairly extended periods of time. For example, a qualitative study of "what actually happens" during a teacher-led reading lesson in a classroom using a specific programming approach might include researcher observations of behaviors of both child and the teacher, interviews with the teacher about his goals and impressions of student involvement, and focus group interviews with all or selected subgroups of the children. Ideally, the researcher would spend many hours in the classroom over a semester, a year, or more. Teacher's logs and notes sent back and forth from home, with appropriate permission, might be reviewed and ideas and needs noted. The researchers would record and transcribe lengthy records of the observations and would not only describe what was observed but also look for patterns linking one kind of activity or characteristic with another. An example of this kind of study was conducted by Williams (1994) who observed pre-literacy behaviors of several deaf students, making observations both at home and at school, collecting numerous samples of their work, and administering informal assessments. She was able to describe the kinds of literacy activities the children experienced as well as many of the things they were learning during those activities. In addition to this kind of descriptive or qualitative information, quantitative (number- or score-based) information is sometimes also collected. With this kind of mixed method, for example, a researcher could relate changes in student reading scores to observations of students' participation during the lessons.

Practice-Based Wisdom

Regardless of the methodology used, evidence of successful practices relies on thorough conceptual grounding in existing literature, documentation of acceptable reliability and validity of all measurements, control of potential intervening variables and threats to design validity, documentation that interventions or practices being assessed are implemented as planned and in uniformly competent ways, use of multiple measures, and (when statistical approaches are used) assurance that the number of participants allows the identification of effects, or provides sufficient statistical power (Gersten et al., 2005). Dependence only on RCT designs, and even on quasi-experimental or correlational designs, is inherently limited with populations in special education, however, not only due to the small number of students identified as having a specific disability but also because of the greater variability in special as opposed to regular education groups. These difficulties are amplified when students who are identified as deaf or hard of hearing are considered.

The accumulated, documented experience of skilled teachers and clinicians also can provide important bases for developing and implementing curricula and educational interventions. Although such reports and documentation of student achievements and activities do not in themselves provide *sufficient* support for any specific practice, they can provide helpful guides for both researchers and practitioners. With appropriate cautions, such reports should be considered in any summary of the evidence base in education, whether general, special, or deaf education. When successful approaches are suggested, more systematic research using designs such as those described above are needed to determine how frequently and under what conditions those results can be reproduced.

CONSIDERATIONS FOR STUDIES INCLUDED IN THIS REVIEW

Not even the very rigorous What Works Clearinghouse relies solely on RCT studies to ascertain practices for which there is evidence of successful use. Instead, the Clearinghouse utilizes a complicated system for determining whether a methodology "meets standards," "meets standards with reservations," or "does not meet standards." The system includes the level or the type of design of the research, the amount of research that has been done on the topic (i.e., is there just one acceptable study? a large number of good studies?), whether all the studies are in agreement or the evidence is conflicting, and other characteristics of the research such as the overall effect sizes (that is, the amount of difference the curriculum or the approach being tested made in student performance) among the studies considered.

Kluwin and Noretsky (2005) noted that given the limitations and complications of conducting research with the deaf and hard-of-hearing student population, it is necessary to look across studies and various study designs to identify convergent ideas as well as to shed light on assumptions that fail to be supported across various studies. This recommendation is consistent with those cited in the above references with regard to the field of special education in general. The chapters that follow, therefore, provide a synthesis of information gathered across a variety of settings and using a variety of research methods to determine what is known about promising and evidence-based practices in deaf education and, perhaps just as important, what continues to need investigation.

The amount of detail provided for individual studies in the following review varies for several reasons. First, although RCT-type studies usually can be described relatively succinctly, qualitative studies and others that go beyond straightforward evaluations of learning following discrete experimental manipulation(s) may need greater explanation for the reader to understand what was done and to appreciate the studies' level of trustworthiness, or validity and reliability. Second, as noted earlier, except for several instances in which specific issues are raised or qualifications noted, all of the material included in the review is drawn from studies we believe to be credible. Toward this end, the vast majority of the research considered comes from peer-reviewed publications, primarily scholarly journals. Some other investigations described in book chapters and conference presentations (e.g., posters with follow-up printed materials) have been reported when there has been sufficient detail to allow evaluation of their credibility. Third, investigations involving creation or relatively long-term evaluation of specific educational programs/interventions, longitudinal studies of development, and large-scale studies that included examination of variables in multiple domains necessarily require greater elaboration. Fourth, it was noted earlier that conclusions and/or claims included in various reports that did not follow from reported methods and results are not included in this literature review.

At the same time, the synthesis in this report of findings obtained over decades of investigation provided clarification of some earlier findings, both positively and negatively, that allowed us to go beyond the original conclusions. This endeavor is inherently risky, because there may be aspects of a study not described originally that could qualify current re-interpretation. To avoid such over-interpretation or misinterpretation and provide sufficient information for others to draw their own conclusions, greater detail was sometimes necessary.

Finally, two other qualifications to the present review are worth noting, insofar as they may assist readers in having a better sense of the true weight of the research reviewed. Most obviously perhaps, it may appear that there are issues either missing from this review or considered in less detail than might be expected. Although oversight on the part of the present authors is certainly possible, often such domains simply lack as much credible research as is commonly believed. For example, as shown below, despite frequent claims for the value of auditory-verbal therapy and sign/bilingual education, each currently lacks sufficient empirical evidence to support broad-based interpretation and implementation. In several other areas of investigation, contradictory findings have emerged from different studies with no clear basis available for accepting one position or another. Wherever possible, likely explanations for such contradictions are provided. There is no way to know, however, how many studies have failed to demonstrate the utility of any particular experimental manipulation or intervention (e.g., cued speech in support of English literacy). Such *null results*, findings of a lack of difference between groups or as a result of an intervention, generally are unlikely to be published unless an investigator provides several convincing replications, either due to lack of clarity in the reasons for null findings or because they fail to support an investigator's theoretical orientation. Both of the latter situations are regrettable, but they do exist.

Because of gaps in the research literature and the difficulties in drawing conclusions from multiple studies at different levels of sophistication and using slightly different approaches, McCall (2009) recommended flexible guidelines for research publication. Those included program descriptions that allow replication, logic models that provide theoretical support for a programming approach, and translation of program and evaluation information so that research professionals, practitioners, and policy makers ("communities of practice") can understand documented program effects or questions about such effects. He called for evaluations across fields or domains of practice that synthesize the preponderance of evidence when effectiveness is considered.

This book alone cannot provide a comprehensive or incontrovertible guide to what should be done in education programs for deaf and hard-of-hearing children. However, our hope is that by providing an objective review of what is known now—and by reporting findings that represent a variety of types of studies—synthesis will be supported. To begin, the following chapter focuses on practices that have repeatedly been found to promote or at least to associate with enhanced development—those of identification of hearing loss and provision of family-focused intervention services during the early days, months, and years of a child's life. A high level of consensus has been reached on this topic across researchers, educators and clinicians, and policy makers. Of course, questions and difficulties continue to exist. Furthermore, subsequent chapters will cover topics on which there is much less agreement and, in some cases, far less evidence.

SUMMARY: HOW DO WE KNOW WHAT WE KNOW?

A variety of approaches have been employed in research on the development and achievements of deaf and hard-of-hearing students. These general methods are similar across general, special, and deaf education and provide varying levels of confidence that their findings can lead to advances in programming.

- Randomized experimental group designs in which participants are picked at random and randomly assigned to different treatments or interventions can provide the strongest evidence of the effectiveness of specific programming efforts. However, these designs are difficult and in some cases impossible to implement in real-life situations and, even when used, careful procedures must be followed if their results are to be valid.
- Other research and evaluation designs, including quasi-experimental, single-subject experiments, correlational studies, qualitative designs, and even less formal teacher and clinician reports, can indicate successful educational and therapeutic practices if findings are consistent across a number of studies. However, an individual study using one of these designs cannot firmly establish cause and effect relations between specific interventions and their outcomes. Multiple studies and reports using varied designs and participants are necessary to provide strong evidence of successful practice.
- Educational research involving deaf and hard-of-hearing students is made more difficult by the low incidence of childhood hearing loss and great diversity in this population. The challenges faced by researchers and other professionals who work with these children, however, are not very different from those faced by anyone who works in general and special education.

It is important that the field of education and services for deaf and hard-of-hearing students continue to develop a strong evidence base for effective practices. This will necessitate investigations by professionals from multiple fields of study. Assumptions and "beliefs" about what we do and what is best for those children need to be targeted in research and evaluation, so that future practices can be justified.

4 Early Identification of Hearing Loss and Early Intervention Services: Implications for Language and Learning

Early identification and specialized audiological, language, and educational interventions to ameliorate the consequences of congenital or early-onset hearing loss represent the expected standard of care in much of the "developed" world. Without such interventions, deaf and hard-of-hearing children are likely to experience significant delays or disruption to their language and communication development, social and emotional development, and ultimately their educational achievement and life options (Leigh, Newall, & Newall, 2010). Leigh et al., pointed out that "the notion that children will develop their language and communication, cognitive, and social skills more effectively if intervention is commenced very early is grounded in the premise that there is an optimal period for the development of certain cognitive and linguistic abilities." In the absence of early services for deaf and hard-of-hearing children and their families, countries pay a much higher monetary price for rehabilitation and support services than they would pay for universal newborn hearing screening (UNHS) and early intervention. The price levied against children's futures cannot be estimated.

NEWBORN SCREENING AND FAMILY REACTIONS

As late as 1990, the average age for identification of congenital hearing loss in the United States was around 24 months (Culpepper, 2003). At that time, identification efforts primarily utilized birth registries and hospital-administered questionnaires designed to identify infants who were at high risk for hearing loss based on family history or events occurring during pregnancy or birth. When individual children were deemed at risk, parents were asked to bring them back for hearing tests after having left the birthing center or hospital. Through such methods, many infants who were at high risk for hearing loss were "lost" to the health care system when parents failed to return for follow-up testing (Mahoney & Eichwald, 1987). As a result, this approach is estimated to have identified only about half of the infants who actually had a congenital hearing loss (Mauk, White, Mortensen, & Behrens, 1991). In the United Kingdom, hearing screening used to be conducted at an 8-month well-baby check by a health visitor watching for the infant's reaction to sounds from an unseen source. A similar system was used in Australia (Ching, Dillon, Day, & Crowe, 2008). Eventually, it was recognized that this *distraction test* did not prove to be sufficiently reliable in identifying infants with significant hearing loss (http://www.ndcs.org.uk/, accessed March 16, 2009).

By the end of the 20th century, technology for assessing infant hearing had advanced sufficiently to allow more definitive identification of hearing loss during the neonatal period. In the United States and the United Kingdom, screening now typically occurs before infants leave the birthing hospital (Culpepper, 2003; http://www.ndcs.org.uk/, accessed March 16, 2009), although UK screening can occur in the family home or in a health clinic in some geographical areas. Where UNHS has been implemented, the average age of identification has dropped to the early months of life (Yoshinaga-Itano, 2006)—for example, to 2 months of age, on average—in England (Young & Tattersall, 2007).

Neonatal (or newborn) hearing screening is based on either the *evoked otoacoustic emissions test* (EOAE) or an *auditory evoked (potential) response* test (AEP). Both tests are quick, non-invasive, painless, and carry no risk to the infant. Typically, the EOAE test is used as the initial screening test, with AEP used for follow up if the first test is inconclusive or indicates the likelihood of a hearing loss (Cone-Wesson in press). The goal in the United States is for the more detailed AEP testing to be conducted by the time the infant is 3 months old, with intervention services provided before 6 months of age.

Despite the effectiveness of hearing assessment during the neonatal period, gaps remain in identification. Beyond those infants whose parents do not return for follow-up testing, some proportion of infants are born without evidence of hearing loss but progressively lose hearing over the first months or years of life. Testing protocols must allow for identification of these children as well as those with mild hearing losses (16–25 dB), some of whom are not identified using current methods, and those with unilateral hearing losses (Moeller, Tomblin, et al., 2007).

Some practitioners initially questioned whether identification of hearing loss at such an early age might interfere with development of positive parent-infant bonding (Gregory, 1999, 2001; Yoshinaga-Itano & de Uzcategui, 2001) or whether potential advantages in development would justify the effort required (Bess & Paradise, 1994). The antagonists suggested that mothers' anxieties about their babies' health might create emotional barriers between them. In a study involving 86 children with hearing loss identified between birth and 6 months of age, however, Pipp-Siegel, Sedey, and Yoshinaga-Itano (2002) found no evidence that early intervention resulted in any increased parental stress that might lead to problems with parent-child attachment. Although that finding represents a null result (see chapter 3), Meadow-Orlans et al. (2004) similarly failed to find any differences in secure versus insecure parent-child attachment between a group of hearing mothers with hearing children and another group of hearing mothers whose children were identified as deaf or hard of hearing before the age of 9 months. (Most of the children's hearing losses were identified well before they were 6 months of age.) In 1998, the European Consensus Development Conference on Neonatal Hearing Screening concluded that the risks of anxiety due to early screening were acceptable, given evidence of the benefits to developmental outcomes (Grandori & Lutman, 1999).

One of the concerns raised about parental anxiety associated with early screening is the wait that usually occurs before the follow-up testing can be performed, a period in which parents may be hesitant or overly cautious in interactions with their child (e.g., Clemens, Davis, & Bailey, 2000; Vohr, Singh, Bansal, Letourneau, & McDermott, 2001). In a carefully designed and conducted qualitative study in England, Young and Tattersall (2005) interviewed 27 families whose infants had received an early diagnosis of hearing loss. The focus was on parents' reactions to and evaluation of processes of screening infants' hearing and referral when hearing loss was suspected. About half of the families reported not having any strong concerns when initial screening resulted in a referral. Even after the diagnosis was confirmed, parents expressed the belief that the screener was right to initially reassure them that false readings were possible and that initial screening is often inconclusive. Most parents placed great value on their personal interactions with the screening professional, on positive aspects of the screener's personality, and on the reassurance that the professional gave them. In contrast, some parents were not reassured by the screener's explanation that the test was not conclusive. Some of these families had other reasons to suspect a hearing loss (e.g., a family history or birth difficulties). Several parents failed to fully understand the screener's message, and some did not understand the difference between initial screening and a definitive diagnosis. They thought that the screening test showed conclusively that their infant was deaf and that, nevertheless, no immediate assistance had been provided.

Another carefully conducted, qualitative study involved parents of 17 early-identified children in Ontario, Canada (Fitzpatrick, Angus, Durieux-Smith, Graham, & Coyle, 2008). Parents were asked to identify their own needs following their child's diagnosis and were asked what they would include in the system of diagnosis and intervention if they could redesign it. Age of identification among the children ranged from birth to 42 months, with nine having their hearing losses identified before 12 months; none of the children were identified as having additional disabilities. Hearing losses in the sample ranged from mild to profound, and all families elected to participate in programs using an oral communication approach (spoken language without signing). The majority enrolled in programs based on auditory-verbal therapy (AVT; see chapter 5). All of the parents involved in the study agreed that neonatal screening is beneficial, and several parents whose children had been diagnosed after 1 year of age were particularly vehement about the need for earlier diagnosis. Overall, most parents expressed satisfaction with audiology and oral therapy (listening and speech) services. At the same time, they reported the need, first, for more information specific to their own child's prognosis for spoken language skills and, second, for more opportunities to interact with other parents of deaf and hard-of-hearing children. Many parents recounted a lack of coordination of services and of information provided across specialists and agencies. Like the parents in the Young and Tattersall (2005) study, the Canadian parents thought that professionals' abilities to communicate and the manner in which information was delivered were important determinants of their overall experience.

Young and Tattersall (2007) explored reactions to and the effects of British parents' knowing about their child's hearing loss so early in life. Although the majority of parents had positive feelings about receiving that information early, they reported that the timing did not prevent their sense of grief about the ultimate diagnosis. Most parents thought that being able to access appropriate assistance so early was a great benefit to their child and, by extension, to themselves. A minority (five) of the families, however, failed to share this positive opinion, indicating that they had not received appropriate and timely help from professionals. At the same time, Young and Tattersall suggested that some parents' rushing into activity at the diagnosis while feeling stressed by timetables can indicate avoidance—an unwillingness to accept their child's hearing loss. They therefore emphasized that it is important for early interventionists to "be mindful of the need to create the space for parents to feel their responses to their child's deafness...and not for that psychological process to be disallowed" (2007, p. 217). Young and Tattersall also noted that most of the parents in their study held expectations that early identification and intervention would provide for normal or near-normal speech and hearing (2007, p. 217). That is, they assumed that the early intervention would be sufficient to make their child be like a hearing child, although that expectation is not supported by the data. Progress is being made in the effectiveness of support for development of young deaf and hard-of-hearing children, but it must be admitted that there are many uncertainties about any individual child's developmental and educational outcomes.

ENHANCED DEVELOPMENTAL OUTCOMES RELATED TO EARLY IDENTIFICATION

Some investigators have pointed out that studies of the efficacy of early identification and intervention have rarely employed appropriate experimental designs (e.g., Ching et al., 2008), although researchers generally have found significant developmental advantages for children following earlier, compared to later, diagnosis and intervention services. Most prominent among those benefits is a reduction in the developmental lag typically observed in deaf and hard-of-hearing children's language development, regardless of whether they are acquiring spoken language or sign language. Children who are identified early and receive early intervention have been found to demonstrate language development in the "low average" level compared to hearing children (e.g., Yoshinaga-Itano, 2003)—not ideal, but better than is the case without early services. McGowan, Nittrouer, and Chenusky (2008), for example, reported that speech development of 10 carefully selected 12-month-olds with hearing loss was significantly less mature than that of a comparison group of hearing 12-month-olds, despite identification shortly after birth and extensive use of hearing aids. Identification and intervention may decrease the effects of hearing loss on development, but they do not eliminate them. One goal of early intervention, therefore, is to assure that parents have positive but realistic expectations for their children's progress (Young & Tattersall, 2005).

Yoshinaga-Itano and her colleagues (Mayne, Yoshinaga-Itano, & Sedey, 2000; Mayne, Yoshinaga-Itano, Sedey, & Carey, 2000a; Snyder & Yoshinaga-Itano, 1998; Yoshinaga-Itano, Coulter, & Thomson, 2001; Yoshinaga-Itano, Sedey, Coulter, & Mehl, 1998), for example, working with the Colorado Home Intervention Project (CHIP), compared the language development of samples ranging from 54 to 72 children whose hearing losses were identified early to that of samples of 59 to 78 children whose hearing losses were identified later. Multiple regression analyses took into account variables such as degree of hearing loss, gender, family socioeconomic status, age at testing, communication mode (sign or speech-focused programming), and nonverbal play levels (as a measure of cognitive development). Results indicated a significant inverse relation with age of identification of hearing loss—that is, younger ages at identification resulted in higher levels of functioning. Positive effects on language development were particularly noteworthy for children whose identification and start of intervention occurred by 6 months of age. The average child with this or earlier age of identification performed in the "low average" range on measures of language relative to children with normal hearing, a level that considerably exceeds the level of language skills for same-age children who do not receive early identification and intervention (Leigh et al., 2010).

Yoshinaga-Itano and her colleagues also have found positive effects of early identification and intervention on social-emotional development and on the development of play in deaf and hard-of-hearing children (Yoshinaga-Itano, Snyder, & Day, 1998). Unlike reports of earlier cohorts of children with hearing loss (e.g., Geers & Moog, 1989; Levitt, McGarr, & Geffner, 1987), children who entered the Colorado program during the first 6 months of life showed no significant differences between levels of performance on language measures and measures of nonverbal cognitive development, regardless of whether they were acquiring sign language or spoken language. Based primarily on this finding, 6 months of age has been established in the United States as a critical deadline for the establishment of intervention services. Interestingly, Becket et al. (2006) also identified 6 months as a critical age for effects of early deprivation, but their study involved normally hearing children. Children who were removed from non-supportive institutions (orphanages) and provided normal environmental supports before that age did not show the negative effects on cognitive and social-emotional development common in children who were institutionalized beyond 6 months of age.

How Early Is "Early Enough?"

Six months of age does not always emerge as critical for positive effects of early intervention for deaf children (e.g., Hogan, Stokes, White, Tyszkiewicz, & Woolgar, 2008). Some studies have reported that children with hearing loss identified and intervention provided up to 1 year of age perform significantly higher than expected compared to children identified later(e.g., Calderon, 2000; Calderon & Naidu, 1999; Kennedy et al., 2006; Meadow-Orlans et al., 2004; Moeller, 2000). Moeller, for example, assessed the language development of 112 children with hearing loss and, using multiple regression techniques, found a significant effect for age at diagnosis and intervention: Children who had intervention beginning before 11 months of age acquired language significantly better than those with a later start of intervention services. At 5 years of age, the children who had received the earlier services were functioning in the "low average" range relative to norms for hearing children on a number of standardized language tests. In addition to the finding related to age of first intervention, Moeller found that children of those parents who were most involved with their child and the intervention program (in the top 25%) had significantly higher levels of language development. DesJardin (2006) also reported that parent involvement had a significant impact on language development of children identified early on as having a hearing loss. Importantly, this finding "comes full circle" with studies of parental responses to early identification and intervention, with a report from Fitzpatrick et al. (2008) that parents' satisfaction with experiences soon after their children's diagnosis is related to their ongoing degree of involvement in programming.

In a longitudinal study of 80 children, Calderon and Naidu (1999) found that age of first intervention services predicted deaf children's receptive as well as expressive language and speech scores. Earlier intervention also resulted in greater mother-child interaction. Meadow-Orlans and her colleagues (Meadow-Orlans et al., 2004; Spencer, 1993a, 1993b), conducted a longitudinal study of development from 6 or 9 months to 18 months of age involving 20 deaf and hard-of-hearing children with hearing parents, a comparison group of deaf and hard-of-hearing children with deaf parents, and a group of hearing infants who had hearing parents. All of the children with hearing loss had their losses identified before 9 months of age. Results indicated that approximately one-third of the children with hearing loss and hearing parents used expressive language at 18 months that was equivalent in level to that of "on age" or average performing deaf and hearing children who shared a first language with their parents. Convergent evidence from various studies, therefore, has indicated positive effects on child language development from early identification of hearing loss followed immediately or soon after by intervention services. A "critical period" for early intervention has not been definitively identified, but given the heterogeneity of deaf and hard-of-hearing children, this situation is not surprising. At the same time, there has been no indication of any negative effects from early identification and intervention on social-emotional functioning or any other aspect of development.

CHARACTERISTICS OF EARLY INTERVENTION THAT SUPPORT POSITIVE DEVELOPMENTAL OUTCOMES

Yoshinaga-Itano (2003) pointed out that positive effects of early identification have been found only when accompanied by early intervention. This conclusion was echoed by Hogan et al. (2008), who studied the early language development of 37 children in England. Unfortunately, data-based comparisons of development across intervention programs, if conducted, tend not to focus on specific pedagogical or parental support approaches—although it is generally agreed that successful early intervention needs to be aimed at parents and the entire family, not only on the deaf child (Bodner-Johnson & Sass-Lehrer, 2003; Brown & Nott, 2006; Sass-Lehrer, in press). Instead, many researchers have focused on identifying effects of the specific approach to communication and language that is used—that is, whether strictly oral (auditory-spoken language) or visual (sign language) or a combination of the two approaches is utilized. This issue is addressed at length in chapter 5.

For guidance about characteristics of successful intervention practices, it is instructive to review characteristics of the programs from which evidence of benefits of early identification have been obtained. The work of Yoshinaga-Itano and her colleagues (e.g., Mayne, Yoshinaga-Itano, & Sedey, 2000; Mayne, Yoshinaga-Itano, Sedey, & Cary, 2000; Yoshinaga-Itano, Sedey et al., 1998), for example, has been conducted primarily in the state of Colorado, which had specific intervention approaches in place for deaf and hard-of-hearing children (CHIP) prior to the advent of UNHS. As described by Yoshinaga-Itano (2003, 2006), CHIP has the following characteristics:

- Providers of early intervention services are trained professionals, usually with graduate degrees in their fields (including deaf education, early childhood special education, speech/language pathology, audiology, counseling/social work, and psychology). These professionals are provided additional in-service training on a regular basis.
- Services are provided to parents, not directly to the infants, 1 to 1.5 hours weekly, with the focus including information about child development, communication strategies, and so on.
- First contact with the family is made immediately after the diagnosis of hearing loss, and the professionals who work first with parents are specially trained to provide emotional support, as needed, to deal with parental responses to the diagnosis.
- Regional coordinators provide information and the guidance necessary to assist parents in evaluating the various language alternatives that are available and choosing an initial approach to language use.
- Children's developmental progress is assessed twice yearly and results are used to help parents make or revise decisions about how to support their child's development.
- On the basis of these assessments, initial language decisions can be modified or changed, as appropriate.

In the United States, the Boys Town National Hospital program (Moeller, 2000) and SKI*HI (Watkins, Pittman, & Walden, 1998) also have shown positive effects on child development after early identification of hearing loss, while emphasizing family-centered approaches in which professionals and parents are seen as partners, and the interventionists work only indirectly with the children (see also Bodner-Johnson & Sass-Lehrer, 2003, and Brown & Nott, 2006). The strong family counseling and support components of these programs may be especially important given comments by parents who participated in the Young and Tattersall (2007) study; many of these parents said that knowing early in their child's life about the hearing loss did not prevent their feelings of grief. Staff at both the Boys Town and SKI*HI programs present information to parents about communication and technological options potentially helpful for individual children, and the program staff adopt a non-judgmental and supportive approach to family decisions. In addition, the SKI*HI program uses an in-depth curriculum (Watkins, Taylor, & Pittman, 2004) that shares information with parents about child development in general and specifically as related to those with hearing loss.

Mohay, Milton, Hindmarsh, and Ganley (1998) reported implementing an early intervention program in Australia that also adopted a modality-neutral position while supporting early language development. The "Deaf Friends" project teamed deaf women in the community with hearing families that had deaf children. Through videos, workbooks, and home visits, parents learned a variety of techniques for visual attention-getting and visual communication useful regardless of whether their children were acquiring sign or spoken language. Mohay and her colleagues reported that such experiences both enhanced parent-child interactions and reduced parental anxiety about their children's deafness. However, empirical evaluations of language as well as social and educational outcomes apparently have not been undertaken.

For families that have decided to use sign language with their children, programs such as the SKI*HI deaf mentor program have shown positive effects on parent and child communication. Watkins et al. (1998), for example, compared outcomes for a group of 18 families receiving services from a deaf adult (who provided sign language instruction and experience as well as information about hearing loss and the deaf community) and another group of 18 families who received weekly intervention visits but without the deaf mentor. Children whose families worked with the deaf mentor showed faster rates of language growth (including vocabulary and English syntax) than those in the comparison group. Further, parents who worked with the deaf mentor were more knowledgeable about aspects of deaf culture and became more proficient users of both American Sign Language (ASL) and Signed English (see chapter 5) than those who did not.

A similar finding was reported by Delk and Weidekamp (2001), who evaluated a program in which specially trained deaf adults demonstrated book sharing for hearing parents. In response to a questionnaire, participating parents reported increases in use of sign language and in satisfaction with interactions around books with their children. None of the above studies involved direct assessment of children's skills following intervention, but experiences that increase parents' confidence and feelings of competence in communicating with their child with a hearing loss generally have shown positive effects on their interactions and the child's language development. This has been reported for families who have chosen to use only spoken language (DesJardin, 2006) as well as those using signs (Meadow-Orlans et al., 2004).

SUMMARY: EARLY IDENTIFICATION AND INTERVENTION ARE COST-EFFECTIVE

A variety of studies, most of which are based on correlational approaches or quasi-experimental group comparisons, indicate that early versus later identification of hearing loss and the provision of early intervention services generally provide a host of developmental advantages. Whether there is an exact age of identification that is critical is still unclear, but 6 months and 1 year both have been found to represent boundaries delineating ages that provide significant boosts in development. Further analyses have failed to find an earlier age (e.g., 2 months, 4 months) that results in another significant boundary related to outcome benefits. Early identification and intervention are not developmental panaceas, however, as research continues to show that language performance of early-identified children overlaps with but does not match typical performance of hearing children. Effectiveness of interventions provided may interact with age at diagnosis and cognitive development in ways not yet fully understood.

Several major questions thus remain with regard to early identification of and intervention for hearing loss relevant to educational outcomes as well as personal and social-emotional growth:

- Is there a "critical age" during the first year of life before which diagnosis needs to occur and intervention needs to begin to optimally support the development of deaf and hard-of-hearing children?
- Why does the average development of deaf and hard-of-hearing children continue to lag that of typical hearing children even in the case of early identification and intervention?
- What are the specific characteristics of intervention procedures that will optimally support the children's development and how might these characteristics interact with those of families and children?
- What are best approaches to protocols for identifying children whose hearing loss develops during infancy but after the neonatal period, and

how, if at all, do intervention efforts need to differ from those for families who receive their child's diagnosis during the neonatal period?

None of the above questions should be taken to minimize the importance and potential benefits of early identification and intervention. All of them, however, are in need of answers, and the sooner the better. Key in this research effort will be longitudinal and cross-sectional studies examining developmental and educational outcomes of children whose hearing losses were identified early and/or who received early intervention relative to those who did not. Such findings will need to be considered in the context of various developmental domains, and these are addressed in the following chapters.

5 Language Development, Languages, and Language Systems

Age-appropriate language development is often taken as a given when regular education programs for hearing children are considered (with special attention, of course, paid to children for whom either organic or environmental differences cause delays), but language acquisition has long been recognized as the central difficulty facing most deaf and hard-of-hearing children (Marschark et al., 2002; Moores, 2001). Deaf children born into deaf families that use sign language develop that language at a rate roughly equivalent to hearing children, although that group (in the United States) comprises less than 10% of deaf children (Mitchell & Karchmer, in press).

Unlike the issues of early identification and intervention, questions about the choice and implementation of methods for supporting the language development of deaf and hard-of-hearing children continue to be hotly, even emotionally, debated. It is generally agreed, however, that if children with hearing loss are not provided rich visual language models that they can process or provided with special programming and assistive listening devices that allow effective access to auditory-based language input, they can reach pre-school and even the primary school years with severely impoverished (if any) language skills (Moores, 2001). And although early identification and intervention are known to be able to lessen those delays, they still do not provide a "level playing field," as most children with hearing loss have continued to reach pre-school age with significant language delays (e.g., Meadow-Orlans, Mertens, & Sass-Lehrer, 2003; Marschark & Wauters, 2008).

Delays and relative deficits in language affect social-emotional, cognitive, and academic growth and outcomes in a number of ways. To the extent that children's communication with parents, peers, and other adults is limited, development in these children of social skills and abilities—and potentially self-esteem and identity—will be negatively affected (Greenberg & Kusché, 1998; Vaccari & Marschark, 1997). Access to information and opportunities to learn about and from others also will be limited (Carney & Moeller, 1998). This limitation is thought to have negative impact on acquisition of such skills as vocabulary, syntax, and the accrual of basic knowledge that are typically gained from "overhearing" conversations and interactions occurring in the environment. Cognitive growth also will be affected if a student lacks sufficient language sophistication to allow "thinking about" learning (i.e., metacognition), organizing and coding of information to support memory, inferencing, and the drawing of logical conclusions based on understanding nuance (Marschark & Hauser, 2008).

Delays or deficits in the language being used in a classroom further limit the academic experiences of these children in that they complicate the teacher's job of communicating information to students, as well as the student's job as a learner. When communication is a struggle, the student must expend energy and attention on communicating that might otherwise be devoted to acquiring information, concepts, and skills. A connection therefore can be made, at least theoretically, between the language development challenges faced by most deaf and hard-of-hearing children and the poor literacy and academic achievement levels that continue to be reported (Marschark & Hauser, 2008; Martin, Craft, & Sheng, 2001).

Recognizing the critical role of language skills in learning as well as socialization, language development has traditionally been the major focus of most programs for deaf and hard-of-hearing children—sometimes to the exclusion of attention to content areas such as social studies, science, and mathematics (Moores, 2001). Yet, despite the development of numerous approaches to support language development and recent advances accruing from early intervention, the use of more effective amplification devices, and greater appreciation for the early use of signed languages, language growth in most deaf and hard-of-hearing children remains problematic. These new developments are resulting in significant progress, but the long-standing debate regarding the best way to support language development of deaf and hard-of-hearing children continues.

This fruitless argument usually centers on the extent to which the primary goal should be acquisition of the spoken vernacular versus an emphasis on acquisition of a fully functional language system regardless of the sensory modality in which it is received and expressed.

Programming alternatives aimed at fostering the language development of deaf and hard-of-hearing children usually are compared along a continuum that ranges from depending solely on auditory input to solely on visual input. Throughout the following review, however, it will be useful to keep in mind Hauser and Marschark's (2008) warning that "our convenient division between individuals who use spoken language and those who use sign language is largely a fiction. Regardless of the hearing status of their parents, their hearing thresholds, and their educational placements, most deaf students are exposed to both language modalities [and] hard-of-hearing students are in a similar situation" (p. 450).

PERSPECTIVES ON LANGUAGE DEVELOPMENT AND DEAF CHILDREN

Approaches to language development in deaf children, that are typically referred to as "oral" or "auditory-oral," focus on promoting production and understanding of spoken language and minimize, to various degrees, visual support for language.[1] Types of oral education (see Beattie, 2006, for a review) include auditory-verbal methods, which aim to build attention to and understanding of language solely via hearing or audition (e.g., Eriks-Brophy, 2004; Hogan et al., 2008), as well as traditional oral methods that include an emphasis on using visual information provided by context and lip/speechreading along with auditory information. A method called natural auralism stresses learning to use audition in naturally occurring interactions instead of through a more structured approach for building spoken language skills (Groht, 1958; Lewis, 1996). The maternal reflective method (van Uden, 1977; Watson, 1998) combines the use of written text with oral methods while stressing a naturally occurring conversational approach. Cued speech (Leybaert, Aparicio, & Alegria, in press) is also considered an essentially oral method even though it uses visual signals presented through specific hand shapes produced in specific locations to represent

---

[1] "Oral" is a misnomer because spoken language involves more than just the mouth, just as "manual" is overly restrictive with regard to sign languages. Because both terms are in common usage, we will use them occasionally here.

auditory phonemes (i.e., language sounds) to supplement and disambiguate information available from lipreading and residual hearing.

"Manual" or sign-based education approaches (Fischer, 1998; Mayer & Akamatsu, 1999) have been prevalent in deaf education settings since their resurgence in the 1970s. Types of signed communication within this general approach include natural sign *languages* and "artificial" or created sign *systems*. Examples of natural sign languages are American Sign Language (ASL), British Sign Language (BSL), and Australian Sign Language (Auslan), which are primarily based on production and processing of visual symbols and which developed, in general, without input from the spoken language of the surrounding culture. "Artificial" or created sign systems include Signed English (e.g., Anthony, 1972; Bornstein, Saulnier, & Hamilton, 1980; Gustason, Pfetzing, & Zawolokow, 1980) and Signed French. In these systems, signs are produced to match the word order of the local spoken language and are usually produced in conjunction with spoken language. Created signs or fingerspelling may be used to represent grammatical meanings in a linear fashion to match the way they occur in the spoken language. Fingerspelling involves production of hand shapes that represent the individual letters of written language and are used to "spell out" words or meaning units. Fingerspelling is used quite frequently in ASL, for example, to represent English words for which there are no generally agreed-upon signs, but it is used less often by deaf persons in other countries (Padden & Gunsals, 2003). American deaf mothers have been noted to use fingerspelling occasionally with even very young (pre-literate) children, and some researchers have suggested that it can provide a bridge to understanding print (Padden, 2006; Puente, Alvarado, & Herrera, 2006; but see Mayer & Wells, 1996).

Forms intermediate between the natural sign languages and the created systems have developed, in part due to interactions between deaf adults and hearing adults who are late learners of sign language. Such intermediate forms (called "contact signing" by Lucas & Valli, 1992) are often used by hearing parents and professionals, but their efficacy as a basis for literacy skills and learning has been questioned theoretically (e.g., Johnson, Liddell, & Erting, 1989) because they do not fully represent the lexicon or grammar of either the spoken language of the hearing culture or the sign language of the corresponding deaf culture. Contact signing typically includes some but not all of the non-manual meaning units (such as specialized facial expressions) of natural sign language and omits many of the grammatical morphemes expressed in the spoken language.

At this juncture, it is necessary to point out a "disconnect" implicit in the preceding paragraphs. We described "oral" approaches to language acquisition by deaf children which involve intensive instruction and drill aimed at providing the child with spoken language skills (hence frequent references to "speech therapy" in the field). Signed communication, in contrast, was mentioned in terms of education and classroom instruction, even if earlier we described its importance for all aspects of development. It may well be that this difference in focus, and the lack of intensive sign language instruction for deaf children in particular, is part of the reason that sign language–based education (including sign/bilingual programs, described later in this chapter) has been less successful than its proponents (and we) have expected. Sign language cannot be an optimal language of instruction if 95% of deaf children enter the classroom lacking age-appropriate fluency.

The following sections address approaches to language development that are currently in common use across programming for children with hearing loss. In each case, findings available about the rate and course of early development are presented; in some cases, implications for both literacy and learning in other educational domains are mentioned. (More detailed discussion of literacy skills is provided in chapter 6.) In the discussions that follow, it is important to note that research in the latter part of the 20th century was strongly influenced by and intensely focused on first, the reemergence of sign language and, then, the development and use of cochlear implants in children with the more severe and profound hearing losses. Unlike hearing aids, which essentially strengthen the volume or loudness of various frequencies of sound so that it may be more perceptible to wearers, cochlear implants are devices with both internally and externally worn components that use sophisticated information-processing software to transform signals originating from auditory stimuli into electrical signals that can be processed neurally (see, e.g., Ackley & Decker, 2006). Due to the increasing focus on cochlear implants and their impact on spoken language, some non-speech-focused language methods—as well as the progress of children with lesser hearing losses—have been relatively neglected by researchers. The research summarized below concerning the current state of knowledge regarding language development in deaf and hard-of-hearing children therefore will include a range of publication dates, and the quantity of recent studies will vary across language approaches.

APPROACHES EMPHASIZING AUDITORY-ORAL ASPECTS OF LANGUAGE DEVELOPMENT

Proponents of the various oral methods for deaf children stress the potential social, linguistic, and academic benefits children gain by being able to comprehend and produce the surrounding culture's language. The primary goal of an oral approach is to build speech perception, production, and general spoken language skills. In addition, spoken language is thought by many (e.g., Mayer & Wells, 1996; Perfetti & Sandak, 2000) to provide an optimal basis for acquisition of literacy skills in that children are expected to make the transition to reading and writing more easily if they are able to move directly from spoken to printed forms of the same language. Given that most young hearing children apply phonological (letter sound) knowledge as a major way to decode print, it is assumed that a thorough grounding in the phonology of the spoken language will enhance deaf and hard-of-hearing children's acquisition of literacy skills. For children using cochlear implants (i.e., with severe or profound hearing losses), oral programming outcomes tend to be improved compared to children with similar hearing levels who are using only hearing aids (e.g., Blamey & Sarant, in press; Geers, 2006). However, significant variability in outcomes remains.

Auditory-Oral Methods and Language Development

Historically, some children make age-appropriate progress using oral approaches to language development (with no one particular approach favored); however, even proponents note that many, if not most, of these children have failed to keep pace with their hearing peers (see Spencer & Marschark, 2006, for reviews). Even when children have mild to severe hearing losses (and thus most frequently attend oral programs), the risk for speech and language delays is higher than typical for hearing children (e.g., Elfenbein, Hardin-Jones, & Davis, 1994; Goldberg & Richburg, 2004; Moeller, Hoover et al., 2007a, 2007b; Nicholas & Geers, 1997). Children with profound hearing losses participating in oral programs were reported as recently as the turn of the 21st century to develop spoken language at only 50% of the rate of hearing children, with average delays of up to 5 years at high school age (Blamey et al., 2001; Boothroyd, Geers, & Moog, 1991), even when cochlear implants were used. Deficits have been noted in a wide range of language development, including phonology, vocabulary, syntax, and morphology (e.g., Griswold & Commings, 1974; Moeller, Osberger, & Eccarius, 1986). Delays have been traced back to the initial stages in acquisition of language and are evident in differences in the frequency and the age of emergence of vocal babbling (Oller, 2000, 2006) as well as in production of first words. These differences continue to be reported, although they are typically less pronounced in young children who have received cochlear implants early in life (Dettman & Dowell, 2010; Nicholas & Geers, 2007, 2008) and in children who have early-identified hearing losses in the moderate to severe range and who receive early intervention services (Moeller, Tomblin, et al., 2007).

Differences also have been noted for children in oral programs compared to hearing children in the emergence of pragmatics, or the functions for which communication is used, during the pre-linguistic and early language stages. Lichtert and Loncke (2006), Nicholas (1994), and Nicholas and Geers (1997) all reported that pre-school children in oral programming rarely expressed a heuristic or "information sharing" function in their communications. Although this pattern differs from that of same-age hearing children, the difference is not limited to deaf and hard-of-hearing children in oral programs. It may simply reflect delayed language level, as opposed to modality of communication (cf. Day, 1986), but there is insufficient evidence at this point to be sure (see Marschark, Sarchet, Rhoten, & Zupan, 2010, for findings from older students).

Nicholas and Geers (1997) found that at around 3 years of age, when the hearing children in their study were using spoken language consistently, deaf children in oral programming continued to use frequent pre-linguistic vocalizations and gestures. These children, whose hearing loss had been diagnosed on average at 12 months of age, were said to use speech in only a minority of their expressive communications (about one-third of the time). Most speech productions were imitations and not spontaneous communications. Importantly, the deaf children's use of speech at age 3, especially to make comments as opposed to requesting or directing others, predicted their spoken language skills at 5 years of age. Early delays, therefore, tended to be predictive of later language achievement levels. Their tendencies to use gesture at age 3, in contrast, failed to predict language levels at 5 years.

Cochlear Implants and Progress in Oral Programs

Nicholas (1994) noted that the tendency to use speech communicatively, that is, speech *production*, is associated with speech *perception* abilities, so it might be expected that children with earlier diagnoses and use of advanced amplification or cochlear implants would show more rapid spoken language development. The literature on language development of children using cochlear implants provides useful information on the relation of audition and language, because it provides evidence of spoken language development when auditory or auditory-like information is increased.

In a comprehensive review of the relevant literature, Geers (2006) reported that use of cochlear implants, especially with the more sophisticated implant technology recently developed, has significantly increased the average rate of language development and the average rate of speech development among profoundly deaf children in oral programming compared to that of their peers who use hearing aids. Evidence of increased success in promoting spoken language with cochlear implants also is evident in reports of child-led changes in the language modality used in parent-child communications after implantation, from signing to speech (Watson, Archbold, & Nikolopoulos, 2006; Watson, Hardie, Archbold, & Wheeler, 2007; Yoshinaga-Itano, 2006).

Even when cochlear implants were unavailable until ages now considered to be late—that is, ages 3 to about 5 years and older—Geers and Moog (1994) found advantages for children using implants compared to those using hearing aids on expressive vocabulary, receptive syntax, and measures of speech production. These and associated language and speech benefits generally have been found to increase as the age at which cochlear implants are first used decreases, regardless of the type of language programming (oral or signing) in which children are participating (e.g., Connor et al., 2000; Dettman et al., 2007; Fryauf-Bertschy et al., 1997; Holt and Svirsky, 2008; Schorr, Roth, & Fox, 2008; Spencer, 2004). However, most of these same (and other) investigators report that even with early implantation, language abilities remain on average below those of hearing peers (e.g., Chin, Tsai, & Gao, 2003; Geers, 2002; Holt & Svirsky, 2008; Schorr et al., 2008; Spencer, 2004). Schorr et al., for example, pointed out that the 5- to 14-year-old children in their study, whose performance was compared to that of an age-matched group of hearing children, were significantly delayed in morphology and syntax, on average, even though they did not show an overall delay in speech articulation skills. Only 13% of the children with cochlear implants scored within the age-appropriate range on tests involving the understanding of idioms and figurative or non-literal spoken language. The children also demonstrated deficits of auditory working memory (see also Pisoni et al., 2008).

In contrast with these reported delays, several researchers have presented evidence that children who receive cochlear implants before 2 years of age and participate in either traditional oral programs or auditory-verbal programs can develop spoken language abilities by the age of 4.5 years (prekindergarten age) at levels within the typical range documented for hearing children (e.g., Nicholas and Geers, 2007, 2008; Svirsky, Teoh, & Neuburger, 2004). Nicholas and Geers (2007), for example, examined vocabulary and syntax skills in a group of 78 children who had received cochlear implants by age 3. They found that an earlier age of implantation benefited vocabulary growth and two aspects of syntax: understanding of bound grammatical morphemes (or meaning units) and mean length of utterances measured by the number of morphemes produced. These benefits were evident for children who were in oral programming, but only those who had at least average nonverbal cognitive skills and did not have any developmental or medical disabilities. Children who met these criteria and had received their implants by 12 months of age achieved higher language levels at 3.5 years than children who received the implants between 12 and 18 months (after duration of implant use was controlled). Children who began using cochlear implants at or around 2 years of age did not catch up with hearing children's age-level expectations for language development by 4.5 years of age, but the younger-at-implantation groups did so.

Some researchers have not found initial bursts of growth in language skills to be maintained at the same rate as time beyond implantation lengthens (e.g., El-Hakim et al., 2001; Geers, 2005); therefore, it is unclear whether the advantages found by Nicholas and Geers (2007) will continue at older ages (see also Marschark et al., 2010). Nicholas and Geers also warned that the measures they used do not encompass all of the aspects of language skill and "may not fully reflect normal language development" (2007, p. 1058). Furthermore, there is contradictory evidence from other researchers as to whether implantation by 1 year of age provides significantly more benefit to development of spoken language than does implantation between 1 and 2 years of age. For example, Dettman et al. (2007) found an advantage for implantation before one year, but Holt and Svirsky (2008) and Duchesne, Sutton, and Bergeron (2009) did not. Nevertheless, the findings of Nicholas and Geers suggest that more children with severe and profound hearing loss may be able to progress through early stages of spoken language development at typical or near-typical rates if they receive early implantation and intensive intervention.

Consistent with results of Nicholas and Geers (2007), other researchers have found that development of speech and spoken language skills after cochlear implantation are related to the degree of aided hearing prior to receiving the cochlear implant: Better hearing before implantation was associated with better language after implantation (e.g., Svirsky, Robbins, Kirk, Pisoni, & Miyamoto, 2000). Across studies, factors such as nonverbal cognitive abilities and parent education or socioeconomic status also have been found to correlate with and predict later spoken language functioning of children, regardless of their type of language programming (Spencer et al., in press). In many cases, including the studies by Nicholas and Geers, only children with nonverbal cognitive functioning in at least the low-average range have been included. Geers (2002), in an analysis of 181 children (ages 8–9) using cochlear implants, showed a small but significant effect of communication mode on spoken language and literacy outcomes, with children in traditional oral (or in auditory-verbal) programs doing better than those in which combined or simultaneous speech and sign (SimCom) was used. Other researchers (e.g., Connor, Hieber, Arts, & Zwolan, 2000), however, have documented an opposite effect, and studies involving Geers's sample generally have not found earlier implantation to be facilitative for literacy.

It seems that the best outcomes of oral education, whether or not cochlear implants are used, are obtained when there is a consistent emphasis on the oral approach, when effective amplification is obtained early in life and used consistently, when early intervention and education is provided, and when there is strong parent support for both the language approach chosen and for their children's language development (e.g., Beattie, 2006; Geers & Moog, 1992; see also Geers, 2002). The studies reviewed above also indicate that nonverbal cognitive skills, the level of aided hearing that is available to the child, general resources of the parents, and the absence of disabilities beyond hearing loss are important predictors of successful spoken language development in oral programs. Beattie (2006) noted, however, that the quality of the language and educational program provided, and not only the particular language approach used, influences outcomes in oral programming.

An Example: Outcomes of Children in a Traditional Oral Program

One well-structured curriculum approach that can provide an example of contemporary oral programming has been described in a qualitative report by Wilkins and Ertmer (2002). In discussing their private, non-profit oral school in the United States, they defined their approach to language development as including "auditory information...supplemented by visual and tactile cues" (p. 198), especially during the early stages of language development. The visual information referred to included lip/speechreading, attending to facial expressions, and other visual cues that are implicitly part of the language reception process of hearing children and adults. This approach, beginning as multisensory (although never with the use of signed language) but with gradually decreasing input from vision and tactile senses as spoken language skills build, has a venerable history and has perhaps been most systematically presented in the EPIC (Experimental Project in Instructional Concentration) curriculum described by Moog and Geers (1985). EPIC includes attention to and monitoring of amplification devices (hearing aids or cochlear implants) and individualized but tightly sequenced goals for spoken language skills. Assessment instruments have been developed to track student progress, and results are used to define continuing goals. Vocabulary, morphology, and syntax are taught through direct instruction, with interactive conversational activities used for practice, while a modeling and repetition approach is used in structured sessions. Group sessions typically have a low student-to-teacher ratio (e.g., four to six students per teacher in the program described by Wilkins and Ertmer) and often use ability grouping based on language skills.

Appropriate placement in the program described by Wilkins and Ertmer (2002) is said to depend upon a careful assessment of potential for success in the program, which skews any outcome assessments, but by design. Variables considered in that assessment are nonverbal cognitive functioning (and lack of disabilities other than hearing loss), parents' support for and children's dependence upon spoken language at home as well as at school, aspects of child behavioral functioning such as attention and distractibility, and initial results on communication and language measures. In this particular program, a trial period initiates enrollment, and recommendations for continuing in the program, changing communication modality (and thus program), or moving to a mainstream program are made after a 6-month period. In addition to the focus on language development, the program includes activity-based work in early literacy and quantitative concepts.

Wilkins and Ertmer reported that of the first 60 students who entered the program, seven children later transferred to a different school using a "total communication" approach (sign accompanied by speech and amplification; see below). These transfers indicate that some of the children were not deemed to be successfully acquiring spoken language, even given apparently optimal oral programming. Research comparing groups of children as well as qualitative case studies thus indicates that oral approaches to language development can support adequate language development by some but not all children with hearing loss, even given technological advances and early identification.

Auditory-Verbal Therapy

The approach referred to as auditory-verbal therapy (AVT, Estabrooks, 1998) is similar to an approach called acoupedics or unisensory (Pollack, 1964; Pollack, Goldberg, & Coleffe-Schenk, 1997). Although AVT is one of the methods subsumed under the "oral education" umbrella, it is addressed separately here because there has been a resurgence of interest in its use since the advent of enhanced hearing aid technology, cochlear implants, and higher expectations resulting from early identification of hearing loss. It differs from traditional oral approaches discussed above in decreased attention to visual accompaniments of auditory input such as speechreading, that is, lipreading (Beattie, 2006; Hogan et al., 2008; Wilkins & Ertmer, 2002).

AVT is a therapeutic approach that typically is conducted by highly trained specialists working with children during the pre-school years (Eriks-Brophy, 2004). Parents are expected to reinforce AVT programming techniques at home, and a major goal is for children to acquire spoken language skills appropriate for their chronological age by the time they begin traditional schooling at age 5 or 6 years (Eriks-Brophy, 2004; Rhoades, 2001, 2006). AVT therefore is not a general classroom practice but instead is expected to prepare deaf and hard-of-hearing children to participate in general education classrooms. If AVT is continued through school ages, it is usually provided in "pull out" sessions or clinical settings.

Much written material is available about conducting AVT (e.g., Estabrooks, 1994, 1998), but only recently have measures of its outcomes been available. Both Eriks-Brophy (2004) and Rhoades (2006) undertook reviews of available evidence and concluded that although there is case study and descriptive-level support for the approach, no existing studies have employed designs rigorous enough to produce evidence-based judgments of effectiveness (see chapter 3).

In a descriptive study, Duncan (1999) found that pre-school-age children in AVT were able to engage in appropriate conversational turn-taking, but that their contributions tended to be shorter and had linguistic content less frequently than those of hearing peers. Duncan and Rochecouste (1999) also found evidence of delay in children in AVT compared to hearing peers on expressive spoken utterance length and use of grammatical morphemes. The deaf and hard-of-hearing children were acquiring English grammatical forms but at a slower rate than is typical for hearing children. Overall, they performed at about 1 year below expectations for their chronological age.

Rhoades (Rhoades, 2001; Rhoades & Chisholm, 2000) administered three standardized language tests (Pre-school Language Scale-3, Sequenced Inventory of Communication Development, Oral-Written Language Scale) to 40 children, ages 50 to 120 months, who participated in AVT for 1 to 4 years; 27 of the participants used cochlear implants. The results of repeated testing showed increasing scores with age and length of time in the program on all of the measures. "Some" of the children were reported to have attained a 100% rate of language growth, that is, their scores advanced the equivalent of 1 year of language growth with 1 year of chronological age. Receptive language generally grew fastest in the first 2 years of programming, followed by growth in expressive language skills, including use of grammatical morphemes and syntax. Interestingly, approximately three-fourths of the participating children in the Rhoades (2001) study were diagnosed to have either or both sensory integration or oral-motor coordination problems, and 30% of the children did not continue use of AVT. Although there was no control or comparison group, these findings indicate that, at least in some cases, spoken language progress is made by deaf and hard-of-hearing children in AVT at rates similar to that of hearing peers. The large dropout rate, however, suggests that significant numbers of children and their families failed to experience success in AVT programming.

In a short-term longitudinal study, Hogan et al. (2008) documented the rate of change in spoken language skills of 37 children in England who participated in AVT in addition to programming provided by their local educational agency. Their parents were highly motivated to participate in AVT and some traveled considerable distances to attend therapy sessions. Twenty-two of the children had profound hearing losses, 10 had severe losses, and 5 had moderate losses. When data collection began, 5 of the children were using cochlear implants, and during the course of the study, an additional 18 children obtained implants. Children's spoken language skills were repeatedly assessed, at program entry and then at intervals of at least 6 months, on the U.K. version of the Pre-school Language Scale-3. Growth over time was plotted, and the ratio of language-age (i.e., age equivalent scores on the language scale) and chronological age was determined at each testing time. That ratio was termed the "rate of language development" or RLD.

Hogan et al. compared RLDs before AVT intervention to rates observed after at least 1 year of participation. An RLD equal to 1.0 would show language growth equal to change in chronological age. In fact, 34 of the children had an RLD less than 1.0 at initial testing, and 11 still had an RLD of less than 1.0 at the end of the study. This result indicates that language growth rates of the majority of children accelerated during the AVT program and were as fast as or faster than expected for hearing children. (But note that because AVT programming was not begun at birth, the children began the program with delayed language, and it would require an RLD beyond the average rate of hearing children for them to catch up with age expectations.) Interestingly, children who switched from using hearing aids to cochlear implants during the study showed two periods of acceleration, with one occurring when therapy was initiated and another after the cochlear implant was obtained. Overall, 23 of the 37 children in the study showed RLDs greater than would have been predicted by their performance levels before AVT was started. Twenty of the children, approximately one-half of the participants in AVT, had language test scores that were within the 90% confidence band of scores expected for chronological age at the end of the study. Some of those who did not achieve at this high level had been identified to have additional disabilities. At 5 years of age, 30 of the participants were in mainstreamed educational placements, 6 were in regular schools but had additional assistance through a resource unit, and 1 was attending a special oral school.

Hogan et al. (2008) pointed out that their study did not compare results from AVT with those of any other specific type of intervention program, and outcomes are potentially confounded because the children were simultaneously receiving other services from their local agencies. The researchers also noted that parent involvement with AVT in their sample was strong—a factor that also has been shown to predict successful language development using other approaches (e.g., traditional oral, sign; Moeller, 2000; Spencer, 2004). In addition, there are some questions about the validity of interpretations of the RLD as it was used in the study, in that a statistical assumption was made that growth will be linear. In fact, rates of growth tend to change over time for most children.

Taken as a whole, the above studies indicate that AVT is a viable approach for some but not all deaf and hard-of-hearing children whose families choose to emphasize spoken language development and do not want to use sign language or signing systems to support their growth. AVT seems to be most successful for children from fairly highly educated families that remain intensely involved with the training approach and who have high expectations for spoken language development. In addition, children without any learning challenges beyond hearing loss seem to have a greater chance of success using AVT. Increases in auditory input from cochlear implants also appear to enhance the positive effects of AVT. Despite reports of children who acquire spoken language at near-typical rates, however, many children in AVT programming do not do so. Hogan et al. concluded that AVT is among the viable choices, but certainly not the only one available to families based upon their own goals for their children.

Cued Speech

Cued speech was developed by Orin Cornett (1967) to provide deaf and hard-of-hearing children access to the phonology of spoken language denied by their hearing loss and thus to promote acquisition of literacy skills. (He assumed that natural sign languages would continue to be used for classroom and social communication and that cued speech would be a specialized intervention employed much like AVT.) Recognizing that only about 20% to 30% of the sounds of English can be reliably determined from watching the lips, Cornett developed a set of manual signals differing in hand shape and in the location of production that would effectively supplement and disambiguate information available from observing lip shape and movement. Unlike sign language or sign systems (see below), cued speech signals represent auditory-based phonemes (sounds) and not semantic characteristics or meanings. Cued speech is meant to be produced concomitantly with spoken language and understanding it requires the "listener" to integrate information from the manual cues with lipreading and auditory information available from speech. Together, these indicate a single, unambiguous "phonological percept" (or, linguistically significant speech sound) that cannot be obtained from any one source alone (Hage & Leybaert, 2006, p. 195). One would expect that the advent of improved hearing aids, earlier intervention, and early use of cochlear implants would increase interest in the cued speech method by providing deaf and hard-of-hearing children generally enhanced but imperfect auditory information. However, there are surprisingly few recent peer-reviewed research reports on its use with spoken English.

Modifications or additions have been made to cued speech signals to accommodate at least 56 different spoken languages and major dialects (Cornett, 1994), and relatively recent data are available from children learning French and Spanish (LaSasso, Crain, & Leybaert, 2010). Researchers in Canada and Belgium have reported gains in speech perception at the syllable, word, and simple sentence level for children using cued English and cued French (Nicholls & Ling, 1982; Perier, Charlier, Hage, & Alegria, 1988). For children in environments consistently emphasizing cuing from an early age, these gains are larger than those typical for perception based on audition and speechreading alone. Kipila (1985) also reported gains from use of cued speech in the rate of acquisition of American English morphology, typically an area of special difficulty for deaf and hard-of-hearing children. In a single case study of a child whose family used cued speech from 18 months of age, Kipila documented 100% correct use by about age 5 of the grammatical morphemes typically learned earliest by hearing children (present progressive, plural, irregular past tense, possessive, uncontractable copula, and prepositions "in" and "on"). Although this child's acquisition process was delayed compared to that of hearing children, it was accelerated compared to that typically reported for contemporaneous groups of deaf children in oral programming in which cuing was not used.

Similarly advanced morphemic knowledge has been reported in a single case study of a child whose parents consistently used cued French with him from the age of 11 months (Perier, Bochner-Wuidar, Everarts, Michiels, & Hage, 1986, cited in Hage & Leybaert, 2006), and in a larger study in which 27 students, tested at ages ranging from 8 to 20 years, in cued French programs were compared to

41 other deaf and hard-of-hearing students who had roughly equivalent levels of parent involvement and program intensity (Hage, Alegria, & Perier, 1991). The cued speech group in the latter study showed higher scores on print measures of vocabulary, prepositions, and grammatical gender—although only the preposition contrast reached statistical significance. Increased age was associated with knowledge of grammatical gender in the group from oral programs, but students in this group were surpassed by the cued speech users, who achieved near-ceiling levels by the age of about 11 years. Hage and Leybaert (2006) concluded that increased phonological knowledge gained from use of cued speech led to this advantage.

Use of prepositions in Spanish was studied by Hernandez, Monreal, and Orza (2003), who compared deaf children using cued Spanish, deaf children in traditional oral programs, deaf children using Spanish Sign Language, and a group of hearing children. Statements were presented in written form and children were to choose a preposition from among several choices to correctly fill in a blank to make the sentence represent a pictorial representation provided with each item. The average age of the 35 deaf children was 11–12 years and that of the 17 hearing children was 8–9 years. Most of the children in cued speech programs had been in traditional oral programs until age 3 years. Despite their late start with cued speech, the average percentage correct for that group (88%) came close to matching that of the hearing group (93%). Both groups scored significantly higher than children in the sign language and traditional oral groups, who averaged only between 57% and 61% correct and did not differ significantly from each other. Hernandez et al. concluded that the combination of visual cues from cued speech and speechreading made these small but important Spanish grammatical morphemes perceptually salient for deaf children and thus allowed them to develop higher levels of competence. The cued speech participants were considerably older than the hearing students (3–4 years on average), however, and therefore the performance of the cued speech group actually represented delayed development.

Bowey and Francis (1991) proposed that rhyming allows children to form sound-based categories of words and later make connections between these categories and printed forms, and several researchers have specifically investigated rhyming skills of cued speech users. LaSasso, Crain, and Leybeart (2003), for example, showed that deaf college students who had experience with cued speech before the age of 5 were more likely than deaf non-cuers to attend to auditory rather than orthographic or speechreading representations when supplying rhymes for a written list of words.

Leybaert and Charlier (1996) reported on a series of studies investigating the degree to which visual information from cued speech can promote development of French phonological representations that typically emerge primarily from audition. They noted that previous investigators had found that deaf children were able to identify rhymes when lip shapes were the same or when rhyming words have similar spellings (e.g., Campbell & Wright, 1988; Dodd & Hermelin, 1977). Thus, deaf children in the earlier studies tended to base their understanding of rhyme on visual information. Leybaert and Charlier (1996) compared groups of school-age deaf children who used cued speech at home and at school or only at school, with groups that used sign language at home and school or only at school, and with hearing children. The average age across groups was 11 to 12 years. Among the deaf groups, children with home plus school exposure to cued speech showed less reliance than the other groups on lip shape and orthography (printed letters) when identifying rhyming words. That is, those children had apparently internalized and generalized phonological knowledge based upon their experience with the combined lip shape/cued speech signals (and perhaps partial audition) of spoken words.

In an additional analysis, Leybaert and Charlier (1996) used pictures instead of written stimuli and included a group of oral-only deaf children and a group of deaf children who were native users of sign language. They found that both the oral and sign language groups, as well as a group of late users of cued speech, tended to depend on patterns of spelling similarities to identify rhyming words. In contrast, the early users of cued speech performed like hearing children and were more likely to base their rhyme judgments on the sound patterns or phonology of the pictured item's labels. In a study of pre-school-age deaf children, Leybaert and Charlier found that even children who did not yet have reading skills, but had both at-home and at-school exposure to cued speech, were able to understand the idea of rhyme as well as hearing children did. The researchers concluded that the deaf children with extensive cued speech exposure were able to develop phonological concepts even before reading skills had been acquired and that such concepts were, therefore, not merely a reflection of reading experience.

Early and intensive exposure to cued speech may be critical if children are to obtain significant benefits from it. In addition to the above discussion of rhyming, Leybaert and Charlier (1996) reported that children with early home plus school exposure to cued speech, unlike their peers with lesser experience, made spelling errors based on phonological rules much as hearing children do. This is additional evidence of an amodal, internal phonology and of the potential for visual input (accompanied by some auditory input for most children) to support development of auditory phonological rules. Nevertheless, as with conclusions about the viability of traditional oral and auditory-verbal methods for supporting language and literacy development, positive outcomes of use of cued speech seem to depend upon early experience and a great deal of parent motivation and support. Cued speech may be easier for hearing parents to acquire than a natural sign language (LaSasso & Metzger, 1998; Strong, 1988), and some case studies have documented rich parental cued speech input to toddlers and pre-schoolers (e.g., Kipala, 1985; Perier et al., 1986; Torres, Moreno-Torres, & Santana, 2006), but there are no studies directly comparing parents' acquisition and use of the various visually based systems.

In an early study, Nash (1973) pointed out that cued speech requires relatively fine motor movements and production of hand shapes in locations that may not be visible to the person who is cueing. Indeed, there are contradictory reports about young children's ability to use cued speech expressively, and all of these reports are of individual or small group case studies. This issue is important because it is generally accepted that sharing a communication system with parents provides interactive and linguistic experiences needed to support language development, especially cognitive aspects of later language development. Nash (1973), Spencer (2000a), and Mohay (1983) all reported cases in which deaf children with extensive exposure to cued speech failed to use it in their own communications. Both Nash and Spencer reported that the children's hearing parents then turned to use of signs, which the children learned to use expressively with ease. In contrast, Cornett (1973) described one child whose first cued speech exposure was at 8 months of age as having an expressive cued vocabulary of 300 words by 2 years of age. Similarly, Moseley, Scott-Williams, and Anthony (1991) presented a case study of an almost 4-year-old child who used extensive cues expressively, producing age-appropriate English syntactic morphemes and vocabulary, and engaging in appropriate turn-taking and initiation and response patterns in cued speech interactions. In discussing these divergent reports, LaSasso and Metzger (1998) indicated the need for comparison studies of children using cued speech and those using sign language or signed communication. Additionally, they suggested that the conflicting reports may reflect a tendency toward a lack of emphasis on children's expressive use during the early years of implementation of cued speech programming, consistent with Cornett's (1967) early formulation of cued speech as an adjunct support for language development but not a communication system.

Using Cochlear Implants and Cued Speech

Hage and Leybaert (2006) discussed the use of cued speech with children who use cochlear implants and thus, in general, have more auditory access to spoken language than was typically the case when the system was first developed and used. This increased access often extends to some auditory awareness of grammatical morphemes and finer discrimination of phonemes, or the individual sounds in spoken language words (e.g., Spencer, Tye-Murray, & Tomblin, 1998). A number of researchers have pointed out that the signals received from cochlear implants are not as clear as those received by hearing children (e.g., Holt & Svirsky, 2008;

Pisoni, 2000; see Spencer et al., in press, for a review). This limitation is even more evident when children are in noisy environments that interfere with receipt of clear signals from the implanted devices. In at least one study, however, children using both cochlear implants and French cued speech were found to have better speech reception skills than those not using cued speech (Cochard, 2003, cited in Hage & Leybaert): The children using cued speech were found to have nearly 100% correct performance on understanding auditorally presented sentences in an open set condition (repetition of sentences as opposed to recognition in a multiple-choice format) after 5 years of cochlear implant use. This was not true for children who had not used cued speech.

A similar result was reported by Descourtieux (2003, cited in Hage & Leybaert, 2006), who found that addition of cued French signals to speechreading information increased children's understanding of spoken French. This trend was notably evident in younger children, who had received their cochlear implants before the age of 3 years. Cochard, as well as Vieu et al. (1998), also found better speech production intelligibility in children using cued French in combination with cochlear implants. Perhaps importantly, however, Hage and Leybaert noted that a potential negative effect of children using cochlear implants is that the increased auditory reception may lead children to pay less attention to the cued speech hand signals that they continue to need to obtain information about the grammatical words and morphemes that are difficult to hear.

APPROACHES EMPHASIZING VISUAL-MANUAL ASPECTS OF LANGUAGE DEVELOPMENT

The approaches to language development described above are all essentially oral methods. Their focus is on developing spoken language skills of deaf and hard-of-hearing children and basing literacy abilities directly on the use of spoken language elements, whether those elements are received auditorally or visually through speechreading and manual cues. Even with the early use of amplification and cochlear implants, the average spoken language skills of deaf and hard-of-hearing children has continued to trail levels typically expected for age. One reaction to the ongoing difficulties in language development among deaf and hard-of-hearing children using oral methods was a return to the use of manual or signed communication beginning in the 1970s. These communication approaches include what has been termed "total communication" (TC; Holcomb, 1970), that is, a combination of speech and a manual code for expression of spoken language, signing with the word order of the vernacular, and natural sign languages produced without spoken accompaniment, all depending on the needs and strengths of the individual child.

Manually Coded Sign Systems Used in Total Communication Programs

Although the language approach used in many schools since the 1960s has often been referred to as total communication, such an approach has rarely been implemented fully. The original TC philosophy assumed that a school would vary communication practices to meet the needs of individual children in individually occurring contexts (Moores, 2001). This could mean that spoken language, natural sign language, manually coded sign systems, fingerspelling, and other methods could be used at various times with different students who also took advantage of assistive listening devices. In practice, however, most so-called TC programs employ a system consisting of signs produced in the same order as spoken words and at the same time as the words are spoken. This is more accurately described as *simultaneous communication* or SimCom (Moores, 2001) or as *sign supported speech* (Johnson et al., 1989). In the United States, the United Kingdom, and Australia, such sign systems have generally been referred to as "signed English" or "manually coded English," even though several different systems have been developed to represent the grammatical morphemes that are so difficult for deaf and hard-of-hearing children learning spoken language or acquiring literacy skills.

It was never claimed that the above sign systems were natural languages themselves. Rather their use in combination with spoken language was intended to provide visual support for both signed and spoken language skills. Systems such as Seeing Essential English (SEE1, Anthony, 1971) Signing Exact English (SEE2; Gustason et al., 1980), and Signed English (SE; Bornstein, 1990) revisited traditions from France (Stokoe 1960/2005), where such approaches had been promoted by Charles Michel Abbé de l'Épée at the National Institute for Deaf-Mutes (now the National Institute for Deaf Youth) in Paris as early as the 18th century. Similar systems were developed in Australia (Australian Signed English or ASE), the Netherlands (Signed Dutch), and many other countries around the world. These systems incorporated invented signs and fingerspelling to represent grammatical morphemes indicating number, verb tense, pronouns, prepositions, and adverbials in the spoken language. Early reports showed that when hearing parents learned and used this form of sign plus spoken language with their young children, patterns of parent-child interaction improved, as did the children's ability to communicate with others (e.g., Day, 1986; Greenberg, Calderon, & Kusché, 1984; Meadow, 1980).

As use of these systems grew, researchers began to document linguistic and socio-emotional advantages for deaf children as their ability to communicate with their parents and deaf peers increased (e.g., Meadow, 1980). Because one hoped-for outcome of the use of the TC approach was to provide more accessible models of the syntax of the spoken language, a number of researchers focused on that aspect of language development. Akamatsu and Stewart (1998), Luetke-Stahlman (1988), and Maxwell and Bernstein (1985), for example, provided data which showed that the manually coded English systems used in TC programs, even when produced in a "relaxed" form in which not all English grammatical morphemes were represented, were effective communication mediums and also provided effective bases for English language development (Mayer & Akamatsu, 1999). By the 1990s, however, there was evidence from numerous descriptive studies that use of the systems was often limited by slow learning of signs by hearing parents, inaccurate productions by both parents and teachers, and difficulties experienced by hearing adults in adjusting to the timing and visual attention needs of young children who were dependent upon visual communication input (Johnson et al., 1989; Spencer, 1993a, 1993b; Spencer, Bodner-Johnson, & Gutfreund, 1992; Swisher, 1985; Swisher & Thompson, 1985; Wood et al., 1986). That is, patterns and rates of communicative turn-taking have to be altered in such systems to allow children to look back and forth between the signed message and its referent (Swisher, 2000). In addition, some researchers proposed that differences in the basic processes of visual and auditory perception could preclude effective matching of manual with spoken language, making it almost impossible to provide an accurate model of the spoken language in accompanying sign (Kluwin, 1981; Strong & Charlson, 1987; Wood, Wood, & Kingsmill, 1991). Thus the signed productions of hearing adults, parents, and teachers, have been referred to as ungrammatical—capturing the grammatical forms of neither the spoken language nor a natural sign language (Marmor & Pettito, 1979).

Other investigators (e.g., Hyde, Power, & Leigh, 1996; Maxwell & Bernstein, 1985; Wilbur & Petersen, 1998) have argued that effective models of the syntax and semantics of a spoken language (i.e., English) can be provided by signing systems, and that the ungrammaticality that has been noted is a result of poor training and expectations for teachers' use of the signed systems. Clearly there is much variation in the degree to which the spoken grammar is made visually accessible by users of manually coded language systems who have diverse signed English or SimCom skills. Luetke-Stahlman and Nielsen (2003), for example, reported that teachers' sign-to-voice ratios (that is, the proportion of language elements spoken that were also signed) in several TC programs for deaf children ranged from 76% to 99%.

Although it is evident that grammatical morphemes in spoken productions are frequently not signed by teachers or parents, Bornstein et al. (1980) found that deaf children in signed English systems did learn and produce those morphemes, albeit less consistently than hearing children and with a significantly later age of acquisition. Geers, Moog, and Schick (1984) reported similarly delayed acquisition of English articles, prepositions, and negation by children in TC programs. However, a careful descriptive study by Schick and Moeller (1992) gave both positive and negative evidence of the ability of deaf children to acquire English from manually coded English (sign/speech combined) input. They analyzed data on the English language skills of 13 adolescents attending schools in the United States whose teachers provided fluent models of SEE2 (Gustason et al., 1980). Although the study included relatively few participants, language samples were copious and analyzed in depth. Schick and Moeller (1992) found that the students' English skills were comparable to those of hearing students of the same age in the use of simple and complex sentence structures and use of embedded clauses. However, the deaf students' productions had much higher error levels on bound grammatical morphemes, such as markers for tense and number, use of auxiliaries and copulas. Schick and Moeller proposed that these latter aspects of spoken English were difficult to acquire from the use of combined sign and speech, but that overall the use of the SEE2 system provided a useful base for English acquisition.

Power, Hyde, and Leigh (2008) conducted a similar study in Australia with 45 deaf students, ranging in age from 10 to 17 years, who had extensive exposure to Australian Signed English in instructional settings. The students' teachers completed self-rating questionnaires indicating their own skills in using Signed English and their attitude toward its use. The Test of Syntactic Abilities (TSA; Quigley, Steinkamp, Power, & Jones, 1978), normed on deaf students in the United States, was administered to the Australian students. These test items are presented in written form. Two potentially interesting findings resulted. First, although Australian scores ranged from 52% to 86% correct, the scores were not associated with age, as was expected, and no significant difference was found between younger and older students. Second, the average score of 62% correct was higher than the mean reported for the U.S. norming group (56% correct). Both of these findings may be explained by trends toward earlier identification and provision of intervention services for hearing loss over the three decades between the norming of the TSA and the Australian research. In addition, the fact that the TSA normative sample included students in oral programs as well as those using signs makes it difficult to compare the Australian students' scores with the earlier American normative group.

Despite this limitation and the lack of a comparison group of hearing or of deaf students using other communication approaches, Power et al. (2008) appear to have found positive effects from students' participation in TC (or SimCom) programming. Significant correlations were found between students' scores on the TSA and teachers ratings of the students' proficiency in the Signed Australian English system. Significant correlations also were found between test performance and ratings of the students' spoken language skills and written English skills. Furthermore, analysis of written language samples showed an error rate of only 18% on common inflectional morphemes, including verb tenses, number, and possessives. This was lower than the 28% error rate on these linguistic markers reported earlier by Schick and Moeller (1992). A criterion of sentences in which 80% of the elements were represented correctly was reached by 15% of the children in both the Power et al. and the Schick and Moeller studies, and Power et al. noted that there are many points of agreement between the two studies (e.g., the relative difficulty of grammatical morphemes). Power et al. concluded that "teachers using any form of signed communication to teach English... (should) pay special attention to the more difficult structures, devising special lessons along the lines of those used by teachers of English as a second language" (2008, p. 45). They also commented that there was "no evidence in the present study that the use of SimCom adversely affects students' spoken language" (2008, p. 44). In short, results from several studies that have looked at classroom learning have indicated that in the hands of a skilled user, use of a TC approach based on signed English is as communicatively effective as other forms of signing (specifically ASL, see below) at middle school through university levels (e.g., Hyde & Power, 1992; Marschark, Sapere, Convertino, & Pelz, 2008; Newell, 1978). Similar studies have not been conducted with younger students, however.

Although the research described above focused on children's acquisition of grammar or syntax when combined sign/speech is used by teachers and parents, it is clear from studies of both hearing and deaf students that vocabulary development is a critical foundational element in the growth of language comprehension and, in turn, in the development of literacy skills (LaSasso & Davey, 1987; Paul, 1998). In a review of studies examining lexical or vocabulary development, Anderson (2006) noted that relatively few data are available about children who are learning language using a "manually coded" system of English. In an early study using a parent diary approach, Griswold and Commings (1974) found that the proportions of word types (i.e., nouns, verbs, propositions, question words) used by their small sample of deaf children (n = 12) were highly similar to those reported for young hearing children. Anderson compared the first words acquired by the children studied by Griswold and Commings with first words learned by hearing children and found that, although they were learning the words significantly later, the deaf children tended to acquire early-learned words in much the same order as hearing children.

Other investigators have reported similar findings of delayed vocabulary development by children in programs using manually coded English relative to hearing children (e.g., Bornstein, Selmi, Hayes, Painter, & Marx, 1999; Lederberg, Prezbindowski, & Spencer, 2000; Mayne, Yoshinaga-Itano, & Sedey, 2000; Mayne, Yoshinaga-Itano, Sedey, & Cary, 2000). An in-depth analysis of the lexicon and vocabulary-learning processes of approximately 100 deaf and hard-of-hearing children ages 3 to 6, about half of whom were in programs using manually coded English and half in oral programs, revealed that the vocabulary development of both groups was only approximately half of that expected from hearing children's norms (Lederberg & Spencer, 2001, 2009). Further analyses indicated that the cognitive skills and processes for quickly acquiring new words (*cognitively mediated word learning*) were achieved by these deaf and hard-of-hearing children, even though the age of acquisition was considerably later than is observed among hearing children. After a still-limited vocabulary was established, it was striking that most of the children were able to learn linguistically valid nonsense signs or nonsense words spoken simultaneously with signs with only three exposures in a context that promoted attention to the labels and the objects they represented. Informal follow-up after a 3-month interval showed that many of the children not only still recognized the newly learned "words" but could produce them when they were again shown the object with which they were associated. Lederberg and Spencer concluded that the vocabulary delays characteristic of most deaf and hard-of-hearing children, including those in TC environments, resulted from lack of sufficient exposure to the words/signs, not to any inherent cognitive or symbolic limitations.

The suggestion that many children in TC programs are exposed to relatively limited or inconsistent signed vocabulary is consistent with findings from Spencer (1993a, 1993b; Meadow-Orlans et al., 2004), who found that the expressive vocabulary size of deaf children (with intervention started by 9 months of age) during the toddler years was significantly associated with the quantity of signs that their hearing mothers produced (see Hart & Risley, 1995, with regard to hearing children). At 18-months of age, the deaf children with hearing parents, who performed at the language level characteristic of the "middle" group of hearing children, all had parents who were using forms of TC with manually coded English. This included one child with a moderately severe hearing loss who, although his mother used signs frequently as she spoke to him, produced only spoken words himself. The other five children also had mothers who produced signs fairly frequently, although with fairly low accuracy, and three of the children produced signs expressively by 13 months of age. Despite their age-appropriate acquisition of initial vocabulary, none of these children performed at the level of the highest functioning children in the hearing comparison group. Furthermore, at 24 to 30 months of age, all of the children whose hearing parents were using a combination of signs and speech scored significantly below their hearing age-mates on the Toddler version of the Communicative Development Inventory for English (Fenson et al., 1994). Results of this relatively small-scale study were in agreement with the larger studies summarized above indicating that parent use of manually coded English provides significant support for lexical development, but that the average functioning of deaf and hard-of-hearing children—even when early identification and intervention are provided—remains in the "low average" range, somewhat below that of hearing children of the same age.

Using Cochlear Implants in TC Programs

Because total communication and SimCom include spoken as well as signed components, considerable research has focused on effects of cochlear implant use among children using these devices and participating in TC programs. For example, Spencer, Tye-Murray, and Tomblin (1998) compared 25 children using cochlear implants and 13 using hearing aids. All of the children were in TC programs. The cochlear implant users obtained the devices after 31 months of age, with a mean of 5 years and 7 months—relatively late compared to current practice. Spencer et al. found that the children with cochlear implants exceeded those using hearing aids on use of grammatical morphemes as well as measures of speech perception and production. Of particular interest is the finding that the children with cochlear implants frequently used voice-only to produce grammatical morphemes (91% of the time) but predominantly used either signs or signs plus speech to express the content words in a phrase or sentence. For example, one child signed "my dad work on a farm" but said "dad works on a farm" (p. 312). Although the group of children using hearing aids sometimes produced the manually coded English sign for an inflectional or bound grammatical morpheme, and several children used devices in ASL to note the semantics of such morphemes, the group using cochlear implants produced the grammatical morphemes (including verb tenses, possessives, and plurals) significantly more frequently, more accurately, and more often through the speech mode. These spoken grammatical productions typically accompanied signed production of the base or key words in the sentence. Thus, the children were able to coordinate and synthesize information from the two modalities. The degree to which visual-manual and implant-facilitated auditory input can be integrated and accessed automatically in the perception and production of language needs to be further investigated.

Tomblin, Spencer, Flock, Tyler, and Gantz (1999) reported that children with cochlear implants enrolled in TC programs performed better than a comparison group of deaf children with hearing aids on the Index of Productive Syntax (Scarborough, 1990) and the Rhode Island Test of Language Structure (Engen & Engen, 1983). They also found that performance increased with age and duration of device use for the cochlear implant but not the hearing aid users.Spencer, Barker, and Tomblin (2003) found that children using cochlear implants in a TC program performed within one standard deviation of their hearing peers on standardized tests of language comprehension, reading comprehension, and writing. In a review of available studies, Spencer and Tomblin (2006) concluded that there is much individual variation in language and literacy achievement of children in TC environments related in large part to age of identification of hearing loss, degree of sophistication of the hearing technologies used, and consistency of exposure to a "fully developed language system." Noting that children using SimCom and signed English tend to continue to use signs for at least several years after they receive a cochlear implant, the investigators suggested that children in TC programs who use cochlear implants may learn to code-switch between modalities and thus communicate fluently with both hearing and deaf peers. Aside from benefits to children's quality of life and their self-esteem from being comfortable across hearing and deaf cultures (Bat-Chava, 2000), this flexibility potentially supports cognitive and linguistic development as children are exposed to a greater variety of ideas and perspectives.

Although Geers (2006) reported that participating in oral programming makes a small but statistically significant contribution to levels of spoken language, Yoshinaga-Itano (2006) argued that it is the general level of language development and not the primary modality used in the program that most strongly affects speech and spoken language acquisition. For children with severe to profound levels of hearing loss and early intervention, Yoshinaga-Itano and Sedey (2000) found that equal numbers in oral programs and sign language programming attained intelligible speech during childhood. In detailed case studies, Yoshinaga-Itano reported on two children in TC programming who, after obtaining and using cochlear implants, initially represented new vocabulary in sign but later in speech. She concluded that expressive use of signs is supportive of and not detrimental to children's use of speech when diagnosis and intervention occur early in life, and that there are advantages from TC experiences in which children have the opportunity to receive language symbols in two modalities simultaneously.

Sign, Sign Bilingual, or "Bilingual/Bicultural" Programming

Studies of children raised in rich sign language environments by (usually deaf) parents who are fluent signers of natural sign language show that sign language skills are acquired at much the same pace and in much the same sequence as hearing children achieve spoken language skills (Bonvillian, Orlansky, & Folven, 1990/1994;[2] Emmorey, 2002; Meier & Newport, 1990; Schick, 2006; Spencer & Harris, 2006). Native-signing children typically are reported to give evidence of sign language comprehension by 6 to 8 months of age and tend to use single signs expressively by 12 months.

Like hearing children learning a spoken language, deaf children learning a natural sign language from fluently signing parents start combining signs in multi-unit expressions by about 15 to 18 months of age. At first, these expressions are unmodulated, that is, without grammatical markers/morphemes indicating time (tense), pronominalization, or number. The grammars of natural sign languages differ significantly from those of spoken languages, however, making it difficult to closely match the steps toward full grammaticality. Nevertheless, general grammatical progress occurs at similar ages despite differences in form

---

[2] The Bonvillian et al., studies involved native-signing hearing children of deaf parents and were later shown to overestimate vocabulary growth due to the counting of some gestures as well as signs.

(e.g., sign languages express many grammatical relations through specific hand shapes called classifiers that serve almost like pronouns to represent entities, shapes, and how objects are held and handled).

By 2 years of age, deaf children raised in natural sign language environments have been observed to produce forms of noun-verb agreement, to understand representations of location, and to produce classifiers (Lindert, 2001). They also demonstrate role-playing in communications during play activities (Morgan & Woll, 2002). Increasingly correct use of classifiers and other aspects of grammar is seen by 3 or 3.5 years of age (Lillo-Martin, 1988), and some children begin to repeat or to tell short stories by that age, albeit frequently with "baby grammar" that prevents their being fully understood by communication partners. Use of pronominal reference and cohesion or coordination across sentences continue to develop through at least age 5 years (Lillo-Martin, 1991), and many aspects of complex sign language grammar are not developed until about the ages of 8 or 9 years (Schick, 2006).

One of the largest studies of language development in deaf children of deaf parents focused on vocabulary development. Anderson and Reilly (2002) tracked 69 young deaf children of signing deaf parents using a modification of the Communicative Development Inventory (CDI; Fenson et al., 1993) created to represent American Sign Language (CDI-ASL). Up to 18 months of age, average sign vocabulary size was somewhat larger for the deaf children than for hearing children in the norming group for the CDI for spoken American English. This phenomenon is often referred to as the "sign language advantage" (Abrahamsen et al., 1985; Meier & Newport, 1990). By 2 years of age, vocabulary sizes of the deaf children were quite similar to those of hearing children, a finding consistent with previous studies indicating that the sign language advantage is short-lived (Abrahamsen et al., 1985; Meier & Newport, 1990). The content of the lexicon was also similar between the two groups, although some differences were observed. First, after the first few signs, the deaf children tended to use somewhat more verbs than do hearing children. A similar phenomenon has been reported by Hoiting (2006) for children acquiring the Sign Language of the Netherlands (NGT). Second, although the spoken English version of the CDI includes animal sounds (e.g., "woof") as well as animal names, the former were not learned early by the deaf children for obvious reasons. Third, because body parts are typically referred to by pointing in ASL, there was no equivalent for those spoken words on the ASL version of the test. Finally, and perhaps of more interest, the trajectory of vocabulary development documented by Anderson and Reilly was essentially linear and failed to indicate the presence of a "burst" or period of rapid acceleration in vocabulary acquisition that has been reported to occur for hearing children (e.g., Dromi, 1987; Goldfield & Reznick, 1990).

There is not universal agreement on the occurrence of a vocabulary burst for hearing children, and its explanation remains to be understood fully (Lederberg

& Spencer, 2001, 2005). Nevertheless, Marschark and Wauters (2008) argued that the failure to observe the phenomenon in the Anderson and Reilly study is consistent with a variety of other results in the literature concerning the development of deaf children that suggest differences in cognitive strategies and patterns underlying language development and learning (i.e., lesser use of automatic relational processing, Marschark et al., 2006; Ottem, 1980). It remains to be determined whether the lack of a vocabulary burst in the Anderson and Reilly (2002) study reflected cognitive differences between deaf and hearing children, reduced availability of incidental learning during vocabulary acquisition, differences in the language provided by parents, (because the vast majority of the deaf parents would have had hearing parents themselves), or was simply an artifact of the study design.

The Sign/Bilingual Approach as an Educational Model

Similarities in developmental progressions of spoken and natural sign languages, as well as continuing reports of below-expected performance on literacy and other academic achievement by children exposed to TC or SimCom,[3] led to the establishment of programs in which natural sign languages are expected to be the first language of deaf children (e.g., Simms & Thumann, 2007). This approach, often called "bilingual/bicultural" or "sign/bilingual," is predicated at least in part on Cummins's (1989) linguistic interdependence theory, which posits that all languages share core proficiencies and that skills developed in a first language will transfer to skills in a second language. When applied to education of deaf and hard-of-hearing children, acceptance of this theory suggests that it is most important for them to learn a natural, complete language during the early years of life. Sign/bilingual programs provide rich language environments in the expectation that children's language skills will develop through natural interactions with fluent signers, and written representations of the surrounding culture's spoken language will become their second language.

Most sign/bilingual programs provide some training in spoken language, usually in pull-out or special sessions. Learning of written forms of spoken language is assumed to be facilitated primarily by productive knowledge of a natural sign language, although evidence to support this notion is scarce. In addition, age-appropriate development of a natural sign language will ideally allow children access to information through interactions with adults and other children in the classroom and at home and, therefore, provide opportunities for supporting

---

[3] Importantly, the quality of language and support for cognitive development/academic achievement in such programs has not been documented, and conclusions have been based on general findings such as norming studies of the Stanford Achievement Test (e.g., Allen, 1986; Traxler, 2000).

cognition as well as further language learning. Such a result, of course, is dependent upon the availability of adults and other children who are fluent in sign language (Johnson et al., 1989). One of the difficulties in interpreting research on education is that published papers often fail to specify the activities that actually happen in the classroom. Several detailed descriptions of bilingual/bicultural or sign/bilingual programs in action are available in Bailes (2001), Evans (2004), and Swanwick and Tsverik (2007). Unfortunately, these studies do not provide information about the children's language growth over time.

Andrews, Ferguson, Roberts, and Hodges (1997) provided some limited outcome data on seven children in an ASL-based sign/bilingual program in a location in the United States where few resources were available. That is, the community did not have a large deaf adult population, and there were relatively few students in each age cohort. The children did not begin bilingual programming until after age 2 (most not until after age 4); more than half were from non-White ethnic groups, and almost half were identified as having multiple disabilities. Over the pre-kindergarten through first grade years, the program had one deaf teacher and several hearing professionals who were fluent in the native sign language. Home visits were provided during the first 2 years by hearing professionals who were fluent in sign language and knowledgeable about the abilities and culture of deaf people. Professionals provided sign language demonstrations and other support to parents and, importantly, demonstrated and encouraged the reading of books using sign language. Information was provided to parents about the accomplishments of deaf people and assistive devices that would be helpful at home (e.g., closed-caption decoders, door-bell flashers, etc.).

The curriculum followed the state-mandated curriculum for all students, with an additional supplement designed specifically for deaf and hard-of-hearing children. During pre-kindergarten, the teachers focused on children's acquiring basic concepts and language through play activities, group discussions, and daily storybook reading using sign language—assuring that the children saw English print in meaningful situations. Additional reading and writing were emphasized during kindergarten and first grade, with stories and other information being presented in spoken language by one teacher and in sign by another. This "whole language" approach, including story-reading, was continued during the first grade when most children were 6 years old but several were older. Activities included keeping a daily journal and "computer literacy, mathematics, science, and social studies, organized around thematic units" (p. 19). Aspects of English grammar (e.g., pronouns, grammatical morphemes) were also directly taught as examples occurred in story reading and in poems that were written by students and the teacher. Andrews et al. reported each child's progress over a school year, as measured by a set of standardized tests of basic concepts, receptive sign vocabulary, the Stanford Achievement Test, and the Woodcock-Johnson Psycho-Educational Battery. Most children for whom data were available raised their scores by at least a grade-level equivalent over the school year, a noteworthy achievement for deaf children. However, the researchers indicated that there was no way to determine to what extent the bilingual programming approach actually contributed to these gains.

Cochlear Implants and Sign/Bilingual Programming

Given the frequent lack of emphasis on spoken language in sign/bilingual programs, it is not surprising that there is a paucity of studies documenting children's speech and spoken language development in such settings, with or without use of cochlear implants. In one case study, Yoshinaga-Itano (2006) discussed a child who was learning ASL before getting a cochlear implant, prompted in part because of a gradual loss of vision. This child used hearing aids from the age of 6 months, but just prior to getting a cochlear implant at 20 months of age, her 183-word expressive vocabulary was produced in sign only. She gave no evidence of spoken language development. Her sign vocabulary continued to increase after implantation, but by 35 months of age, she often accompanied signs with vocalizations. At 51 months of age, she was considered to be an intelligible speaker by hearing people who knew her well, including parents, teachers, and the person who coded her videotaped communications. In one language sample at 51 months, the child produced 226 utterances, but only 6% of them included signs, so she was clearly making a transition to spoken language. Yoshinaga-Itano (2006, p. 323) concluded that spoken language "gets a piggyback ride on language in any modality" although she also indicated that level and amount of hearing experience have additional effects. Her conclusion agrees with that of Wilbur (2000) that, despite the lack of emphasis on speech, there is no evidence that focusing on natural sign language actually decreases the speech skills attained by deaf students.

Early exposure to natural sign language is mandated in Sweden, although it is not certain to what degree this occurs at home. Preisler, Tvingstedt, and Ahlstrom (2002) studied the spoken language development of 22 pre-school-aged children who received cochlear implants between the ages of 2 and 5 and who continued to be exposed to sign language at home and at school. Overall, the children who developed the best sign language skills also had the highest level skills in spoken Swedish. Increases in the two abilities *tended* to occur in parallel, although the researchers noted that achieving higher levels of sign language skills did not assure a parallel advance in spoken language skills. These findings replicate a similar, earlier finding for Swedish children who were hard of hearing (Preisler & Ahlstrom, 1997). They are also consistent with a report by Yoshinaga-Itano and Sedey (2000) that children in the United States with higher levels of language skills at early ages, regardless of modality, had the best speech skills at later ages.

A program at Clerc Center at Gallaudet University in the United States provides special programming for children using cochlear implants and also learning ASL in a school with a sign/bilingual approach. The students interact with other deaf children, many of whom use sign exclusively, but also have opportunities for small group and individual work focusing on spoken language development. No peer-reviewed publications are available that report the progress of these children, but a conference presentation (Seal et al., 2005) provided profiles of development of individual children that indicated correlations ranging from .67 to .97 between growth in sign and spoken language. Seal et al., noted that children entering the pre-school program who have little or no formal language in either mode begin to communicate with sign before beginning to use speech. The researchers noted that decisions about encouraging an individual child's transition from sign to spoken language should take into account any discrepancy between modes of functioning and that children should not be put in a position of suddenly depending on their weaker communication mode. On the basis of educational records, Seal et al. reported that most of the children in the program eventually transition to at least partial dependence upon spoken language—but the transition may be extended in time.

SUMMARY: LANGUAGE LEARNING IN SPEECH AND SIGN

Considerable disagreement continues about the efficacy of various methods and modalities for supporting language development of deaf and hard-of-hearing children, despite centuries of application and research. Although some children using each of the methods succeed in developing age-appropriate language, this is not the norm; deaf and hard-of-hearing children generally continue to fall farther behind the language accomplishments of hearing children as they increase in age. Early identification and use of current technology have raised language levels, but the average difference between children with and without hearing loss has not been eliminated. Much more work is needed, but at this point we can summarize what we know and what we don't know about language development in deaf and hard-of-hearing children fairly succinctly:

- Differences among the approaches to language programming focus on the degree to which they depend primarily on auditory-oral versus visual-manual modalities. Regardless of modality, language delays result from lack of complete access to a language model. This may be due to inability to receive auditory information or, in other cases, to a lack of adults' providing a complete and consistent model of visual language.

- Across language methods, levels of parental involvement and resources (socioeconomic and educational), children's nonverbal cognitive abilities, the presence or absence of multiple disabilities, and the intensity or consistency of programming all are associated with outcomes achieved. Regardless of the language approach used, deaf and hard-of-hearing children tend to have significant delays in the acquisition of vocabulary, the understanding and use of grammatical morphemes, and other aspects of syntax (at least in English).

- With the exception of a limited number of recent studies indicating that the combination of early intervention and use of cochlear implants before 2 years of age predicts age-appropriate spoken language during pre-school years, children (with average cognition and no additional disabilities) in oral programming tend to develop language later and less completely than hearing children. Even children with mild-to-moderate or severe hearing loss levels are at greatly increased risk for language delays and difficulties.

- Insufficient data are available to indicate efficacy of auditory-verbal therapy, a clinical approach that aims for children to develop age-appropriate spoken language before entering first grade—different from the expectations of other methods. However, positive descriptive reports are available, and some children have been shown to develop at chronologically appropriate rates when participating in AVT.

- There is evidence that cued speech supports some aspects of language, especially phonological development, in children learning French and Spanish when they have early and consistent exposure at home and at school. Researchers investigating cued speech have tended to focus on selected aspects of language rather than providing information about overall functioning. Outcomes have indicated, however, that children are able to integrate and synthesize information available through visual and auditory processing.

- The potential of total communication programming using manually coded versions of the spoken vernacular has apparently been compromised by the fact that adults tend to use the signing systems inconsistently and often incorrectly. Both American and Australian studies, however, show that TC effectively supports some aspects of language, including understanding and use of English word order in sentences. Studies of children using TC along with cochlear implants indicate that (as was said for cued speech) children are capable of synthesizing visual and auditory representations of language.

- Children exposed to rich natural sign language models from birth acquire language as readily and completely as hearing children in similarly supportive spoken language environments. Sign/bilingual programming, in which a natural sign language serves as the first language and medium of communication in the classroom, has a strong theoretic basis but to date lacks sufficient evidence to allow evaluation of its language development outcomes. With only a few exceptions, available peer-reviewed publications focus on the method of program implementation instead of children's language accomplishments.

Despite the tendency of many professionals (and parents) to compare one type of approach to deaf and hard-of-hearing children's language development with another, it is clear that no method has succeeded in "leveling the playing field" for deaf and hard-of-hearing children compared to hearing children. Our inability to "prove" a best method can be seen as a negative finding but also can be interpreted in a more positive light: Some children have been shown to achieve relatively rapid and high levels of language development in each of the approaches surveyed. Comparison studies of the various approaches may be inherently flawed because children (and their families) with various characteristics trend toward one or another approach. In addition, some available studies have limited their participants to children who are most likely to succeed, that is, children who have no disabilities in addition to hearing loss and whose families are intensely involved in the program. Future research might more profitably focus on a wider range of characteristics and experiences that predict success *within* each approach (or combination of approaches). This may lead to the acquisition of more information that will be of direct help in program planning and in supporting families' choices of methods and programs.

6 Acquisition and Development of Literacy Skills

Perhaps the most long-term and vexing challenge in deaf education is the continuing difficulty experienced by students with regard to print literacy. Despite the availability of alternative language approaches described in chapter 5, continuing delays and challenges in language development, problems in accessing other kinds of environmental information, and perhaps our lack of understanding about how best to teach deaf and hard-of hearing students reading and writing typically create barriers to the normal acquisition of literacy skills. Some students with hearing loss, of course, demonstrate excellence in these domains (e.g., Padden & Ramsey, 2000; Toscano, McKee, & Lepoutre, 2002), but most lag significantly behind their hearing age-mates. As a result, the median level of reading achievement among deaf and hard-of-hearing 18-year-olds in the United States is roughly equivalent to that of 9-year-old hearing students (Traxler, 2000). Further, despite claims to the contrary, those lags are found regardless of the language approach or modalities employed. There also is no evidence that this delay generally is resolved by cochlear implants or advanced hearing aids, even in combination with early intervention, although with this assistance outcomes do tend to be improved (see Marschark, Rhoten, & Fabich, 2007, for a review).

FACTORS PROPOSED TO INFLUENCE READING SKILLS

Numerous investigators have documented the difficulties of deaf and hard-of-hearing students in reading and writing, and those studies are reviewed elsewhere. The pervasiveness of this apparent barrier to print literacy, however, emphasizes the need to identify the characteristics and skills of those students who are more successful so that we can promote higher achievement among the students who continue to struggle. This chapter therefore addresses several major factors that are thought to influence the development of literacy skills. Most of these ideas are based on research involving hearing children, although there are increasing data available about the patterns of skills of deaf and hard-of-hearing children that allow us to evaluate the usefulness of various approaches to support their literacy development. At the outset, we can identify several of these factors that also are central to understanding the acquisition of literacy skills by deaf and hard-of-hearing children, even if they do not all have sufficient evidence to support their direct role.

- Early experiences in which adults read to and with children in a pleasurable context support the children's literacy skill development.
- Phonological knowledge, often as expressed through *phonics* skills, provides an important component of literacy skills and is typically advanced in more fluent readers.
- Vocabulary knowledge is critical for the development of literacy skills, and reading and writing are facilitated when many words are mastered through conversation prior to being confronted in text.
- Knowledge of the syntax of the written language provides important support for literacy development and, along with vocabulary knowledge, promotes more fluent, "automatic" reading and writing skills.
- Knowledge of one language, especially at a core or conceptual level, may facilitate acquisition of literacy skills in another language.

The following sections will address each of these points, presenting available evidence that supports and, in some cases, fails to support them as they pertain to deaf and hard-of-hearing children. In addition, available information on the effectiveness of specific teaching approaches and the impact of general cognitive skills underlying print literacy will be presented. Later in the chapter we will summarize information about deaf and hard-of-hearing students' development of writing skills, an area in which much less information is available.

Early, Interactive, Pre-Literacy Experiences Support Literacy Development

There is a clear literacy-learning advantage for children who arrive at school with age-appropriate language skills (Musselman, 2000). However, it is no longer assumed that language development must precede the emergence of literacy skills (e.g., Roberts, Jurgens, & Burchinal, 2005; Valdez-Maenchaco & Whitehurst, 1992; Yaden, Rowe, & MacGillivray, 1999). A case can be made that among hearing as well as deaf and hard-of-hearing children, literacy activities themselves promote language development, and the two can be mutually supportive (Teale & Sulzby, 1986; Williams, 2004). This recognition has led to a focus on early parent-child and teacher-child reading experiences as a context for building both language and print awareness skills.

One activity that has been proposed to support emerging literacy skills is *shared reading*. Utilizing guidelines requiring the highest level of causal evidence (see chapter 3), the Institute of Education Sciences in the U.S. Department of Education (www.whatworks.ed.gov) has concluded that studies have demonstrated positive effects of early shared storybook reading on emerging literacy of hearing children who are at risk for literacy difficulties (e.g., Crain-Thoreson & Dale, 1999; Justice & Ezell, 2002; Whitehurst et al., 1994). Shared reading is just what the name implies—books or other written material become the shared focus of an interaction between an adult, typically a parent or caregiver, and a young child. At the earliest stages, this may consist of merely looking at pictures together and allowing the object of shared attention to be labeled or become the communication topic. For example, looking at a picture of a car, a parent might label it and then ask the child something about "Mommy's car." At later stages, stories in the books, as reflected by the pictures, may be "told" without regard for the actual text. Intermittently, or at a later stage, parents may actively lead the child to recognize associations between printed and either spoken or signed words (Roberts et al., 2005; Senechal, LeFebre, Hudson, & Lawson, 1996). The initial purpose of such activities is to introduce children to the idea of books and print, and shared reading progresses more smoothly when parents follow the children's lead regarding the focus of attention and the duration of time spent on the activity (Bus, 2003; Bus, van Ijzendoorn, & Pelligrini, 1995; Whitehurst et al., 1988).

Shared reading occurs often in many families, but rarely if at all in others. Hearing parents of deaf children have often commented to researchers and educators that their children do not enjoy books, and that they themselves do not know how to create interest and sustain attention in the activity (Delk & Weidekamp, 2001; Swanwick & Watson, 2007).[1] Although some studies of deaf children (for whom literacy typically emerges at a somewhat later age than for hearing children) have reported positive results from shared reading activities, these studies have tended to have few participants, qualitative or case-study designs, and/or no comparison groups (Ewoldt & Saulnier, 1992; Gioia, 2001; Williams, 2004).

In one exception to the above generalization, Fung, Chow, and McBride-Chang (2005) conducted an experimental comparison involving three groups of 5- to 9-year-old deaf and hard-of-hearing children enrolled in oral programming in Hong Kong. They examined the effects of a specific approach to shared reading, the Dialogic Reading Intervention (DR; Whitehurst et al., 1988). Dialogic reading emphasizes the parent's role as a listener and responder rather than a teacher during shared reading activities and has been shown to have positive effects with hearing children from various ethnic-cultural groups (e.g., Jimenez, Filippini, & Gerber, 2006; Hargrave & Senechal, 2000; Zevenbergen & Whitehurst, 2003). The program is relatively structured, as parents are taught to use a specific sequence of prompts, feedback methods, expansions, and repetitions to increase children's contributions to the interaction. Children are prompted to complete a sentence or idea, remember something from the story and relate it to an event that has been experienced, and to answer both *wh-* and open-ended questions.

In the Fung et al. (2005) study, deaf children and their hearing parents were randomly assigned to one of three treatment groups. The first group, with nine children, received the dialogic reading DR intervention. A specific set of books was given to the parents to read, along with guidebooks that explained the procedures, rationale, and goals of the program. Notes were attached to specific pages to remind them of opportunities to use particular prompts and questions. Fung et al. prepared picture cards for the children to use when discussing the stories or responding to questions and for parents to use in prompting the children to retell the stories. Parents also were provided with a calendar indicating when the reading activities should be done, and they were called by program staff twice in the first 2 weeks of the 8-week program to ensure that the procedures were clear. A second group of nine parents was given the same books to read with their children and was also provided the calendar indicating when the books should be read. However, those parents received no other materials or

---

[1] Research involving the large number of deaf parents who themselves lack fluent print literacy skills apparently has not been undertaken; the Shared Reading Program (Schleper, 1997) was developed based on observations of literate deaf parents reading to their children.

training. Parents of 10 other children did not receive materials or training, although the set of books was given to them after the 8 weeks had passed.

Preintervention testing showed no statistically significant differences among the groups of children in average age, hearing levels, or performance on the Raven's Colored Progressive Matrices test (Court & Raven, 1995), a nonverbal intelligence test. A Cantonese version of the Peabody Picture Vocabulary Test (PPVT; Dunn & Dunn, 1997) also was administered prior to the intervention. Although differences failed to reach statistical significance, the group that was to receive the DR intervention started with a higher average score on the Raven test (91) than the other two groups (70 and 68, respectively). Because such small numbers of participants in each group limit the statistical power of the study, this difference represents a potential confound in the results. However, post-intervention testing showed that the Raven scores of the DR group had increased to even higher levels, with an average of 114 (100 is average), while the other two groups' scores stayed essentially the same (66 and 65, respectively). Change scores on the PPVT also were greater for the DR group, with a statistical effect size in the "large" range, indicating that one can have confidence in its behavioral impact. In responses to post-intervention questionnaires, parents expressed the belief that the DR program had benefited them and their children. Although it is unclear to what extent the findings of this study can be generalized to other deaf and hard-of-hearing populations, it appears to be an approach worthy of further study. In particular, the structured nature of the DR program may be of special benefit in building hearing parents' confidence in their ability to participate in and guide shared reading with their deaf or hard-of-hearing children.

A major difficulty faced in shared reading with deaf and hard-of-hearing children, one that is not specifically addressed in the DR program, is the children's need to divide visual attention between communication and the book being shared (Spencer, 2000b). This difficulty arises in parent-child dyads using any language approach that requires visual attention, whether through speechreading, cued speech, or signing. This difficulty can be attenuated by appropriate seating so that the child easily can look at the parent, by pacing communicative input to match the child's natural attention changes from the book to the parent, and by use of manual or gaze attention-getting signals when speech-based signals are ineffective. A number of studies have indicated, however, that hearing parents generally do not intuitively make such adjustments for their deaf and hard-of-hearing children and that specific demonstrations of these adjustments are helpful (e.g., Spencer & Harris, 2006; Swanwick & Watson, 2005, 2007).

Visually sensitive strategies do appear to be intuitively employed by deaf, signing parents, and these strategies have been described by several researchers (e.g., Lartz & Lestina, 1995; Schleper, 1997; Waxman & Spencer, 1997). Schleper, for example, described 15 principles of effective, early shared reading based on his observations of deaf parents, and he created the Shared Reading Program

(SRP) to facilitate hearing parents' use of those principles. Many of the SRP principles echo those identified to promote shared reading with hearing children and are not dependent upon the language modalities used. These principles include promoting positive interactions by following the child's interests, reinforcing attention to books, making print meaningful by elaborating on the text and providing related language input, adjusting the level and amount of input to match child language levels, and connecting story concepts to events in the child's life. Schleper identified other strategies specific to use of sign language in shared reading. These include adults' producing signs near pictures or print in the text so that the child can see them simultaneously, using tapping and other physical signals to redirect child attention to communication or back to the book, and using sign language translations for the text in the book—only later connecting the story and the actual written text.

The SRP has been implemented in a number of locations in the United States. It is designed as a 20-week intervention in which a tutor (usually deaf but always a fluent signer) visits individual families to demonstrate the strategies and signs appropriate for a given book and provides a corresponding instructional videotape. Delk and Weidekamp (2001) surveyed parents of 116 deaf and hard-of-hearing children ages 1–11 years (average age 4.5 years) who had participated in SRP. They found that parents reported increased quality and enjoyment of shared reading, with 97% reporting that their use of sign language had increased. Unfortunately, no observational or direct assessment data were collected, and parent reports were not compared to those of families not utilizing SRP. To date, it appears that no published, peer-reviewed studies have provided evidence of the efficacy of the SRP approach in promoting deaf and hard-of-hearing children's literacy.

Shared reading activities have been incorporated into early intervention programs for deaf and hard-of-hearing children and their families in the United States, England, and the Netherlands, and there is additional descriptive evidence of parent satisfaction with the process from those countries. Increased enjoyment of shared parent-child reading, as well as more productive communication, for example, were reported by hearing parents of three deaf children in the Netherlands who participated in an SRP-like intervention stressing visual attention, expansion of text, and responding to children's interests (Van der Lem & Timmerman, 1990). Additional evidence that repeated book sharing provides an avenue for the relating of sign language to print was reported in case studies by Maxwell (1984) and Rottenberg (2001), in which children and their parents read books from the Signed English series (Bornstein et al., 1980). These books provide a picture, related text, and line drawings of the sign hand shapes that would be used to produce signs for the printed words. Children in both studies began "reading" by producing the signs pictured on the page and later progressed to reading (by signing) the printed words themselves.

Positive reports of gains from parent-child shared reading are supported and extended by qualitative studies of shared reading activities in the early school years between teachers and individuals or small groups of students (Andrews & Mason, 1986a, 1986b; Gioia, 2001; Rottenberg & Searfoss, 1992). In addition to reports of increased linguistic and emergent literacy skills, researchers have reported that deaf and hard-of-hearing children who participate in these activities show high motivation for reading and writing activities, sometimes using these skills spontaneously to assist when "through-the-air" spoken or signed communication fails (see, e.g., Williams, 2004).

Aram, Most, and Mayafit (2006) studied both the shared reading and mediated (assisted) early writing activities of 30 mothers and kindergarten-aged deaf and hard-of-hearing children in Israel. The families participated in an after-school program which provides information and guidance to parents about managing their children's hearing losses, but the parents had not been provided specific guidance on early reading or writing activities prior to the study. All children were attending mainstream school classes during the day, and early literacy experiences were provided during the school day. It appears that the children used spoken language, because the authors do not mention use of signs or signed language. The families were videotaped at home as parents and children shared a wordless story book and engaged in a writing activity in which mothers assisted their children in writing words that they knew the children could not write on their own. A variety of background information was obtained, and the interactive reading activity was assessed using both the Adult/Child Interactive Reading Inventory (DeBruin-Parecki, 1999, back-translated to Hebrew) and the Dialogic Reading Cycles (Whitehurst et al., 1988, 1994). A measure of mothers' use of *wh-* questions during the story book activity also was obtained. These measures were combined to represent a "storybook telling" variable. In addition, a 6-point scale was used to rate the mothers' scaffolding of the writing activity, the degree of autonomy the mother allowed the child, the degree of precision the mother demanded in the child's production of alphabetic letters, and the degree to which mothers gave evidence of perceiving the activity as mutual or shared rather than adult-directed. These ratings were collapsed to produce a "writing mediation" variable.

Six measures of early literacy were obtained from children in the Aram et al. (2006) study, including measures of the ability to write spoken or pictured words, word recognition, letter knowledge, phonological awareness, receptive vocabulary, and general knowledge. The first three measures were considered to represent alphabetic skills and the remaining three measures to represent language skills. A series of hierarchical multiple regression analyses showed that when child age, degree of hearing loss, and the maternal storybook-telling measures were controlled, mothers' writing-mediation ratings contributed significantly to explaining differences in child alphabetic skills. An additional analysis showed that after controlling child age, degree of hearing loss, and mothers' writing mediation ratings, the mothers' storybook-telling ratings contributed significantly to explaining variance in child language skills. The quality of mothers' mediation of writing and of storybook telling thus had independent effects on children's development of print knowledge versus general language skills. No comparison data were obtained from children who did not participate in the intervention, however, so causal conclusions cannot be drawn.

In summary, there is a convergence of data indicating that shared reading is fruitful in early at-home intervention and early school years for supporting development of hearing children, with positive effects on developing vocabulary, building phonological knowledge, and increasing motivation for attention to books. Studies of hearing children also have shown reading comprehension advantages from early shared reading that extend into the elementary school years (Zevenbergen & Whitehurst, 2003). Evidence is limited for deaf or hard-of-hearing children, although available reports suggest similar effects. Easterbrooks and Stephenson (2006) concluded that shared reading has a stronger evidence base as a support for beginning than for more mature readers.

Phonological Awareness, Phonics, and Literacy Skills

The National Reading Panel (2000) in the United States identified *phonemic awareness* and *phonics* as two of five essential components of reading instruction. *Phonemes* are the smallest units specific to a language (e.g., the [k] sound in English, regardless of whether it is made by /k/ or /c/), and phonemic awareness includes knowing the rules for combining and sequencing those units to produce meaningful larger units such as words and sentences. *Phonics* refers to the knowledge of rules that allow associating the sounds or phonemes of a language with the *graphemes* or printed form of those sounds (i.e., letters). Both phonemic awareness and phonics are aspects of what is generally referred to as phonological awareness or phonological knowledge. The panel pointed out that phonemic awareness and phonics are important tools both for beginning readers and for older readers with lower levels of literacy skill. It indicated that both of these tools need to be supported by specific lessons and should not be expected to develop without structured input. In addition, the panel stressed that acquiring literacy requires more than simply phonological knowledge, despite its benefits.

The National Reading panel used the term "phonemes" exclusively to refer to the sounds that make up a spoken, or auditory-based, language, although the work of Stokoe (1960/2005) and others have shown convincingly that natural sign languages consist of visually received units that serve the same linguistic functions as the phonemes of spoken language (for a more in-depth discussion, see Lucas & Valli, 1992). This chapter is primarily concerned with literacy as it relates to the ability to read and write the print form of a spoken language, and thus references to phonemes and phonology will indicate auditory or sound-based phonemes even when they are at least partially expressed in a form that can be received visually through speechreading or systems like cued speech.

Like skilled hearing readers, skilled deaf and hard-of-hearing readers frequently are found to have and to apply considerable phonological knowledge during reading in order to decode and unlock the meaning of words. Trezek, Wang, and Paul (in press), Perfetti and Sandak (2000), and other investigators have emphasized that such knowledge is best acquired through hearing and speaking, although Leybaert (1993) concluded that many deaf children are able to utilize representations that are functionally equivalent to phonological codes by integrating information obtained through varying combinations of sign, fingerspelling, orthography, articulation, speechreading, and limited audition. Educators and investigators nevertheless continue to struggle with determining the best way(s) to "teach" phonology to children with significant hearing losses so that they utilize it in appropriate contexts.

Trezek et al. (in press) reviewed evidence indicating that phonological knowledge not only can be an aid in word identification but also can support syntactic knowledge—especially the ability to understand grammatical morphemes such as tense and number, which typically are not stressed in speech. Phonetic decoding may be even more important in word identification processes of deaf and hard-of-hearing students than hearing students because the former typically are found not to use context effectively for determining word meanings (Andrews & Mason, 1986a; deVilliers & Pomerantz, 1992). Questions remain, however, about the degree to which preexisting phonological knowledge is a necessary, as opposed to merely a particularly effective, method of entry into reading. For example, learning of whole words (*sight* words), understanding morphology, and deriving meaning from context can provide alternative or supplemental paths to understanding. The National Reading Panel (2000) pointed out that not only do reading skills develop from phonological knowledge but, in turn, the activity of reading also strengthens and expands that knowledge.

Goldin-Meadow and Mayberry (2001) noted that associations that have been demonstrated between phonological skills and reading ability generally fall short of showing causal effects and they, along with Musselman (2000), proposed that engaging in reading may be the *source* of the phonology-literacy relationship observed in effective deaf readers, rather than the other way around. Andrews and Mason (1986b) and Harris and Moreno (2006) also argued that deaf and hard-of-hearing students' knowledge of signs and their meanings can be associated with printed words without the students' having knowledge of the sound-print relationship. Finally, Padden and Ramsey (1998) suggested that fingerspelling, providing visual-manual representations of the graphemes or printed letters that make up a word, can serve as a direct aid to decoding print.

The above claims are hopeful, but they remain in need of empirical verification. Harris and Beech (1998) described two deaf children with good reading skills who were skilled signers but had no evident auditory phonological awareness. Izzo (2002) conducted a correlational study of 29 deaf students, ages 4 to 13.5 years, and also failed to find a significant association between phonological skills and reading. Overall, the children in Izzo's study, who used either Signed English or American Sign Language (ASL), obtained low scores on a picture-based test of phonemic awareness. Their reading scores on an independent reading and retelling task, however, ranged from low to moderately high and were associated significantly with both age and sign language ability. Regression analyses indicated that 40% of reading variance was accounted for by the three variables of language, age, and phonological awareness, but when language scores were controlled, age was no longer a significant predictor.

Emphasizing Auditory Information to Build Phonological Knowledge and Literacy Skills

Despite evidence that auditory access to the sounds of a spoken language is not always necessary for effective reading and writing, much effort has focused on building just such awareness. Auditory-verbal therapy (AVT) and other oral programs are grounded at least in part on an assumption that literacy skills will be promoted by speech and listening skills which, in turn, can be expected to assist in the development of phonological knowledge (see chapter 5). Access to auditory information conveyed through hearing aids and cochlear implants may further be expected to encourage phonological development. Despite several reports indicating that students in oral programs tend to show higher levels of skill in both reading and writing compared to students in signing programs (Geers & Moog, 1989; Moores & Sweet, 1990; Musselman & Szanto, 1998), a causal relationship has yet to be identified in available studies. The lack of a consistent relationship likely is due primarily to the preferred language modality being confounded with background factors including family socioeconomic factors, presence or absence of additional disabilities, and the child's use of assistive listening devices. Geers (2006), for example, pointed out that literacy problems remain even in programs using the newest technology combined with oral education approaches.

Much of the research involving children with cochlear implants has focused on the degree to which they develop speech perception and production skills, both of which would suggest the presence of phonological knowledge (see Boothroyd & Eran, 1994; Kirk, 2000; Spencer et al., in press). Several studies have indicated that children who receive their cochlear implants early produce phonemes more accurately (achieving approximately 70% correct) after 3 years of implant use than has been reported for previous cohorts of children with the same levels of hearing loss who used hearing aids (Peng, Spencer, & Tomblin, 2004; Spencer & Bass-Ringdahl, 2004). Earlier implantation also has been shown to result in greater phonological awareness (James, Rajput, Brinton, & Goswami, 2008). Palmer (2000), however, noted that phonological awareness does not assure that knowledge will be used in decoding written words. She reported that a 12-week program (Phonographix) based on reading of books plus *explicit* teaching of phonics was successful for two 9-year-old deaf children who initially had very delayed reading skills. The children made significant gains in phonological and word decoding skills. With only two participants, however, the generality of these findings is unclear.

Despite the fact that cochlear implants generally increase access to auditory-based language, findings to date have failed to demonstrate that they eliminate the children's delays in literacy development. In an initially positive assessment, Geers (2002, 2006) reported that over half of 181 orally trained children using cochlear implants scored within the average range (at 8–9 years of age) on reading tests for hearing children. This suggested that increased auditory experience provided a basis for development of phonological and other abilities that supported reading skills. However, when a subsample of these children was retested between 15 and 16 years of age, their reading scores averaged approximately 2 years behind grade level expectations (Geers, 2005). Increasing lags with age among children in the sample also were reported by Geers, Tobey, Moog, and Brenner (2008) in a longer term follow-up study with more participants, although levels achieved by the older students using cochlear implants compared favorably with the average achievement levels cited historically for deaf and hard-of-hearing children as a group (e.g., Traxler, 2000).

Because of the early, intense auditory focus of AVT, it might also be expected that children in those programs would attain high levels of literacy if auditory-based phonology is a critical element in development. Robertson and Flexer (1993) provided a qualitative report of positive AVT literacy outcomes. The majority of their participants were said to have average to high literacy levels and be enrolled primarily in mainstream school environments. Wray, Flexer, and Vaccaro (1997) and Lewis (1996) also reported that AVT participants tended to achieve higher level literacy skills than are typically found among deaf and hard-of-hearing students in the United States. A survey of Australian students produced similar findings (Roberts & Rickards, 1994a, 1994b). The above reports, however, either provided no information from hearing children with which to compare the AVT participants or used non-standardized instruments for data collection. Although these studies suggest satisfaction of participants with AVT, a high incidence of mainstreaming, and age-appropriate reading skills consistent with the aims of the AVT approach, the samples in all cases were self-selected and the survey data obtained were retrospective and inherently subjective.

Literacy achievements were also quite varied in a group of 62 American children in AVT programming studied by Easterbrooks and O'Rourke (2001). The children attended a program that provided one-to-one language therapy, parent instruction, and expectations of parent follow-through at home. Participating families generally were financially affluent, highly educated, and "highly involved" (p. 313) with their children's education. Children's ages at assessment were not clear from the published article but were based on reports from educational testing. Language and literacy scores of the boys fell, on average, 3.8 years below what would be predicted from a nonverbal measure of their cognitive abilities. Girls' language and literacy scores fell 2.7 years below predictions based on the nonverbal measure. Easterbrooks and O'Rourke, who were primarily interested in gender-related differences, noted that language and literacy performance was also associated with aspects of child attention behaviors and aided (amplified) hearing levels.

Phonological Knowledge and Literacy When Visual Language Input Is Increased

The potential for eventual positive effects of cochlear implants on deaf children's literacy was demonstrated in a retrospective study of 72 children in total communication (TC) programs provided by Spencer and Oleson (2008). They found evidence of increased phonological knowledge as measured by speech perception and production after 48 months of cochlear implant use. These skills, in turn, related significantly to later reading skills. The children's use of signs along with speech and spoken language experiences did not appear to interfere with their using the information provided by their cochlear implants (Spencer, Gantz, & Knutson, 2004).

A number of researchers (e.g., Harris and Beech, 1998; Harris & Moreno, 2006; Schorr, Fox, van Wassenhove, & Knudsen, 2005) have shown that deaf and hard-of-hearing children are able to coordinate visual information with the partial auditory information they receive and utilize speechreading to obtain information about the sounds of spoken language. Therefore, increases in speechreading ability may support reading as well as understanding of spoken language. It is well known, however, that speechreading fails to disambiguate among the majority of sounds produced in English, and additional information may need to be provided.

As described in chapter 5, cued speech was developed in an attempt to add visual information beyond that available from speechreading to enable deaf and hard-of-hearing students to develop full phonological knowledge of spoken language and to use it to support reading skills. Colin, Magnan, Ecalle, and Leybaert (2007) reported a study of 21 hearing children and 21 deaf children in France and Belgium who participated in programs emphasizing spoken French with cueing.

The time and extent of exposure to cued speech varied among the deaf children, with some but not all having parents who used the system consistently at home and some being in a school environment using cued speech longer than others. Colin et al. found that the children's ability to make automatic (non-conscious) phonological comparisons at kindergarten age—as indicated by the ability to recognize rhymes—was predictive of their ability to consciously make decisions about rhymes at the end of Grade 1. In addition, both the early phonological skills and the later ability for consciously made phonological decisions predicted children's recognition of printed words in first grade. Age of exposure to cued speech related to both the first-grade phonological skills and first-grade reading skills: Children who started to use cued speech when they were younger had higher skill levels. These associations were maintained even when chronological age and nonverbal I.Q. were controlled. Colin et al. noted that children did not overtly use cued speech hand movements when performing the kindergarten-level rhyme recognition tasks, but they did so when making judgments about rhyming words when they reached first grade. Colin et al. (2007) thus concluded that the effects of early exposure to cued speech may become apparent only when cognitive levels are reached that allow children awareness of and the ability to manipulate information that previously had been implicit.

The Colin et al. (2007) findings and results from several other studies indicating facilitation in the development of literacy skills among children exposed to cued French are encouraging (e.g., Leybaert, 1993; Leybaert & Charlier, 1996). Marschark (2007), however, noted that in contrast with reports of effective literacy development by deaf and hard-of-hearing children using cued speech in French- and Spanish-speaking environments, there is an insufficient database from which to draw any conclusions about its outcomes in English-speaking environments. Alegria and Lechat (2005) suggested that the situation might be the result of the dependence of cued speech on the regularity of sound-to-spelling correspondence within languages, a correspondence that is lower in English than in French or Spanish.

Another system that uses visual representation of the phonemes of spoken language to supplement auditory information is Visual Phonics (VP; International Communication Learning Institute, 1996). Several investigators have suggested that VP can be a helpful aid in phonological development among deaf and hard-of-hearing children, regardless of the language modality they use for communication purposes.

Visual Phonics is based upon the concept that it is more critical to understand phonemes as building blocks of language and to develop the ability to use and manipulate them than to actually hear or produce the sounds (Trezek & Wang, 2006). It utilizes a system of hand signals that are produced in conjunction with spoken language in order to disambiguate those that either cannot be seen or cannot be differentiated through speechreading. VP can be used in speech therapy sessions in bilingual or sign/bilingual school settings (Waddy-Smith & Wilson, 2003) as well as with children using other language approaches (e.g., oral, TC, etc.) during the rest of the school day. It differs from cued speech in three ways. First, cued speech is often used as a routine communication system and is most beneficial when produced at home and school as a regular means of communication (along with spoken language); VP is used primarily in the school setting and for specific purposes of teaching phonics. Second, cued speech provides information about the sounds themselves but not their production, whereas VP hand shapes incorporate iconic elements that remind students of the articulatory movements necessary to produce the sounds orally. Third, cued speech represents sounds at the syllable level; VP represents individual phonemes.

Trezek and Wang (2006) reported on the outcome of a VP program for a small number (ranging from 9 to 13 on various subskills assessed) of deaf children in kindergarten and first grade in a TC setting. The school had adopted the Reading Mastery curriculum (Englemann & Brunner, 1995), a direct instruction approach that has been used successfully with hearing readers with and without reading problems. Teachers were trained in the use of VP and used it to implement the reading curriculum with their deaf and hard-of-hearing students. Pre- and post-intervention testing using the Wechsler Individual Achievement Test II (Psychological Corporation, 2002) indicated that during the 8 months of the study, students significantly increased their skills in word reading, pseudoword (word-like letter strings) decoding, and reading comprehension. Gains were not correlated with levels of hearing loss, but students with profound hearing losses seemed to benefit as much as those with losses in the severe range. Further, teachers gave anecdotal reports of children's spontaneously using the VP hand shapes when working to decode words on their own.

Another study of the effects of using VP was conducted by Trezek, Wang, Woods, Gampp, and Paul (2007). The approach again accompanied a structured curriculum approach designed to teach general literacy skills in kindergarten and first grade. This study included 20 children in two classes using manually coded English (TC) and in one oral class. Hearing loss levels ranged from mild to profound, and 10 of the students had cochlear implants. The districtwide reading curriculum had been developed by professionals in the local school district, and daily lessons included 90 minutes of literacy instruction including explicit instruction in phonemic awareness and phonics, a "read aloud" session in which teachers read to the children, vocabulary instruction, and general guided reading activities. Teachers were given initial and follow-up training in use of the VP method, and researchers' observations documented that the program had been implemented as planned.

Teachers initially expressed difficulties presenting the phonics portion of the county's reading program to students with hearing loss, but they reported that use of VP had removed that difficulty. Testing before and after the two-semester program showed that the children had made gains in the abilities targeted by the curriculum. Significant gains were found on subtests of the Dominie Reading and Writing Assessment Portfolio (DeFord, 2001) on written representation of sounds (phonemes) and spelling accuracy. Statistically significant gains were also reported on a subtest of phonemic awareness segmentation, in which the student must indicate the number of syllables in words that are presented orally, as well as on subtests of phoneme deletion (indicating what word remains after a particular sound is deleted), of word onset sounds, and of rhyming skills. The investigators were not specifically able to connect gains made by the children with the use of the VP method, however, because they failed to include a comparison group of deaf and hard-of-hearing students who did not receive the intervention. In addition, despite the observed gains, Trezek et al. (2007) found that students' stanine scores, which can be translated roughly into percentile scores for comparison with a norming sample, decreased over time on the subtests of reading skills. That is, although the deaf and hard-of-hearing participants had improved their phonics and reading skills, they had not kept up with the progress expected on the basis of initial levels.

In addition to speechreading, cued speech, and VP, other methods have been devised to make the phonology of spoken language more perceptible to deaf and hard-of-hearing students. Among these are computer-assisted systems such as the vocabulary tutor Baldi, that displays images of articulation from both inside and outside of the head together with lessons on speaking and reading words (Barker, 2003; Massaro, 2006). A series of multiple-baseline, single-subject studies involving hard-of-hearing students has shown increased outcome scores in recognition and production of spoken words. One advantage of the system is that the program can be used individually by students at various times and in various settings during the day. The degree to which such a tool will be accepted and used widely in educational settings for deaf students has yet to be fully explored, however, and more evidence of successful outcomes is needed.

Regardless of the approach used, it is evident that most deaf and many hard-of-hearing readers continue to have only tenuous knowledge of phonology during the early school years—and sometimes fail to apply that knowledge when it is available. Compared to hearing children, deaf and hard-of-hearing students are more dependent upon visual characteristics of words, indicated by their tending to rely on orthographic similarities when asked to write words that rhyme even in cases in which orthography misleads about phonology (e.g., *cave*, *have*). Nevertheless, there is evidence that at least some deaf and hard-of-hearing children can and do combine visual and auditory information in developing a phonological system and that this combination supports the development of reading skills (see Leybaert, 1993).

Vocabulary and Literacy Development

One of the reasons for interest in developing phonology is its use in decoding and identifying printed words that are represented in a child's lexicon, or vocabulary. Vocabulary size among deaf and hard-of-hearing children has consistently been found to be smaller on average than that of hearing children, both reflecting their language delay and providing a barrier to reading and writing that could otherwise enhance further language development. Such delays likely have multiple causes, including children's lack of experiences overhearing conversations occurring around them—and frequently insufficient skills to take advantage of those conversations they can access. Parents and other adults also are likely to use restricted vocabularies in interactions with deaf and hard-of-hearing children, sometimes because of lowered expectations concerning a child's knowledge or hearing and sometimes due to the adults' own lack of skills in producing sign language or unambiguous oral communication (Calderon & Greenberg, 2003; Easterbrooks & Baker, 2002). As with other aspects of development, deaf children's vocabulary development also reflects their parents' degree of involvement with them and their learning experiences and, in many cases, limited opportunities to interact with peers, siblings, and older children (Marschark et al., 2002; Moeller, 2000). Lederberg and Beal-Alvarez (in press) concluded that vocabulary growth of children with hearing loss is related to the frequency with which they are exposed to a word, the visual accessibility of the representation of the word, and the degree to which the word's use is contingent upon or related to the child's interest and focus of attention.

As might be expected by this point, the reading abilities of deaf and hard-of-hearing children have been found to associate especially strongly with their vocabulary skills (Hermans et al., 2008b; Kyle & Harris, 2006; LaSasso & Davey, 1987; Marschark et al., 2002; Paul & Gustafson, 1991). They typically have restricted diversity of words in word classes, as shown by the overuse of a limited number of familiar verbs and concrete nouns in their writing (de Villiers, 1991; Trezek et al., in press). Furthermore, because their vocabulary knowledge tends to be less rich or complete than that of hearing children, and because they have probably seen or heard the words in fewer contexts than the average hearing child, many deaf and hard-of-hearing children have a particular weakness in comprehending multiple meanings for the same word. To overcome this problem, Paul (1996) suggested that vocabulary instruction should deviate from the traditional practice of learning definitions in relative isolation prior to use in assignments and should instead involve encounters with new words in multiple situations. He argued that discussion and schematic representations of aspects of a word's meaning, along with repeated experiences with a word in varied meaningful contexts, is a better way to support vocabulary development. Restricted vocabularies mean that, more often than is the case with hearing children, children with hearing loss must learn a word's printed form without having known and used a label for that meaning in conversational language (Hermans et al., 2008a). Hermans et al. (2008b), however, indicated that learning of written vocabulary is easier when children already know a sign for the concept or entity represented. They posited that the initial stage of a printed word's recognition occurs when it is paired in memory with a sign. When the printed word is repeatedly encountered, understanding of its meaning is strengthened as it is used in varied syntactic and pragmatic contexts. This proposal is consistent with Kelly's (1996) assertion that syntax and semantics (the meaning of words) work reciprocally to build reading comprehension (see below). The third stage of understanding described by Hermann et al. involves a word's meaning becoming automatically available upon being encountered, so that excessive cognitive resources are not required to identify it when it is found in a new context (see also Bebko, 1998, and Kelly, 2003a). When opportunities for generalization and deepening of understanding of a word's meaning are not provided, Hermans et al. (2008a) suggest that the meaning can "fossilize" and fail to include all the features which it typically would include.

Automaticity in word recognition and comprehension is enhanced when children have multiple means of representing a word's meaning, that is, when they know its printed, spoken, and signed expression. Wauters, Tellings, van Bon, and Mak (2008) also found that increasing the number of senses through which children experience the meaning of acquired words (e.g., hearing, seeing, smelling, touching) increases the strength of acquisition and subsequently makes comprehension of the words quicker and more automatic. Interestingly, although this approach was generally found to be more effective than acquiring word meaning through purely linguistic means, hearing children profited more than deaf children.

One method that provides opportunities to teach multiple representational forms to deaf and hard-of-hearing children has been referred to as "chaining" and has been noted to occur frequently in classes taught by teachers who are fluent signers (Padden & Ramsey, 1998, 2000). This involves the teacher directly and sequentially demonstrating a word using print, sign, and fingerspelling. Thus the letters in the word, or orthography, appear twice, with the signed form (typically the word's most frequent meaning) always included and often repeated. An extension of this approach has been used in programs that also aim to build spoken representation of the word by adding the spoken form of the word to the chain (Seal et al., 2005). Although there is little or no indication that deaf and hard-of-hearing children directly decode printed words via fingerspelling (Musselman, 2000), its apparently spontaneous use in these chains is an indication that many teachers have learned from experience that it can assist initial learning of words in print.

Vocabulary development has been extensively studied in young children who use cochlear implants, with the frequent goal of identifying developmental predictors rather than establishing age-based expectations for vocabulary size. Typically, researchers find that children using cochlear implants understand and produce more spoken words than those with similar hearing levels who use hearing aids. Connor et al. (2000), investigating the effects of language modality and age of implantation on vocabulary, reported that at the beginning of their study the 66 participating children who were in TC programming had an average expressive vocabulary size larger than that of the 81 children in oral education programs. The children in TC programs were exposed on a daily basis to manually coded English and were also provided intensive auditory and speech training. The vocabulary growth of both groups of children was accelerated compared to that typical for deaf children without cochlear implants. However, both groups of children (oral and TC) with cochlear implants showed less rapid growth in receptive vocabulary (tested using only speech) than is typical for hearing children, and their scores increasingly deviated from hearing norms over time. Vocabulary growth rate was higher for children using TC than those in oral-only programs, however, if they received their implants early—before the age of 5 years.

Connor et al. (2000) concluded that age of implantation, characteristics of the technology used in the implants, and the use of signs to build early vocabulary levels all influenced the children's vocabulary growth. Similar results have been reported by other researchers (e.g., Schorr et al., 2008). Connor and Zwolan (2004) investigated the reading comprehension skills of 91 deaf children (average age = 11 years) who had used cochlear implants for at least 4 years. Using a statistical procedure that allows identification of effects of a single factor while controlling all others (SEM path analysis), they found that vocabulary scores significantly predicted reading skills. Pre-implant vocabulary size tended to be larger for children in TC programs (which included an emphasis on speech and spoken language) and predicted post-implant vocabulary. Post-implant vocabulary size had a direct and positive effect on scores on reading. Direct effects on reading outcomes were also found for age of cochlear implantation (younger ages led to better reading scores) and for socioeconomic status, with lower status predicting lower achievement. Although reading skills tended to increase by age, the gap between deaf children's performance and norms for hearing children also increased with age.

In contrast to frequent assumptions, the use of signing as a support for spoken vocabulary development has shown benefits for children who are hard of hearing as well as those who are deaf. Mollink, Hermans, and Knoors (2008), for example, studied 14 hard-of-hearing children, aged approximately 4.5 years to just over 8 years, who used hearing aids and were in separate educational placements for deaf children using Sign Supported Dutch. Pre-testing showed the deaf children's average nonverbal cognitive functioning to be slightly below the average established on the test for hearing children, and a similar result was found on a test of visual short-term memory. Vocabulary training was conducted under four conditions: a control condition which included no specific training, a spoken Dutch–only condition, a combined sign and spoken Dutch condition, and a condition in which definitions using spoken Dutch were combined with mention of a specific color name associated with the vocabulary item. Children were tested in spoken Dutch before the training sessions began, then 1 week and 5 weeks after the training was completed. The most efficacious condition was that in which both sign and spoken word were used during training. In all except the control condition, the number of words correctly named by the children (in spoken language) increased significantly between pretesting and testing 1 week after training had been completed. Test scores at one week post-training were statistically significantly higher than those 5 weeks after training, but the actual difference was relatively small (means of 39.5% and 36.5% correct, respectively). Thus, significant benefits endured even after the training finished.

Mollink et al. (2008) also analyzed learning and retention of word meanings based on the iconicity of the sign representing each word—that is, the extent to which the sign looks like what it represents. Consistent with earlier findings, they found that iconicity did not have a significant effect overall on learning, but there was an interaction between degree of iconicity and change in scores between 1 and 5 weeks post-training, with lower scores obtained at the 5-week post-test for words with lower versus higher iconicity. More research with larger numbers of individuals is needed to further investigate this phenomenon. Despite some remaining questions, the findings of this study are consistent with others indicating that presentation of words in more than one modality does *not* interfere with deaf and hard-of-hearing students' learning their spoken representations.

Taken together, the above studies indicate that there is a convergence of find-ings showing that development of written vocabulary knowledge continues to be limited for deaf and hard-of-hearing children, despite various interventions, and general agreement that it is an area in which special efforts need to be made if literacy skills are to be increased. It is frequently pointed out that vocabulary instruction needs to occur in meaningful contexts as opposed to simple drill and practice or memorization of definitions. However, it is also acknowledged that vocabulary should be specifically addressed and cannot be expected to develop sufficiently without direct instruction (e.g., Davey & King, 1990; deVilliers & Pomerantz, 1992; Easterbrooks & Stephenson, 2006; Musselman, 2000; Paul, 1998). Kelly (2003a) recommended extensive practice on print vocabulary by providing frequent, repeated but short and focused reading activities to increase automaticity of word recognition and support reading comprehension. Importantly, he emphasized that the activities should be developmentally appro-priate and that feedback on performance is critical for progress. Easterbrooks and Stephenson (2006) further recommended instruction in the use of context for identifying word meanings and provision of specific activities that build understanding about root and base words, prefixes, and suffixes by identifying the print forms of English grammatical morphemes (see also Gaustad & Kelly, 2004). This level of understanding words in print, of course, requires knowledge of phonology, semantics, vocabulary, and syntax, and we now turn to the last of these.

Syntactic Knowledge and Reading

"Syntax" refers to word order in sentences and also to the use of grammatical morphemes that represent and qualify aspects of number, verb tense, prepositions, articles, and in some languages, the gender of nouns, pronouns, and modifiers. Many deaf and hard-of-hearing students face special challenges learning morphological aspects of syntax because the syntax of natural sign languages such as British Sign Language (BSL) or ASL does not match that of the spoken language they are expected to read and write. Adding to the difficulty, users of manually coded systems such as Signed English frequently fail to sign the grammatical morphemes, and these components of words tend to be unstressed in speech productions and thus difficult to hear. Some sentence-level syntactic constructions are more difficult than others, but the difficulties with syntax noted in both reading and writing by deaf and hard-of-hearing students are myriad. For example, Trezek et al. (in press) summarized work by Quigley and his colleagues (see also King & Quigley, 1985) by reporting that deaf and hard-of hearing students have difficulties at the sentence level with negation, conjunction, question forms, pronominalization, verbs and verb tenses, complement structures, relative clauses, disjunction, and alternation (p. 100). Gaustad and Kelly (2004) showed that hearing middle school students had better use and understanding of grammatical morphemes and word segmentation than deaf college students, even when the two groups of students received similar scores on standardized reading tests.

Kelly (2003b) studied 16 skilled and 14 less skilled young adults who were profoundly deaf and predominantly used sign language, concluding that complex syntactic structures in reading stimuli slowed the reading speed of both groups. The decreased automaticity or processing speed was particularly striking for the group with the lower level of reading comprehension skills, who read at approximately a fifth-grade level. Kelly concluded that syntactic complexity was a contributing factor to decreases in working memory for material that was read. This finding was consistent with an earlier study by Kelly (1996) involving 100 deaf adolescents who had been educated in oral programs, 113 from TC programs, and 211 young adults who were entering postsecondary programs. Results of that investigation indicated that when syntactic competence was low, the students could not make full use of advantages they might otherwise have from their vocabulary knowledge. Difficulties and delays in one domain thus affect the ability to employ skills in the other. Kelly concluded that syntactic skills have both direct and indirect effects on deaf students' reading comprehension.

In another study, Kelly (1998) used a single-subject, multiple-baseline design with 11 participants and showed that understanding of complex sentences (with relative clauses or passive voice constructions) could be increased through silent videos in which the sentence meanings were demonstrated, students had to actively choose the sentence represented in the video, and feedback about correctness was provided. Unfortunately, few such interventions have been reported specifically targeting remediation of the syntactic delays characteristic of so many deaf and hard-of-hearing students.

Due to delays in syntactic development, however, those students need to have other strategies and approaches available to aid their understanding and production of print (Bebko, 1998; Kelly, 2003a). A potential compensatory strategy would be application of background knowledge and use of context beyond the sentence level to disambiguate complex syntactic constructions (Ewoldt, 1981; McGill-Franzen & Gormley, 1980; Nolen & Wilbur, 1985). Deaf and hard-of-hearing students' documented limitations in background or general knowledge (Marschark, Sapere, Convertino, Seewagen, & Maltzen, 2004; but cf. Paul, 1998) nevertheless may limit the usefulness of such strategies, unless much pre-teaching is done prior to reading activities.

Another potential strategy to compensate for lack of specific syntactic knowledge involves relying upon the order of the major words in a complex sentence. Students often may assume that the first noun is the sentence subject, followed by a verb and a complement or object. Schick and Moeller (1992) reported that knowledge of English word order was relatively well established for deaf and hard-of-hearing adolescents who had had extensive exposure to a manually coded English system, although the students' use of grammatical morphemes was deficient. This suggests that a word-order strategy can be helpful in some cases. Findings of strengths in deaf students' understanding of word order are not universal, however. Miller (2000), for example, compared the word and sentence reading performance of 19 hard-of-hearing students in Israel (most of whom used signed and spoken Hebrew), 206 deaf students (most of whom used Israeli Sign Language), and 35 hearing students. He found that only about half of the students with hearing loss were able to respond appropriately to a test requiring knowledge of syntax as reflected in word order. The other students tended to identify key content words and use those in attempting to understand the sentences. This strategy was successful when information in the sentences was consistent with students' prior knowledge and experience, but not when it was new or anomalous.

Although lack of phonological knowledge has been blamed for at least part of the syntactic problems evidenced in reading and writing by students with hearing loss (Lillo-Martin, Hanson, & Smith, 1992), it was notable that some of the worst performers in Miller's study were hard-of-hearing students, suggesting that more than the degree of auditory sensitivity (and presumably phonological awareness) determines the application of syntactic knowledge in reading comprehension. Results consistent with this suggestion come from a study by Nikolopoulos, Dyar, Archbold, and O'Donoghue (2004). They assessed the performance of 82 children, all of whom began to use cochlear implants before the age of 7 years, on a test of comprehension of grammatical contrasts in spoken language. The test tapped understanding of nouns, verbs, negative constructions, singular/plural forms, passive sentences, and relative clauses. Nikolopoulos et al. found that before getting their cochlear implants, only one child obtained a score as high as the lowest percentile group of hearing children in the test norming sample. After 3 years of cochlear implant use, 40% attained at least this level and 67% scored at that level or higher after 3 to 5 years of use. Because percentile scores provide a way of making comparisons with same-age hearing peers, this result shows a gain in relative standing over years of use (i.e., longer experience with an implant leads to better grammatical skills), although students who score at only the first percentile have scores below 99% of the norm group and cannot be said to be very accomplished in the area tested.

Looking at the Nikolopoulos et al. (2004) data from another perspective, 18 children (47%) who received implants before 4 years of age scored in percentiles 1–25, two children (5%) scored between the 25th and 75th percentiles, and three (8%) scored between the 75th and 100th percentiles after 3 years of use. In comparison, of the children implanted after age 4, only nine (21%) scored between the 1st and 25th percentiles and one child (2%) scored between the 25th and 75th percentiles; none scored higher than that. In short, benefits accrued from implant experience, but the age at which auditory information became available also affected development (see Marschark et al., 2010, for discussion of the role of cognitive development in such findings). Even considering the effect of age, scores in the above study varied greatly and, overall, remained below scores of the great majority of hearing children.

Knowledge of a First Language as a Basis for Literacy in a Second Language

Cummins (1989, 1991) posited that there is a common underlying proficiency across languages, so that fluency in one language will support the development of fluency in another. This linguistic interdependence theory, plus observations described in chapter 5 showing strong development of a natural sign language by children in an environment rich in that language, provides support for the establishment of bilingual-bicultural or sign/bilingual programming for deaf and hard-of-hearing children. In general, these programs focus on development of a natural sign language and, later, acquisition of a second language through the medium of print. That is, children's second language is the print version of the spoken language of the surrounding hearing community. Accordingly, most available research on the bilingual approach focuses on relationships between children's skills in a native sign language (e.g., BSL, ASL) and their reading and, occasionally, their writing skills.

The applicability of Cummins's (1989) theory to education of deaf and hard-of-hearing children is not universally accepted. Mayer and Wells (1996), for example, claimed in a widely read theoretical paper that Cummins's work was not directly relevant in the context of an ASL to English transfer due to structural differences between the languages at multiple levels (e.g., morphological, modality of perception) and to the fact that there is no written form of ASL from which transfer to another written language can be made. Mayer and Wells's view was consistent with results from a study by Moores and Sweet (1990), who found no relationship between ratings of adolescents' ASL conversational fluency and scores on the Test of (English) Syntactic Abilities (Quigley et al.,(1978), the Peabody Individual Achievement Test (PIAT; Markwardt, 1970), or other measures of English functioning.

Hoffmeister (2000) argued that the ASL assessment used by Moores and Sweet was a general one and that more detailed and sophisticated measures might allow better identification of relationships between ASL and skills in reading English. In addition, the ability to find significant correlations among measures used in the Moores and Sweet study was limited by a ceiling effect on their ASL measure, with a relatively large number of children rated as performing at the top level (Strong & Prinz, 1997, 2000). Nevertheless, Convertino, Marschark, et al. (2008) also failed to find a significant relationship between deaf college students' ASL skills and their learning from print. Classroom learning from both sign and print (i.e., real-time text) was significantly predicted by their reported Simultaneous Communication (SimCom) skills, suggesting that flexibility in dealing with the two languages of the classroom was more important than skill in any one alone.

DeLana, Gentry, and Andrews (2007) summarized a longitudinal study of 25 students participating in a public school ASL/English bilingual program. The study involved six teachers in a single school district where considerable effort was made to provide fluent ASL models. Students ranged from second grade to high school age at the time analyses were performed, so it appears that more data were available for some than for other students. The Reading Comprehension subtest of the Stanford Achievement Test, 9th edition (SAT-9; Harcourt Educational Management, 1996) was the sole reading outcome measure used, but information was collected on a number of background demographic variables. Descriptive data indicated that reading comprehension scores increased with age and that increases continued to be made after students reached the age of 12 years. In most cases, however, the students' reading grade level score was below their actual grade in school. Students' number of years in the ASL program correlated significantly with their reading scores, but it does not appear that student age was controlled in the calculation and no formal measure of ASL skills was available. No statistically significant differences in students' reading achievement were identified as a function of the hearing status of parents and siblings, primary home language, parents' sign language skills, socioeconomic status, age at onset of hearing loss, level of hearing loss, use of amplification technology, or ethnicity (see also Convertino, Marschark, et al., 2009). The level of parent involvement (as rated by teachers), however, was found to correlate significantly with greater gains and higher scores on the reading measure. Although the large number of correlations calculated without compensatory changes in acceptable level of statistical significance makes even this positive finding questionable, it is consistent with earlier reports of deaf and hard-of-hearing children's progress (e.g., Moeller, 2000; Spencer, 2004).

Strong and Prinz (1997, 2000), utilizing a detailed test of ASL skills (Prinz & Strong, 1994), analyzed the relationships between ASL and several tests of English skills (including the Woodcock Johnson Psychoeducational Test Battery-Revised [Woodcock & Mather, 1989, 1990]) for a sample of 155 8- to 15-year-old students at a residential school for deaf children. Results showed that students with higher ASL skills also scored higher on English literacy measures, even after age and nonverbal IQ were controlled. Although students with deaf mothers generally outperformed those with hearing mothers on the literacy measures, this difference disappeared for students with medium to high levels of ASL skills. These results show convincingly that skill in ASL does *not* interfere with development of English skills. However, because Strong and Prinz failed to assess or account for the ability to use manually coded English, spoken language, or benefits of residual hearing, it is not possible to attribute a causal effect of ASL skills on English literacy development based on their analyses.

Hoffmeister and his colleagues (Hoffmeister, 2000; Hoffmeister, Philip, Costello, & Grass, 1997) also found that ASL skill was related to and did not interfere with development of English literacy skills.[2] They investigated the ASL skills (knowledge of synonyms, antonyms, plural and quantifier forms) of 78 students, ages 8–15, in four schools (two day schools and two residential schools) in the United States and related those skills to manually coded English skills and English reading comprehension (as measured on the SAT-HI, the 1973 "hearing impaired" version of the Stanford Achievement Test, 6th edition). The ASL tests included no printed English and used a recognition format to minimize memory

---

[2] Neither these nor related studies by the same team have been published in peer-reviewed journals, and their rigor is thus unclear.

constraints. Students with deaf parents scored significantly higher on the first two ASL tasks than did those with hearing parents and limited exposure to ASL.

Hoffmeister (2000) also examined SAT-HI reading comprehension scores for a subsample of 50 students, divided into those with extensive ASL exposure and those with limited exposure. Knowledge of manually coded English was assessed using the Rhode Island Test of Language Structure (Engen & Engen, 1983), for which a score on complex sentence structure was created. Not surprisingly, the group with extensive ASL exposure scored significantly higher on knowledge of ASL than the group with less exposure; however, the higher exposure ASL group also scored significantly higher on the task of manually coded English. This suggests that the effects of greater sign language exposure were not specific to ASL. Furthermore, the students with more ASL experience also scored higher on the reading comprehension measure, even when age was controlled. Hoffmeister concluded that even children exposed more often to manually coded English than to ASL learn rules of ASL, and that deaf children exposed to ASL also perform well on measures of manually coded English. Thus, he argued that "deaf students can and do transfer skills from one language to another" (p. 160).

On the basis of these findings, Hoffmeister (2000) also concluded that "intensive language exposure in the form of ASL enhanced language functioning, as reflected in the MCE [manually coded English] and reading measures" (p. 158). However, he pointed out that there is an inherent confound in these data—that is, the students with more ASL skills usually had more (and earlier) exposure to language overall than those whose experiences with fluent manual language were limited to the school context. The relations found between ASL knowledge, knowledge of manually coded English, and reading thus may have resulted at least in part from early, consistent exposure to language rather than from exposure to any particular language. There was no way to test whether these advantages would have accrued had that language been fluently signed, manually coded English or spoken language based on effective use of amplification or cochlear implants.

In a study conducted in the Netherlands, Hermans, Knoors, Ormel, and Verhoeven (2008a) reported that setting up and attaining a fluent bilingual system is more difficult for deaf children than for hearing children. They attributed this in part to variation in the quality and quantity of input models provided (i.e., in the sign language skill of teachers and parents) and in part to the fact that most deaf children face learning yet a third representation system, written language, before fluency in either a first (i.e., sign language) or a second (i.e., spoken language) language is fully developed. They noted that studies showing that better reading skills accompany better native sign language skills (e.g., ASL, BSL, Sign Language of the Netherlands [NGT]) give evidence of the transfer of "conceptual knowledge, metacognitive and metalinguistic knowledge/strategies"

(p. 157) between a first- and a second-learned language. However, Hermans et al. emphasized the importance of early and proficient learning of sign language to support deaf children's acquisition of print vocabulary. They concluded that it is important for the children first to have extensive vocabulary repertoires in sign language, so that signs can provide the basis for the association between meaning and printed word. The richer the understanding of the sign, the richer will be appreciation of the meaning of the written word with which it is associated (McEvoy, Marschark, & Nelson, 1999).

In another analysis of the language and literacy performance of deaf children in special schools in the Netherlands, Hermans, Knoors, Ormel, and Verhoeven (2008b) predicted and subsequently found that sign vocabulary size predicted knowledge of vocabulary in written form, even after age, nonverbal cognitive skills, and short-term memory skills were statistically controlled. They also found that children whose preferred language was NGT had larger vocabularies than those children who showed no such preference. Children with deaf parents, and thus with early and consistent exposure to NGT, had larger sign vocabularies than those without such exposure, and sign vocabulary scores were associated with comprehension of stories whether presented in written Dutch or NGT. Comprehension of stories in NGT and in written Dutch were also significantly associated; however, this association was not significant when vocabulary differences were controlled.

Hermans et al. (2008b) pointed out that earlier studies showing associations between reading and natural sign language skills had not accounted for vocabulary differences. They concluded: "High scores on the sign language tasks are not *necessarily* (emphasis in original) associated with high scores on the written language tests" (p. 527). They further noted that the children in their study who scored above the 90th percentile on the test of written vocabulary also tended to have the highest ratings on their *spoken* Dutch skills, as reported by teachers and shown in their comprehension of stories presented in spoken Dutch. Hermans et al. cautioned, therefore, that researchers need to ascertain whether and to what extent spoken language abilities confound and complicate identification of apparent relationships between sign language skills and literacy measures.

Knowing the spoken form of a word adds the potential for multiple sources of information about its meaning, although this may of necessity happen late in deaf children's stages of reading acquisition. Accordingly, Hermans et al. (2008a) suggested that teachers may use methods like Visual Phonics (Woolsey, Satterfield, & Robertson, 2006) or fingerspelling to "increase children's knowledge of the sublexical structures (letters, graphemes/phonemes, and syllables" (p. 169) or cued speech to transmit information about the spoken language to combine with that based on sign knowledge.

It is apparent that full implementation of a sign/bilingual model of education will require specialized training and skills in the teaching staff. In general, teachers need to have a combination of knowledge about child development, educational practice, strong skills in production and understanding of natural sign language skills, and fluent literacy skills in the second language. Winn (2007) noted that sign language skills are considered by pre-service teacher training students in Australia to be a critical element in their educational preparation. He concluded that ongoing courses in Auslan are needed for teachers if they are to meet the needs of increasingly diverse students in increasingly diverse educational environments in that country.

Simms and Thumann (2007) reported on the components of an undergraduate and graduate program at Gallaudet University in the United States, which aims specifically to train teachers to work in sign/bilingual programs. That program stresses fluent use of natural sign language and understanding of its role in a sign/bilingual approach, appreciation of the culture and history of deaf persons, high expectations for the achievements that can be attained by deaf students, and the ability for collaboration between deaf and hearing education professionals. Simms and Thumann posited that deaf learners typically have strengths in visual processing and that a deaf-centered approach to teaching will place greater emphasis on certain aspects of development and skill development than programs that are based on models of hearing students' learning styles. Although intuitively appealing, such programming lacks empirical tests of its outcomes (see Marschark & Wauters, 2008).

Perhaps the best-known program of this sort for younger children is the CAEBER (Center for ASL/English Bilingual Education and Research) now located at Gallaudet University. According to its website, CAEBER "envisions high academic achievement for deaf and hard-of-hearing students by facilitating proficiency in both American Sign Language and English." Apparently the only outcome information currently available from the program, however, is its 2002 5-year report to the U.S. Department of Education, which funded the project (http://caeber.gallaudet.edu/assets/PDFs/resources/year5.pdf, accessed November 20, 2008). According to the data presented in that report, reading comprehension scores on the Stanford Achievement Test, 9th edition, for 8- to 18-year-olds in their bilingual program were no higher than those reported by Traxler (2000) for all deaf and hard-of-hearing children in the SAT9 normative sample. This finding is particularly noteworthy given that 33% of the students in the CAEBER sample had deaf parents and thus represented a group that frequently is claimed to have higher literacy skills than deaf children with hearing parents.

Given available published data, it is not possible to ascertain whether attaining fluency in a first, natural sign language will provide a means of strengthening literacy skills in a second language for deaf and hard-of-hearing students. This is not to say that signed/bilingual educational programming has been shown to be ineffective, but that positive evidence is lacking despite the appeal of the theoretical perspective. Moores (2008) called not only for additional research but for publication of any information available about deaf and hard-of-hearing children's progress in "Bi-Bi" or sign/bilingual programs. Hermans et al. (2008a) similarly asked why, after two decades of sign/bilingual programming across many countries, deaf children still have not matched the literacy achievement of their same-age hearing peers. They suggested that it is important to keep in mind that the original language (in this case, a sign language) and the language represented in print interact as the children acquire literacy skills. As an example, Hermans et al. reported a reading error in which the signed form of a concept actually seemed to interfere with the child's reading of a sentence (p. 158) and commented (similar to Paul, 1998) that "the role of spoken language in the acquisition of written language" (p. 157) skills may have been underestimated by proponents of sign/bilingual education approaches.

Teaching Approaches and the Development of Reading Comprehension

Comprehension is the central purpose of reading and is the active process of constructing meaning from text (Luckner & Handley, 2008, p. 6). Understanding of messages carried by print requires skill in all of the abilities addressed above. In addition, application of vocabulary, syntactic, and phonological /morphological knowledge must proceed at a fairly rapid or automatic rate to allow memory and cognitive processing of the material decoded. Background information and experiences that result in the reading material being familiar also assist in interpretation of texts.

Luckner and Handley (2008) conducted a review of research published in English (with a focus on publications in journals readily available in the United States) between 1963 and 2003 on reading comprehension of deaf and hard-of-hearing students. They included studies at all levels of evidence: experimental or randomized clinical trials, case study or qualitative studies, correlational or descriptive studies, and single-subject studies. Approximately half of the studies they identified tested an intervention procedure, and converging findings across multiple studies indicated that the following approaches produced positive outcomes (Luckner & Handley, p. 9): (a) explicit instruction in strategies for comprehension, (b) teaching narrative structure or story grammar, (c) using modified directed-reading thinking activities or DRTAs (i.e., reading for specific purposes, guided by questions), (d) using approaches to activate and build background information prior to reading activities, (e) using reading materials that are high interest, well written, and have *not* been simplified grammatically or in vocabulary choice, (f) providing specific activities to build vocabulary knowledge, (g) using connected text instead of sentences in isolation to provide instruction in syntax or grammar, (h) encouraging the use of mental imagery while reading, and (i) teaching students to look for key words to assist in comprehension of text (see also Sartawi, Al-Hilawani, & Easterbrooks, 1998).

Easterbrooks and Stephenson (2006) also surveyed existing research, but they used more rigorous criteria for evaluating the degree of certainty in the evidence produced by the studies. Their analysis used state websites, education administrators at state agencies, and web-based indices of peer-reviewed publications to identify the set of top 10 activities considered to be "best practices" for supporting general literacy skills. They then evaluated the quality and quantity of research evaluating outcomes of those practices. They found little to no research investigating outcomes related to the amount of time provided for independent reading, and a still-developing research base indicating that web-based instructional programs can provide useful visual support for reading (Barman & Stockton, 2002). There was only mixed evidence across studies for the effectiveness of teaching of phonemic awareness and phonics as a path to reading comprehension (Izzo, 2002; Luetke-Stahlman & Nielsen, 2003). Like Luckner and Handley (2008), Easterbrooks and Stephenson found evidence that supported the practice of directed reading: Reading in a content area, such as science or social studies, was also found to have a mutually supportive relationship with general reading comprehension, and Easterbrooks and Stephenson decided it fit the definition of best practice. Shared reading activities were found to meet the criteria for best practice at younger ages but not necessarily for older and better readers. Approaching both vocabulary and morphological knowledge through meaningful activities was also shown to effectively support reading comprehension (e.g., deVilliers & Pomerantz, 1992; Paul, 1996) and thus earned a "best practice" label.

Metacognition and Reading Comprehension

The above surveys of research literature identified practices that prompt application of cognitive processes and promote reading as a problem-solving activity as fruitful approaches to increasing literacy skills. Schirmer and Williams (in press) pointed out that metacognition, or awareness of one's own comprehension and the intentional use of strategies to support it, is an important and positive component of effective reading. Some researchers have found that metacognition is often not spontaneously activated by deaf and hard-of-hearing readers (e.g., Walker, Munro, & Rickards, 1998). For example, deaf students have been reported to be less aware than hearing students when they do not comprehend what they are reading, to rely more on pictures and less on their relevant background knowledge than hearing children do to help them predict and comprehend text, and generally to be "passive" readers instead of actively engaging in comprehension strategies unless prompted by the teacher (Marschark, Sapere, et al., 2004; Schirmer, 2003; Schirmer, Bailey & Lockman, 2004, pp. 6–7).

Schirmer et al. (2004) posited that responsibility for deaf and hard-of-hearing students' relative lack of use of metacognitive strategies is due in large part to methods of teaching that have fostered dependence instead of independence. They summarized existing research showing that teachers' questions encouraging application of background knowledge and using salient details from the reading as a basis for drawing inferences can increase students' abilities to analyze, synthesize, and evaluate what they have read and can increase independence in applying metacognitive processes. Walker et al. (1998) reported that a 30-lesson curriculum designed to encourage deaf and hard-of-hearing students to make both simple and complex inferences resulted in increased reading comprehension.

Schirmer et al. (2004) employed a "thinking aloud" approach like that used by Schirmer (2003) to assess deaf students' use of metacognitive strategies while reading. A total of 16 deaf students were assessed over the two studies. Content analysis was performed on transcripts of the children's verbalizations (mostly in sign because they were in TC programs using a form of manually coded English) to identify the strategies that they used. The students were found to use strategies such as paraphrasing, visualizing, interpreting, and looking for main ideas to construct meaning. On the other hand, students generally did not monitor their comprehension carefully and, consistent with other reports, were often not aware when their comprehension failed. They therefore failed to modify and use alternative strategies when these would have been appropriate. The deaf students, like hearing students, gave evidence of evaluating the material they were reading, but their evaluations were primarily affective, and they did not spontaneously comment on the quality of writing in the story. They also did not give evidence of making decisions such as when to skim a section quickly or when to slow down and reread to enhance comprehension. Although these deaf students often failed to recognize when their lack of comprehension was the result of a lack of background knowledge, they used such knowledge when it was available.

Schirmer et al. (2004) recognized that the limited number of participants in the two studies prohibited firm conclusions. However, based on their own and others' research, they recommended that deaf students be provided "systematic and explicit instruction" (p. 13) on strategies for comprehending text. These strategies would include monitoring characteristics of the text, being aware of their purpose for reading, recognizing their own problems keeping attention focused on the text, monitoring the pace of their reading and deciding when they should reread or read more slowly and carefully, and evaluating both the quality of the text and the ideas that it was expressing. They concluded that use of verbal protocols, or thinking aloud, during reading is a useful method for identifying the strategies used by individual readers and, consequently, for designing individualized instruction.

WRITING

The processes of developing reading and writing skills are intimately intertwined, but it is generally agreed that writing places even greater demands than reading on linguistic and cognitive processing (Mayer, 1999; Moores, 2001). It therefore is not unexpected that deaf and hard-of-hearing students tend to show delays and difficulties in their production of written work. Typical 17- to 18-year-old deaf students have been reported to write at skill levels like those of 8- to 10-year-old hearing students (Marschark et al., 2002; Paul, 1998, 2001). Written productions of deaf and hard-of-hearing students have been described as containing shorter and simpler sentences than expected for age, along with use of fewer adjectives, adverbs, prepositions, and conjunctions (Marschark, Mouradian, & Halas, 1994). Problems with aspects of morphology and grammatical structure are especially prevalent (Yoshinaga-Itano, Snyder, & Mayberry, 1996). Despite these problems of form, deaf and hearing students have been found to produce similar numbers of t-units (propositions or ideas) in writing samples (Musselman & Szanto, 1998; Yoshinaga-Itano et al., 1996) and expression of meaning is relatively unimpaired in the productions of deaf and hard-of-hearing students compared to their difficulties in surface-level forms (Marschark et al., 1994; Svartholm, 2008; Yoshinaga-Itano et al., 1996).

No current approach for supporting language development has been found to resolve deaf and hard-of-hearing students' difficulties with written language. Similar problems have been reported for children across programs utilizing spoken language, manually coded systems for signing, and natural sign languages. Burman, Nunes, and Evans (2006), for example, reported on development and trial of an approach to assessing the written language skills of children whose first language is British Sign Language (BSL). The need for a unique assessment instrument was based on the fact that so many of these children failed to produce writing that could be scored as falling even the earliest or lowest level proposed by the Qualifications and Curriculum Authority for English students. Burman et al. noted that children who use a natural sign language face an extra translation step when writing a spoken language. They pointed out that in addition to syntactic differences, there is not a one-to-one correspondence between many signs and spoken words. (They give an example of "up until now," which is expressed by a single sign in BSL.)

In an extensive study in the United States, Singleton et al. (2004) investigated the written vocabulary use of 72 children in Grades 1 through 6 who had in-school exposure to ASL, comparing their productions with those of 66 same-age hearing students who were monolingual speakers of English and 60 hearing English-as-a-second-language (ESL) students. ASL-experienced students were divided into three groups based on their ASL competency as assessed on the

American Sign Language Proficiency Assessment (Maller, Singleton, Supalla, & Wix, 1999). Proficiency scores (low, moderate, and high) on this assessment have been found to be independent of both age and grade level. All participants watched a video of the "Tortoise and Hare" story and prepared a written retelling of the story in English. Consistent with earlier studies, the deaf children used fewer words overall than hearing students for whom English was a first language *or* those for whom English was a second language.

Deaf children with low ASL skills used a greater proportion of "most frequent words" (Luckner & Isaacson, 1990) than children in the other two groups, although they were not statistically significantly different from the ESL students on that measure. The high ASL group used more non-frequent words than either the ESL or the low-ASL group, a finding that implies that they had more creative use of English vocabulary. When English grammatical or "function" words (e.g., pronouns, prepositions) were compared, however, both typical and ESL hearing children used more than did any of the deaf groups. Among the deaf groups, those with high ASL skills were more likely to use grammatical function words when there was an ASL sign equivalent. However, overall, the low-ASL group (which was recruited primarily from a TC school) actually used more grammatical function words than did the moderate and high ASL groups.

The overall picture is that children with moderate or high ASL skills were as creative and had as broad a use of vocabulary in their written stories as did the hearing students, while the low ASL students were the least productive. However, any transfer from ASL to English appeared limited to semantic or conceptual vocabulary, not the function or grammatical words that are not represented by discrete signs in ASL. The transfer that Cummins (1989) hypothesized was, at least at these age levels, occurring at a conceptual and perhaps cognitive level but not at the level of mechanics of grammar. Singleton et al. (2004) concluded that the model of hearing ESL students' acquisition of literacy skills was not applicable to deaf children. They posited that hearing gives an "advantage in terms of exposure to the probabilistic patterns of vocabulary in English" (p. 100), a reference to the difficulties deaf children face in learning the highly frequent function words and grammatical morphemes. The Singleton et al. data also suggest that deaf children in the study were still in the process of learning their first language and that attaining fluency in a second, written language in a sign/bilingual program would require time beyond the sixth year in school.

The following portion of an example of the written production of a child with *high ASL skills* shows both the conceptual strengths and English grammatical weaknesses indicated by Singleton et al (p. 101):

Turtle and Rabbit Race Try
Who win turtle
Rabbit sleep tiptoe Turtle and Wake Rabbit...

In contrast, the following example they provided from a hearing child learning English as a second language shows that the grammatical system is far from perfected, but the placement of and necessity for function words seems to have been grasped:

One day rabbit and turtle was race.
The rabbit can run fast then turtle.
The rabbit think that turtle is far away from rabbit.
So rabbit sleepy…

Despite differences in the writing products of deaf and hard-of-hearing compared to hearing students, some of the processes have been found to be similar. As with reading, writing skills begin to emerge during the early years and the stages of development progress in the same order as for hearing children, if somewhat delayed, gradually taking on more conventional form (Ruiz, 1995; Schirmer & Williams, in press). Young deaf and hard-of-hearing children are reported to make connections between fingerspelling, signs, and print, and are motivated to use writing in notes and as informal communication means (Conway, 1985; Williams, 1999).

The quality of older deaf and hard-of-hearing students' writing relates to the purpose and genre in which it is produced. In a study by Musselman and Szanto (1998), letters written in response to specific prompts showed more elaboration and more complex expression of ideas than writing in response to a picture. The profile of strengths and weaknesses was similar in both situations, however. The students made relatively few errors on punctuation and spelling; multiple meanings were expressed (showing a command of semantics), but grammatical expressions were problematic.

There are also reports that deaf and hard-of-hearing students' writing lacks sufficient use of cohesive devices (also called discourse rules) to provide coherent messages within and beyond the sentence level (deVilliers, 1991; Maxwell & Falick, 1992; Yoshinaga-Itano et al., 1996). However, Marschark et al. (1994) found that deaf children were just as capable of appropriate use of cohesion and discourse rules as hearing age-mates. They indicated that it was difficulties in vocabulary and syntax that interfered with fluid writing. Others (Mayer, 2010) have noted that problems with syntax interfere significantly with organization of written content, although other sources of difficulty also have been identified. Among these other sources are general cognitive and problem-solving skills (Marschark & Hauser, 2008). Deaf and hard-of-hearing children, for example, have repeatedly been described as having shorter memories for sequence as well as difficulties connecting disparate bits of information (Marschark et al., 2006; Pisoni et al., 2008). Both of these cognitive differences could affect overall structure and cohesion of written productions and, in fact, are not dissimilar to difficulties reported for many hearing children who have learning disabilities (Singer & Bashir, 2004).

Antia, Reed, and Kreimeyer (2005) pointed out that a number of researchers have concluded that some of the problems of deaf and hard-of-hearing children originate with the classroom approaches being used to teach writing skills. They suggested that strong emphases on producing basic sentence structures militate against students' learning to build cohesive and coherent meaning across levels of text. Similar conclusions were reached by earlier researchers (e.g., Ewoldt, 1985; Wilbur, 1977). Disappointment with results of highly structured drill approaches to teaching writing contributed to the turn to "whole language" or more naturalistic pedagogical approaches in the 1980s that stressed the need to approach writing activities as inherently social and communicative, focusing on the expressing and sharing of meaning (McAnally, Rose, & Quigley, 1987). However, Mayer (2010) summed up the result of this pedagogical movement as improving student attitudes toward writing, building abilities to express ideas and content, but resulting in no real improvements in grammatical structure and form.

Although students with hearing loss generally lag behind hearing children in their abilities to produce clearly interpretable written material, researchers have documented great variability in this regard. Antia et al. (2005), in a study of 110 students between third and twelfth grade (ages 8 to 18 years) in public school classrooms found mean scores on the Test of Written Language-3 (TOWL-3; Hammill & Larsen, 1996) to be at the "low average" level compared to norms for hearing students. However, deaf and hard-of-hearing students' scores ranged from above average compared to hearing students to being unscoreable due to the low quality of writing. Consistent with earlier research, the lowest scores of the students with hearing loss were on subtests of vocabulary and syntax, and the widest range of scores was found on the part of the test that taps these areas. An unexpected but hopeful developmental pattern was identified in student scores, however, with deaf and hard-of-hearing students in the upper grades (years 7–12 of school) scoring higher compared to hearing norms than those in Grades 3–6; that is, deaf and hard-of-hearing students tended to increase rather than decrease their relative standing compared to hearing students with advancing age and years in school. Thus, unlike some earlier researchers, Antia et al. found that the gap between students with and without hearing loss narrowed with age and years in school. Other variables that associated with writing skills included gender (with girls performing better than boys on average—see also Musselman & Szanto, 1998), socioecomic status, degree of hearing loss, and use of an interpreter (which predicted lower writing scores).[3] Neither communication mode

---

[3] Antia et al. (2005) suggested that the quality of interpreting varied across situations, and as Marschark and his colleagues (e.g., Marschark, Sapere, Convertino, & Seewagen, 2005) have noted, student understanding of interpreted lessons is often limited, even when interpreter quality is assured.

nor hours routinely spent in a regular education classroom predicted writing scores.

In contrast, Musselman and Szanto (1998) found that adolescents in oral programs produced better grammatical forms in their written work than did students from TC backgrounds. This result is consistent with earlier findings from Geers and Moog (1989) and Moores and Sweet (1990), but, again, it is not clear whether the result reflects background variables associated with choice of language placements or effects of the language training itself. Because the students in oral programming were, at least in theory, exposed to more complete models of the (spoken) language which they were to represent in writing, the connection may have been easier to make.

To the extent that access to spoken language relates to the quality of written language productions, use of cochlear implants could provide benefits. Spencer, Barker, and Tomblin (2003) studied the writing skills of children using cochlear implants who were in TC programs using a combination of spoken language and a manually coded sign system. They administered the Clinical Evaluation of Language Fundamentals-III (Semel, Wiig, & Secord, 1995) to assess expressive and receptive language skills of 16 children, average age approximately 9 years, who had used cochlear implants for an average of 71 months. The language scores were compared to performance on a written language sample. Scores on the language measure, which lagged those of a comparison group of hearing children, were found to correlate highly ($r = 70$) with the score for written productivity. Although the average number of t-units (meaning units) expressed was not significantly different between the deaf children with cochlear implants and hearing children, the cochlear-implant users produced fewer pronouns, verbs, determiners, adverbs, conjunctions, and prepositions. Therefore, use of cochlear implants, which typically result in children's being able to receive increased auditory language input, did not resolve the or the written language difficulties of the deaf participants.

Antia, Jones, Reed, and Kreimeyer (2009) presented data from a 5-year study involving 197 deaf and hard-of-hearing students who participated for 2 or more hours daily in a regular classroom with hearing students. Consistent with the report from Antia et al. (2005), positive growth was shown in writing (and language) skills, with average performance relative to peers improving with time. Average scores remained somewhat below age-level expectations for hearing children, however, and there was, again, great individual variability. In this analysis, expressive and receptive communication, degree of class participation, parent involvement, and communication mode (with an advantage found for children in oral programming) were significantly but moderately associated with progress. Communication variables overall accounted for between 16% and 20% of the variance in writing outcomes.

The data on development of writing, although relatively sparse, indicate that deaf and hard-of-hearing students make progress over time, but Antia et al. (2005)

concluded that "even students who have access to oral English through audition have difficulties in various aspects of writing and probably need instructional support from both the general educator and the teacher of D/HH... [W]riting instruction should be a focus for most students with hearing loss" (p. 254). As with reading, there is a consensus that writing instruction needs to be meaning-based, with more practice in producing work at a less formal level when structural rules are being addressed. However, as with reading, there appears to be need for a balanced approach in which direct instruction and pragmatic, freely produced opportunities for writing are provided (Marschark et al., 2002).

SUMMARY: THE CONTINUING CHALLENGE OF LITERACY

Research continues to demonstrate a pattern of reading and writing achievements of deaf and hard-of-hearing children falling on average below those of hearing students, with concomitant greater individual differences. Efforts to design and implement improved educational interventions therefore continue to be required. The evidence base establishing successful intervention approaches continues to be severely limited, although there is general support for increased provision of background information, directed reading activities, explicit teaching of reading comprehension strategies, use of age-appropriate reading materials, and both reading and writing in content areas of the curriculum. At this point, several issues have become clear:

- There is qualitative evidence that shared reading promotes motivation for literacy experiences in deaf and hard-of-hearing children. At least two quantitative studies are available that indicate increased language growth for children whose parents engage in effective shared reading or story-reading activities. However, there are no such studies that track any such effects to improved reading skills. A shared reading program, which provides demonstration and instruction in visually sensitive reading and interaction behaviors, has been positively reviewed by hearing parents but has no quantitative data to indicate the degree to which it results in changes in parent or child interactive behaviors or child language or literacy growth.
- A variety of methods are available to support the phonological knowledge of deaf and hard-of-hearing children. There are arguments, however, about the degree to which phonological awareness and knowledge are causes as opposed to results of reading experience and skills. Interventions that increase access to audition (e.g., the use of cochlear implants) and those that provide increased visual information to

disambiguate speech sounds (e.g., cued speech or Visual Phonics) have increased deaf and hard-of-hearing students' phonological abilities, but associations between these increases and improved literacy skills remain tenuous. Literacy achievements of children in orally oriented programming continue to trail age-expected levels, although the preponderance of available data suggest some advantages over children in programs with a stronger focus on visual language. However, studies of children in TC and cued speech programs as well as those using speechreading and others receiving Visual Phonics interventions provide consistent evidence that deaf and hard-of-hearing children are capable of combining and synthesizing phonological information received through visual and auditory processes. Regardless of modality, early and extensive experience with phonological input promotes better integration of phonological knowledge and skills and appears to support reading skills.

- Vocabulary continues to be an area of need for most deaf and hard-of-hearing students, and its lack contributes to difficulties for these students in comprehending text to the degree that it slows and complicates decoding and comprehension. Vocabulary development requires both exposure to a rich language environment and, especially in the case of children with hearing loss, direct instruction to build word knowledge. Direct instruction must be meaningful and engaging, and it appears to be most helpful when based on multiple experiences of words in varied contexts and with varying nuances of meaning. Use of cochlear implants has been shown to promote vocabulary development, and studies indicate that sign vocabulary acquired prior to obtaining and using the implant supports rather than impedes acquisition of spoken vocabulary. Introduction of new words in sign as well as speech supports their acquisition in spoken form.

- Despite multiple studies indicating weaknesses for deaf and hard-of-hearing students in spoken (as well as written) language syntax, there are few data available providing guidance on methods to directly increase students' syntactic abilities. Fewer difficulties have been noted in the area of word order than in use of prepositions, pronouns, and bound grammatical morphemes such as those indicating tense and number. Learning such elements is complicated in that they are difficult to hear, are represented by very different mechanisms in natural sign language and in spoken language, and are often omitted in manually coded forms of spoken language. Again, increasing auditory input through use of cochlear implants appears to increase understanding of these morphological units, but the addition of visual information also appears to be helpful. As with vocabulary, strong suggestions have been made that direct instruction on syntax is required but must occur in meaningful situations with segments larger than individual, short phrases. Evidence is lacking on various methods for promoting development in this area.

- Efficient reading comprehension requires a level of automaticity in vocabulary and syntax understanding that is often not reached by deaf and hard-of-hearing students, although they benefit from direct instruction in using metacognitive strategies. These strategies include checking their own understanding, setting purposes for reading, and generating questions and predictions as they read. Use of writing during reading activities also has been found to be useful in helping students organize their ideas.

- Published peer-reviewed data are lacking to indicate that sign/bilingual approaches (in which children's first language is to be a natural sign language that then forms the basis for instruction in a second written language) support literacy development any better than other educational/language approaches.

Acquisition of writing skills by students who are deaf or hard of hearing continues to be challenging. For students writing in English, word order is more often intact than use of grammatical words and morphemes such as pronouns, prepositions, and indicators of tense and number. It has been posited that English conversational skills in one modality or another would promote writing skills, but serious challenges remain regardless of language modality or use of cochlear implants. There seems, therefore, to be little rationale for further research aiming to compare literacy progress made by students using one language approach or modality with those using another. Instead, research is needed to identify methods that enhance literacy skills regardless of the language approach being used.

7 Cognition, Perception, and Learning Strategies

Previous chapters have documented the academic challenges of deaf and hard-of-hearing students. Contrary to claims made in earlier centuries, those difficulties are not a reflection of intellectual inferiority. The average scores of those students do not differ significantly from the scores of hearing students on nonverbal tests of cognitive functioning, when students with multiple disabilities are excluded (Maller & Braden, in press). Deaf and hard-of-hearing students' scores on tests of verbal intelligence, in contrast, tend to fall a full standard deviation below the hearing mean (Maller & Braden, 1993), primarily reflecting differences in opportunities for language development between children with and without hearing loss.

Although it has been argued that deaf students' performance on the verbal scales of intelligence tests can provide helpful information for making programming decisions (Akamatsu, Mayer, & Hardy-Braz, 2008), there is no doubt that such scores are not valid measures of students' cognitive capacities. Indeed, there is no evidence that hearing loss diminishes intelligence or cognitive abilities in general. Marschark and Wauters (in press), however, cautioned that pointing out that deaf people can be every bit as competent as hearing people should not be taken as equivalent to the claim that deaf individuals necessarily think, learn, or behave exactly like hearing peers. Indeed, they argued that differences in the environments and experiences of deaf children and hearing children might lead to different approaches to learning, to knowledge organized in different ways, and to different levels of skill in various domains. Identification of such differences therefore is critical if optimal support for learning is to be provided (see also Hauser et al., 2008).

FOUNDATIONS OF LEARNING: PLAY AND THEORY OF MIND

Play

Marschark and Wauters (in press) described some of the findings from studies indicating that even during the early years of life, the expression of cognitive skills may differ according to hearing status, especially as differences in rate and patterns of language development become apparent. Play behaviors have long been accepted to be an overt expression of the developing cognitive skills of infants and toddlers (Rubin, Fien, & Vandenberg, 1983; Spencer & Hafer, 1998), although with the emergence of language, a reciprocal relation is established. Quittner, Leibach, and Marciel (2004) noted that along with emerging language, play gives evidence of a child's growth in understanding and using symbols and representations. Spencer and Hafer therefore described play as a "window" onto the emerging cognitive development of deaf children as well as a "room" in which such development occurs.

In a longitudinal study comparing three groups of mothers and infants—deaf infants with deaf mothers, deaf infants with hearing mothers, and hearing infants with hearing mothers, all from 9 to 18 months of age—Spencer and her colleagues (Meadow-Orlans et al., 2004; Spencer & Hafer, 1998; Spencer & Meadow-Orlans, 1996) found no differences at 9 months in the amount of time or the types of play in which the children engaged. By 12 months, however, a difference was seen, as hearing children engaged in more play than did either group of deaf children at the *representational* level, where toy objects are recognized and manipulated as though they were the actual object, but with evidence of pretense. This pattern of play had changed when the children were observed again at 18 months of age. At that age, the quantity of play by deaf children with age-appropriate language (in this case, mostly children acquiring sign language from deaf mothers) was comparable to hearing children's play, both at the representational level and at a higher level referred to as *symbolic*. Symbolic play is cognitively more complex than simple representational play in that it typically either demonstrates evidence of pre-planning or of an intentional substitution of one object for another. Both of these behaviors indicate mental manipulation of symbols separate or distanced from immediate perception and, as Quittner et al. (2004) posited, reflect the existence of "inner" or "mental" linguistic symbols that support memory and facilitate comparisons with past experiences.

Although play differences at 18 months did not relate to child hearing status itself, they were different according to children's language level, which Spencer and her colleagues (Meadow-Orlans et al., 2004; Spencer & Meadow-Orlans, 1996) measured by the diversity of vocabulary and complexity of emerging syntax. The general quality of mother-child interaction also was strongly associated with the amount and level of play in which the children engaged. A separate analysis of data from these same groups of participants by Meadow-Orlans and Spencer (1996) additionally indicated that the rate of development of visual attention skills was related to both language and quality of mother-child interaction. Thus a web of interrelationships is suggested.

Analyzing three different groups of deaf and hearing children from 24 to 28 months of age (again two groups of deaf children and one of hearing children), Spencer (1996) again found differences in cognitive play behaviors related to expressive language levels, but not to hearing status. Lower amounts of symbolic play were found for children with lower language levels and, as in the Meadow-Orlans and Spencer (1996) study, the group with lower language skills was composed mainly of deaf children with hearing parents. In addition to more pre-planned play behaviors from children with higher language skills (regardless of language modality), those with more complex expressive language also engaged in more *canonical* play sequences, those representing logical or realistic activity sequences that formed part of a larger whole or theme. Although it has not yet been replicated, this may be an important early finding, because the production of canonical sequences of play behaviors is indicative of sequential order in memory storage and retrieval.

Other researchers also have found that differences between play behaviors of deaf and hearing children have associated strongly with language levels (e.g., Bornstein et al., 1999; Brown, Rickards, & Bortoli, 2001; Snyder & Yoshinaga-Itano, 1998; Yoshinaga-Itano et al., 1998b). Because the ability to engage in complex symbolic play during the early years of life provides opportunities for learning (Spencer & Hafer, 1998), a combination of hearing loss and delayed language development can result in a child reaching the age of formal education with a greatly reduced information and experience base. Meadow-Orlans et al. (2004) suggested that differences in both early language development and early play result at least in part from differences in early interactive experiences of children who are deaf or hard-of-hearing (and have hearing parents) compared to those of hearing children. The former group has been reported to experience less responsive and fewer supportive scaffolding behaviors from their mothers during interactions (cf. Lederberg & Prezbindowski, 2000, for a contrasting interpretation). This may become a self-perpetuating cycle as mothers find it easier to scaffold (or structure) play and other cognitive skills when their children have higher levels of receptive language.

Although the above studies indicated that language ability was a better predictor of play behavior than was hearing status, both language and play likely are indirectly influenced by hearing status. Because deaf children depend primarily upon visual communication (whether for watching signs, cues, or speechreading), the pace and timing of their turn-taking exchanges differ from what most hearing adults expect. Many deaf mothers have been shown to intuitively manage the visual aspects of early communications in positive ways (e.g., moving location of signs to accommodate child's existing attention, using a defined set of attention-getting signals), but such accommodations seem much more difficult for hearing adults (Harris, 2001; Harris & Mohay, 1997; Spencer, 2000b; Waxman & Spencer, 1997). Given that infants, deaf and hearing alike, do not develop the ability to flexibly switch visual attention between objects and people until about 12 to 15 months of age, mothers' roles in managing and accommodating attention during interactions with deaf and hard-of-hearing infants are more important as well as more complex. Play is as much an engine of continued cognitive development as it is evidence of current levels (Spencer & Hafer, 1998), and thus less than optimal early experiences could impede normal cognitive and linguistic development.

Theory of Mind

Another indicator of cognitive development which has been found to emerge during the pre-school years is *theory of mind* (ToM). Theory of mind refers to a metacognitive ability, that is, the ability to think about something in the abstract, removed from the immediately perceptible environment. Peterson, Willman, and Liu (2005) defined theory of mind as "the awareness of how mental states such as memories, beliefs, desires, and intentions govern the behavior of self and others" (p. 502). Al-Hilawani, Easterbrooks, and Marchant (2002) found no differences between deaf and hearing children from two very different cultures (in the Middle East and in North America) on one type of ToM task: recognition of pictorially represented facial expressions of emotion. In earlier research, Odom, Blanton, and Laukhuf (1973) had demonstrated that deaf children aged 7 to 12 years could identify facial expressions of specific emotions as well as hearing children, but the deaf children were significantly worse than hearing peers in their ability to predict which mental state or emotion would result from a pictured sequence of events. Consistent with this finding of a dissociation between recognizing emotions and being able to identify their underlying causes, tasks tapping other aspects of ToM have shown consistent differences between children with and without hearing loss.

The most frequently administered and reported task for assessing ToM, often referred to as the Sally-Anne task, involves the recognition of a false belief. In this task, an object is put in one location, in view of both the child and another person, then moved to another location while the child is watching but after the second person has left the room. The child is asked to predict where the second person will look for the object after returning to the room. This task therefore requires the child to remember the sequence of events and to understand that the second person has not had access to what the child has seen and thus will pick the original location. A second frequently used task involves an unexpected object (such as a piece of candy) being found in a container that is labeled to clearly indicate a different object is inside. Upon discovering this trick, the child is asked whether she was surprised and what a friend would think was in the box.

Both of the above tasks involve complicated language merely to understand the questions, and it is not surprising that language skills are associated with correct responses. Accordingly, although typically developing hearing children often answer the questions correctly by 4 or 5 years of age, a number of studies have demonstrated that children with hearing loss, most of whom have delays in language development, show significant delays in this metacognitive skill (Courtin, 2000; Courtin & Melot, 1998; Moeller & Schick, 2006; Wellman & Liu, 2004). Courtin (2000), however, found that deaf children with deaf parents performed better on ToM tasks than deaf children with hearing parents, regardless of the language modality used. This finding appears to support the view that language delay is a significant cause of ToM delays.

Schick, de Villiers, de Villiers, and Hoffmeister (2007) investigated this issue by using tasks tapping conceptual processes similar to those described above but requiring minimal language to give evidence of ToM. They tested 176 participating children, representing four groups: hearing children, deaf children from oral language programs, deaf children who used American Sign Language (ASL) and had signing deaf parents, and deaf children who used ASL but had hearing parents. The children ranged in age from 4 to 7 years of age. Schick et al. replicated earlier findings insofar as the deaf children with demonstrated language delays, most of whom had hearing parents, performed less well on the false belief tasks (a picture version of the Sally-Anne task and an unexpected contents task) than either deaf or hearing children with better language skills. This difference in performance was found even with low-language ToM tasks (e.g., a hidden sticker game).

Schick et al. (2007) concluded that the children with lower language skills actually have problems *reasoning* about tasks involving people holding false beliefs. The fact that the deaf children with deaf parents, who had been exposed to fluent language interactions since birth, performed like the hearing children on these tasks showed that it was not hearing loss itself that caused the ToM delay observed in the other group of deaf children. On the basis of additional analyses, Schick et al. argued that command of a specific grammatical structure (English complements, like "Daisy said *she would help cook*" and "Johnny wanted *to go to the show*") is important for ToM, but that general syntactic ability is not. However, it cannot be the surface-level structure of that grammatical form that is important, because it is expressed differently in spoken English and American Sign Language, and fluency in ASL also supported age-appropriate performance on the false belief task. Cheung et al. (2004), in fact, studied hearing children speaking Cantonese or English, languages that differ in complement structures at the surface level. They found that correlations between understanding of complement structures and ToM were no longer significant when general language comprehension was controlled. They argued that general language skills and not any specific syntactic knowledge drives the development of ToM.

Schick et al. (2007) found that, in addition to syntax, children's vocabulary knowledge was positively related to ToM performance. This led to a suggestion that it was the opportunity to participate in rich conversational exchanges that was the mechanism for advances in ToM abilities. This conclusion is in agreement with that of earlier researchers (e.g., Lundy, 2002; Peterson & Siegal, 1995) and suggests that the quality of interactions, which was identified as an important facilitative factor for play development, continues to have effects on cognitive growth as theory of mind becomes established.

Mechanisms that build ToM abilities, and differences in ToM performance depending upon task variations, thus are clearly of theoretical importance but have not yet been fully identified. Marschark, Green, Hindmarsh, and Walker (2000), for example, explored ToM by examining stories created by deaf and hearing children aged 9 to 15 years. Overall, 87% of the deaf children and 80% of the hearing children produced mental state attributions in their stories. The first figure is far greater than the success rate on the false belief task reported by Peterson and Siegal (1995) and others for deaf children with hearing parents. More interesting perhaps was the finding that the deaf children produced more mental state attributions than their hearing age-mates, a finding that also held when only the youngest participants were considered. On the basis of their results, Marschark et al. suggested that false belief tasks typically involve both recognizing mental states in others and predicting behavior on the basis of those states. Given their finding that deaf 7- to 12-year-olds showed significant delays in linking emotional states to related behaviors (Odom et al., 1973), they argued that the narrative paradigm was a more straightforward, uncontaminated means of evaluating ToM.

These and other findings from diverse ToM tasks suggest that both the acquisition of theory of mind and the ability or tendency to use it in various situations (either automatically or intentionally) are not simple or unidimensional, but involve various kinds of knowledge and subskills. Meanwhile, findings from a number of relevant studies suggest that many deaf and hard-of-hearing children may not bring to school-age learning situations the range of cognitive skills that hearing children do (see Hauser et al., 2008). Theory of mind skills, in particular, seem likely to be essential to the teaching-learning enterprise insofar as they allow children to place teachers' language in a larger context. Thus far, however, the link between ToM and academic achievement has not been explored.

VISUAL ATTENTION, LANGUAGE, AND COMMUNICATION

Although there is no indication that decreased hearing results in increased visual acuity, there are indications of visual *attention* differences between deaf and hearing persons (Dye, Hauser, & Bavelier, 2008; Meadow-Orlans et al., 2004; Quittner et al., 2004). Deaf people must monitor their environment without having auditory signals to alert them to changes, and in apparent response to this situation, both behavioral and neurological investigations have shown them to be more sensitive than hearing people to objects and movements in the periph-eral visual field (Neville & Lawson, 1987a, 1987b; Swisher, 1993). Perhaps as a result of this peripheral sensitivity, deaf and hard-of-hearing children have often been reported by their parents and teachers as being more visually distractible and even impulsive relative to hearing age-mates (Meadow-Orlans et al., 2004; Mitchell & Quittner, 1996; Quittner et al., 2004). Mothers of deaf children, accordingly, have been observed to use a specialized set of attention-directing and maintaining behaviors with deaf infants and toddlers (e.g., Harris & Chasin, 2005; Spencer, 2000b; Waxman & Spencer, 1997). Convergent results across studies thus indicate that visual attention is an area in which deaf and hearing children demonstrate cognitive differences.

Beyond peripheral sensitivity in the visual domain, performance of deaf chil-dren on tests of sustained, selective visual attention has been shown to be worse than that of hearing children (Dye et al., 2008; Quittner, Smith, Osberger, Mitchell, & Katz, 1994). This finding was interpreted by Dye et al. (2008, p. 253) in a value-neutral way as being evidence of a "redistribution of attention…across visual space," but it clearly has implications for classroom learning. Deaf persons who use sign language also have been shown to have increased face discrimina-tion abilities (Bellugi et al., 1990) and to recognize rotations in three-dimensional block figures better than hearing people (Emmorey, 2002; Talbot & Haude, 1993). Thus, adaptation and experience appear to affect the profile of relative strengths in the visual skills of children with significant hearing losses. This suggestion is supported by data reported by Smith, Quittner, Osberger, and Miyamoto (1998) who reported increased selective attention performance by deaf children who used cochlear implants and thus had greater access to auditory information.

Smith et al. suggested that opportunities for cross-modal integration of stimuli help to develop focused attention skills, but it is also possible that the ability to hear changes in the environment decreases the need for visual vigilance.

Simms and Thumann (2007) argued that educators have focused for too long on deficits assumed to result from lack of hearing and recommended instead that curricula be organized to make best use of visual information and visual processing. It remains, however, that deaf and hard-of-hearing children are prone to distraction in educational environments by activity in the peripheral visual field. Dye et al. (2008, p. 260) therefore suggested that learning can best be served by providing deaf children with a "visually predictable environment" arranged so that students with hearing loss can see the teacher and their peers at all times. In contrast with the views of some proponents of sign/bilingual programs (e.g., Evans, 2004) and the situation in many mainstreamed programs as well, this would argue against large numbers of deaf students in a classroom.

It cannot be assumed that access to visual communication, even in small classroom groups or dyadic conversations, resolves complications arising from the need for visual communication. Just as literacy levels vary, so do receptive and expressive communication skills of deaf and hard-of-hearing students, especially given different ages of language acquisition and, when signing is involved, variability in the consistency and fluency of appropriate models. Communication can be thwarted when language skills are insufficient to support conversation. In addition to this potential difficulty, the differences in patterns of visual attention necessitated by increased dependence upon vision for communication, even if only for speechreading, have potential effects on the optimal pacing of instruction for deaf and hard-of-hearing students.

It is commonly recognized that information presented verbally (in speech or in sign) to deaf students in an instructional situation must be paced to allow learners time to look away from the speaker/signer to attend to any visual aids that are presented as supportive information. For example, time must be given for students to look at and read a whiteboard or a PowerPoint slide and then look back at the instructor to understand the importance of the material in that particular context. In most cases, this necessity results in teachers' progressing more slowly through a given amount of information than in a situation with only hearing students, who can look at a visual display while the instructor speaks about it (a situation that actually results in better learning; Mayer & Morena, 1998). The situation is further complicated by a report from Matthews and Reich (1993) indicating that deaf and hard-of-hearing students visually attended to their teachers less than 50% of the time during teacher-directed lessons. Attention was even less likely to peers who were signing in the context of classroom discussion.

Developmental differences in visual attention and metacognition, especially in combination with language delays, may lead to differences in the amount of information that is understood in conversations and in formal lessons in class-rooms involving deaf and hard-of-hearing students. Marschark, Convertino, et al. (2007), for example, measured understanding as well as requests for clarification between communicative partners, using a dyadic communication task with college students who used ASL, those who used spoken language, and mixed dyads in which one student used sign but the other used spoken language. They found that understanding and being able to repeat back single sentences, even in this optimal one-on-one situation, was quite low across all three groups, although those using ASL performed somewhat better (understanding 66% of communications) than the others. Oral dyads understood each other only 44% of the time, not significantly different from the mixed dyads. In addition, students generally gave no evidence that they appreciated their lack of mutual understanding, only rarely asking for clarification despite the experimenter's encouragement to do so.

Marschark, Convertino, et al. (2007) suggested that deaf students' frequent failure to recognize misunderstandings, both in their study and in the classroom, may reflect metacognitive failures—that is, the students may not be aware that they have failed to understand. On the other hand, lack of requests for clarification may reflect unwillingness to acknowledge communication gaps, perhaps because many students who are deaf or hard-of-hearing have learned from experience not to expect complete grasp of communications in the classroom (Napier & Barker, 2004). Either explanation suggests that teachers of deaf and hard-of-hearing students need to be especially alert to gaps in understanding and learn to respond appropriately.

The ability of deaf and hard-of-hearing students to gain understandings from language used in the classroom has been further investigated by Marschark and his colleagues (Marschark, Sapere et al., 2004, 2005), and they have consistently reported that deaf college students in mainstream classrooms with excellent teachers and highly trained interpreters score lower on tests of learning when compared with hearing students, even when levels of pre-existing knowledge are statistically controlled. Multiple regression analyses have indicated that background variables, such as degree or age of hearing loss, parents' hearing status, and reading level do not significantly predict deaf students' learning outcomes (Convertino et al., 2009). Students' spoken language and sign language skills also have proved to be poor predictors of learning in mainstream classrooms, as has whether interpretations are presented in ASL or signed English.

Marschark et al. (2008) obtained similar findings regardless of whether teachers were deaf or hearing and whether they utilized interpreters or signed for themselves. In contrast to the researchers' earlier studies, however, the teachers in these experiments were all experienced in teaching deaf students, and deaf students gained just as much as their hearing peers relative to pre-test performance, even though they came into and left the classroom with less content knowledge. On the basis of those results, Marschark and his colleagues hypothesized that having a teacher who understands what deaf students know and how they learn may be more important than having teachers who sign for themselves. Further research will be needed to determine whether this hypothesis is correct or, more likely, in which settings it is true for which students.

MEMORY PROCESSES, PERCEPTION, AND LEARNING

Studies spanning more than 100 years have found that deaf individuals remember less from sequential memory span tasks involving both verbal and nonverbal materials than do hearing individuals (e.g., Spencer & Delk, 1989). Although such findings were once considered indicative of general intellectual delays, recent studies have indicated that these findings are affected by the individual's primary language modality and the modality in which he or she is tested rather than on hearing status (Hall & Bavelier, 2010; Marschark, Convertino, & LaRock, 2006). Deaf persons who have relatively strong phonological and speech skills tend to use phonological or temporal coding strategies particularly suited to sequential memory tasks, and they show better memory. Those who depend primarily on visual or sign language are more likely to use visual and spatial coding strategies that are less appropriate for retaining sequences but may be more effective for remembering locations in space. Todman and colleagues (Todman & Cowdy, 1993; Todman & Seedhouse, 1994) thus found that deaf children had better memory than hearing children for complex visual figures, but the advantage disappeared when parts making up the figures had to be remembered in sequence. On the basis of such findings and their own demonstration that visuospatial place memory is as good as or better in deaf signers than in hearing speakers, Hall and Bavelier (2010) argued that sequential memory tasks are inherently biased against deaf signers, emphasizing that memory coding preferences rather than capacity differences are at issue in such studies.

The suggestion that deaf individuals might tend to use visuospatial strategies even when confronted with a sequential memory task is supported by results from a study by Wilson, Bettger, Niculae, and Klima (1997). They found that ASL-signing deaf children (with deaf parents) had similar digit span memories, whether they had to repeat the digits in the original (forward) order or the reverse (backward) order. In contrast, hearing children show a considerable advantage with forward compared to backward repetitions, a direct result of sequential, linguistic coding. A similar explanation would account for results from a series of studies by Pisoni and his colleagues (see Pisoni et al., 2008), showing that memory for digit sequences is shorter for children using cochlear implants than for hearing children of the same age. These children were using spoken language and thus were expected to be using it in the memory task, thus enhancing sequential memory. Because most of them received their implants at a fairly late age (>3 years), however, their performance on the memory tasks may reflect some limits to neurological or behavioral plasticity. That is, the availability of auditory information from their cochlear implants might not (or might not yet) have resulted in changes to the children's previously established information processing habits, and therefore they might not have developed an effective sequential coding strategy. Marschark and Wauters (2008) therefore called for recognition that deaf children, especially those using sign language, may need accommodations or, alternatively, direct instruction in use of sequential processes in tasks such as reading, where they are required.

INTEGRATING INFORMATION AND USING PROBLEM-SOLVING STRATEGIES

A critical aspect of learning is the ability to relate discrete bits of information to form concepts and identify relationships. Difficulties in this aspect of cognition have been shown during reading activities with deaf children (e.g., Banks, Gray, & Fyfe, 1990) and with deaf adolescents (e.g., Marschark, DeBeni, Polazzo, & Cornoldi, 1993). In the Banks et al. and Marschark et al. studies, deaf and hearing children showed similar memory for details and words, but the hearing students were more likely to remember and express complete idea units, cause and effect, and conceptual relationships. These findings may reflect, in part, difficulties with reading, per se, and thus increased cognitive resources required by the deaf students for the process of decoding. Marschark, Convertino, and La Rock (2006), however, argued that the relative lack of automatic relational processing is consistent with similar findings from a variety of memory and problem-solving studies and may represent a general information-processing style characteristic of deaf students—one that can have specific effects on learning. A review by Ottem (1980), for example, showed that deaf children and adults performed less well than hearing peers when cognitive tasks required the relating or integrating of multiple concepts, stimulus dimensions, or bits of information. That is, activities like categorizing by single characteristics were performed similarly by deaf and hearing adults and children, but activities that required keeping more than one characteristic in mind (e.g., color and size or shape), were performed better by hearing than deaf people. More recently, Richardson, MacLeod-Gallinger, McKee and Long (2000) found that deaf students reported more difficulties than hearing students when required to integrate or synthesize information across class lectures and texts.

Other indications of differences in relational processing between deaf and hearing students were seen in responses to a Twenty Questions game utilized by

Marschark and Everhart (1999). They found that naïve deaf participants, aged 7 to 20 years, were unlikely to produce "constraint" or category-based questions (e.g., "Is it an animal?") in the game, and therefore were less successful than hearing participants in discovering the answers. Deaf students who had experience with the game, however, did apply category-based strategies and performed as well as the hearing students. Thus, the group difference apparently derived from the likelihood of students' applying relational strategies in this problem-solving situation and hearing students' faster discovery of the appropriate cognitive strategy through experience. Similar findings with regard to performance are described in chapter 8 with regard to mathematical problem solving (e.g., Ansell & Pagliaro, 2006; Blatto-Vallee et al., 2007).

Findings of differences in the ways that deaf and hearing students approach problem-solving situations also may reflect differences in the background knowledge they have acquired through incidental learning. McEvoy, Marschark, and Nelson (1999) demonstrated significant differences in the organization of concept knowledge between deaf and hearing college students, and Marschark, Convertino, McEvoy, and Masteller (2004) found asymmetries in their category-exemplar relations that were not observed among hearing students. In contrast to the hypothesis of Marschark and Everhart (1999), Marschark et al.'s (2004) results indicated that the category membership of a familiar object (exemplar) is just as salient for deaf as for hearing students, but that deaf students appear less likely to automatically activate high-frequency exemplars in memory when they encounter a category name. This information processing difference would affect not only deaf students' reading comprehension but also their memory and problem-solving performance. That is, the automatic association of incoming information with background knowledge is an essential component of efficient reading, problem solving, and learning. To the extent that the arousal and/or application of prior knowledge is less automatic for deaf and hard-of-hearing children, their performance will suffer in these domains (e.g., Marschark, Convertino, & LaRock, 2006; Ottem, 1980).

RESPONSES TO COGNITIVE INTERVENTION

A number of differences between cognitive functioning typical of children with and without hearing loss have been discussed above. In some cases, such as a child's relative lack of recognizing failures in understanding and subsequent tendencies to fail to request clarification, these differences can be thought of as deficiencies, at least in terms of the tools necessary for academic success. Other instances, such as enhanced memory for visual-spatial versus sequential information and increased attention to peripheral as opposed to centrally situated visual stimuli, may more appropriately be considered differences than deficits. However, the overall picture is of a tendency for students with hearing loss to face difficulties integrating information, often failing to recognize when linguistic or conceptual understanding has broken down, and employing patterns of visual attention that provide them with less information than is available. Indeed, deaf students frequently do not apply knowledge we know they have in situations where it would be helpful (Liben, 1979; Marschark & Everhart, 1999). Fortunately, the fact that deaf students demonstrate such conceptual and procedural knowledge in other contexts suggests the potential for interventions that might enhance problem-solving performance in formal and informal tasks.

Mousley and Kelly (1998) demonstrated the potential of such interventions in an effort to promote metacognition and teach more effective mathematical problem-solving strategies to deaf and hard-of-hearing students. They conducted a series of three experiments involving the Tower of Hanoi problem, a nonverbal task that requires multiple actions to arrange rings on a set of pegs in a prescribed order. In their first experiment, students identified as high- or lower achievement readers were asked to explain (using sign language) their understanding of the Tower of Hanoi problem and the strategy to be followed in solving it; then they were asked to record in writing their goals and the strategies they used. This was followed by presentation of a mathematics word problem, the solution of which required similar logic. Reading ability did not associate with effective solving of the nonverbal problem, but it related to both recording of strategies and to understanding and solving the word problem.

The second experiment introduced a procedure in which the deaf students were to take at least 2 minutes to visualize the steps in solving the Tower of Hanoi problem. One objective in using visualization was to prevent too rapid, nonreflective actions to solve the problem by including enforced thinking and planning time. One group of students was given the visualization instructions and another proceeded as in the first situation described above. Overall, the group using the visualization approach solved the problem in significantly fewer moves than the group not using visualization. Mousley and Kelly concluded that the visualization process reduced the number of impulsive moves.

The third experiment of the Mousley and Kelly study involved the teacher modeling, in detail, strategies for solving a mathematics word problem. He communicated his thinking about the problem and walked the students through the problem's solution step by step. One group of students received this kind of extended, problem-focused presentation while others participated in regularly structured mathematics lessons. Results showed that the students who experienced the modeling were able to generalize the problem-solving steps to similar but different math problems. Mousley and Kelly concluded that although reading levels have some effects on mathematics problem-solving abilities, there are non-linguistic factors that are important. They noted that even at college age, deaf and hard-of-hearing students frequently do not spontaneously apply well-developed problem-solving strategies. More important, they found that structured instruction in strategies and devices to help students take time to visualize problem solutions was effective and could increase successful performance.

A different approach to building deaf and hard-of-hearing students' metacognitive skills was reported by Martin et al. (2001), who replicated and expanded a previous evaluation of effects of the Instrumental Enrichment (IE) program developed by Feuerstein (1980). Two groups of U.S. secondary school students participated in the first study (Martin & Jonas, 1986). Forty-one students made up the experimental group and participated in IE activities (making part-whole comparisons, projecting visual relationships, identifying spatial relations, following directions, setting up classification systems) for a period of 2 years. Teachers incorporated the activities and metacognitively oriented discussions about strategies for problem solving into at least two lessons weekly. Another 41 students served as a comparison group and participated in the regular curriculum without the IE component. The experimental group showed gains in measures of reading, math computation and concepts, and nonverbal cognitive skills as measured by the Raven's Standard Progressive Matrices. Qualitatively, students in the experimental group were reported to improve in sequencing, presentation of details, and thoroughness when asked to write answers to problems presented in print.

The Martin et al. (2001) follow-up study was conducted in China (with deaf students only) and England (with both hearing and deaf students). Participating teachers received 9 hours of training on the concepts of the IE system plus information on creative thinking, multiple intelligences (Gardner, 1984), metacognition issues, and teacher as cognitive mediator. Teachers themselves participated in some of the activities that would be used in the classroom and had the opportunity to reflect upon their own approaches to creative thinking and problem solving. They were asked to incorporate the cognitive activities into lessons two or three times a week but, in contrast with the original study, the intervention lasted only 6 months. Pre- and postintervention assessments were conducted with both experimental and control groups, with a limited number of students from each group taking the Raven's Progressive Matrices test before and after the intervention. In addition, all students were asked to write or narrate their responses to problem situations before and after training, and teachers completed a questionnaire about children's creative and critical thinking skills.

The deaf and hearing students in England made gains on the Raven's test, as did the students in China. The experimental group in England showed advances in their critical thinking for problem solving, although they failed to differ from the control group in creative thinking. Teachers in both countries reported that they had increased their use of questions at higher cognitive levels, students were more attentive, and students were more likely to use cognitively related vocabulary after the intervention. It is particularly interesting to note that hearing as well as deaf students benefited from the program, suggesting that a focus on cognitively based problem-solving curricula may be of significant utility beyond the scope of classes for deaf or hard-of-hearing children.

SUMMARY: ON THINKING AND LEARNING

Although there is no difference in general intelligence between deaf and hearing individuals, differences in use of various cognitive processes are reported as early as toddler/pre-school age in sequencing of behaviors and the ability to distance oneself from one's own perspective. These differences are associated with variations in language abilities and perhaps with differences in early interactive experiences, but they also may be early indicators of specialized processing styles associated with primary dependence upon visual instead of auditory processing.

- Some visuospatial differences, such as increased attention to changes in the peripheral visual field also are manifested in recordings of neurological activity and appear to represent adaptive functioning. The corollary of this—decreased selective and sustained central visual attention—however, can complicate learning in typical classrooms and educational tasks where sustained visual attention is necessary.
- Deaf and hard-of-hearing students generally show poorer memory for both verbal and nonverbal materials relative to hearing peers, especially when information is presented sequentially. Native-signing deaf adults, however, have been found to have visuospatial memory equal to or better than that of hearing adults, likely an adaptation to differing real-world experiences and concomitant brain development. Still to be determined is the extent to which observed memory differences influence learning, particularly among the vast majority of deaf and hard-of-hearing students who grow up using a combination of signed and spoken language.
- Learning in traditional educational situations also seems to be complicated by other characteristics including difficulties in sequential memory and in integrating disparate pieces of information, impulsive and non-reflective responses to problem solving, and often a lack of metacognitive awareness of one's own understanding or misunderstanding of communication. Of course, there is much individual variation in these characteristics, and the issue is more the degree to which particular cognitive processes have become automatic rather than their total presence or absence (Bebko, 1998). What is suggested is

a difference in their distribution across the populations of learners with and without hearing loss, but with greater variability in the former.

Factors that contribute to the distributions of these characteristics across individuals are only now being discovered, and more research is needed to tease apart and identify causal factors. It is especially important to conduct additional research on responses to cognitively focused interventions, some of which have been shown to increase deaf and hard-of-hearing students' use of beneficial learning and problem-solving strategies. Even without awaiting the results of such research, it is important to recognize that deaf and hard-of-hearing learners may bring to the educational setting needs for training in problem-solving and cognitively oriented learning strategies that differ in degree and perhaps in type from modal behaviors and needs of hearing students. Teachers therefore require specialized training if they are to optimally meet the academic needs of students with hearing loss. Ultimately, curriculum and classroom design, as well as approaches to presentation and guidance in teaching and learning activities, should be based on recognition of these differences rather than assuming that when communication barriers are removed, deaf and hearing students have the same knowledge and approach learning in the same way.

8 Achievement in Mathematics and Science

Mathematics and science are topics of special importance in education, both in terms of their content matter and the reasoning and problem solving underlying achievement that they encourage. Accomplishments in these areas will have lasting impacts on students' educational attainment and for their eventual employment opportunities. Unfortunately, students with hearing loss repeatedly have been found to lag behind hearing peers in both mathematics (Ansell & Pagliaro, 2006; Traxler, 2000; Wood, Wood, Griffiths, & Howarth, 1986) and science (McIntosh, Sulzen, Reeder, & Kidd, 1994; Roald & Mikalsen, 2000; see Marschark & Hauser, 2008, for a review). Consequently, there has recently been considerable research into both processes and accomplishments in these areas, although there has been more work, by far, in mathematics. The following questions, among others, have been addressed:

- How does the achievement of deaf and hard-of-hearing students in these areas compare with that of hearing students?

- How can we characterize the foundations of mathematics and science problem solving and reasoning in deaf students, both within the population and as they compare to hearing age-mates?
- What modifications can be made to educational approaches and environments to enhance deaf and hard-of-hearing students' performance in STEM (science, technology, engineering, and mathematics) subjects?

MATHEMATICS

Early Development

Recent investigations have suggested that young, pre-school-aged deaf children have some of the basic knowledge necessary for mathematics learning, but they lag behind hearing peers in other areas.[1] Leybaert and Van Cutsem (2002), for example, found that deaf children between 3 and 6 years of age were comparable to a group of hearing children (who were approximately 1 year younger) in the ability to count an array of objects or group them according to number; however, the deaf children demonstrated a lag of approximately 2 years in the ability for rote counting, or production of abstract numeral sequences. The researchers concluded that the deaf children possessed basic concepts of counting and quantity and were only delayed on the sequential linguistic aspect of counting. Zarfaty, Nunes, and Bryant (2004) reported even more positive findings in a comparison of deaf and hearing children's number concepts. The two groups performed similarly in a task requiring them to reproduce the number of objects that were presented to them sequentially, one at a time; however, the deaf group exceeded the hearing group on a task that involved reproduction of the number of objects presented in a spatial array (O'Connor & Hermelin, 1973).

These reports give evidence that deaf children understand some important basic number concepts, and they may even have a strength when arrays are presented visually. Based on administration of the Test of Early Mathematics Ability (TEMA; Ginsburg & Baroody, 2003) to 28 deaf children, Kritzer (2008, 2009), however, found that 4- to 6-year-old deaf children generally performed below hearing peers in formal and informal mathematics skills beyond that most basic level. Delays were observed in making number comparisons, counting by numbers other than one, and in reading and writing multidigit numbers. Thus, young deaf

---

[1] Findings indicating that even preverbal infants have some recognition of differences in number or quantity suggest an innate basis for later-attained mathematical concepts. This is an active area of research involving hearing children (e.g., Butterworth, 2005; Mix, Huttenlocher, & Levine, 2002), but its implications for deaf and hard-of-hearing children have not yet been explored.

children already were lagging behind hearing peers in the foundations of mathematical achievement even prior to entering school. Finding that five of the six highest scorers on the test had at least one deaf parent who used ASL, Kritzer (2009) proposed that basic language skills as well as aspects of parent-child communication were implicated in the children's acquisition of mathematics concepts. She noted, however, that even the highest scoring children with deaf parents scored only at the "average" level and not above, compared to norms for hearing children on the TEMA.

Kritzer (2008) investigated bases for the differences she found among young deaf children's early mathematics concepts and skills in a qualitative study of parent-child participation in a planned problem-solving activity. She focused on three of the children in her 2009 report who had shown the highest mathematical skills and three who had performed at the lowest level. Both of the high performers for whom data were available (one parent-child dyad had not conducted the activity as planned) had deaf parents and the low performers had hearing parents. The deaf parents used ASL, and hearing parents used spoken English with sign support. Kritzer was interested in ways that the parents referenced, or mediated, quantitative concepts during interactions that required categorization in the problem-solving activity. Her analysis showed that parents of the two highest functioning children referred to math concepts more frequently than did the other parents. In addition, parents of the higher functioning children were exposed to more problem-solving situations requiring critical thinking while quantity was discussed. Kritzer pointed out that abstract terms describing quantities (e.g., "everything," "all") were used more often by the parents of the higher functioning children (Anderson, 1997). Although the three children who were functioning lower in mathematics were exposed to math concepts during the intervention activity, their parents did not produce math-related vocabulary. Parents of the lower functioning children also were more likely to use the categorization activity as a labeling exercise than to prompt the children to use a problem-solving approach focused on identifying categories. Kritzer's observations are consistent with suggestions from Gregory (1998), Bull (2008), and Bandurski and Galkowski (2004) that sharing a first language with their parents provides deaf children with more opportunities for number-related incidental learning, in part because less time will be spent on explicit language training. Therefore, although such a conclusion may be counterintuitive, the development of language abilities appears to have an effect on the development of quantitative concepts and skills even during the pre-school years.

Mathematics Development During School Years

Most studies involving mathematics operations and number concepts in school-aged deaf and hard-of-hearing students indicate delays relative to hearing peers, although they generally show much the same pattern of development (Hyde et al., 2003). Marschark and his colleagues (e.g., Marschark, 2003, 2006; Marschark & Hauser, 2008; Marschark & Wauters, 2008) have proposed that cognitive or learning style differences between students with and without hearing loss likely require modified pedagogical approaches to support academic achievement of those who are deaf or hard-of-hearing (see chapter 7). At the same time, there are widespread indications that the mathematical and problem-solving experiences provided to most deaf and hard-of-hearing students are insufficient in frequency and structure to achieve the desired outcomes (e.g., Hyde et al., 2003; Kluwin & Moores, 1989; Kritzer, 2009; Pagliaro & Kritzer, 2005).

As indicated by outcome data, educational approaches to date have failed to optimize mathematics learning in deaf and hard-of-hearing students, and data collected over at least 40 years show that they face obstacles to age-appropriate development of math skills (e.g., Allen, 1986; Kelly, Lang, Mousley, & Davis, 2003; Serrano Pau, 1995). Bull (2008), for example, noted that deaf students generally have delays in developing measurement concepts, fraction concepts, and operations. In her detailed analysis of a national sample in the United States, Traxler (2000) found that deaf and hard-of-hearing students (ages 8–18 years) achieved below hearing students on the standardized mathematics problem-solving subtest of the Stanford Achievement Test, 9th Edition, functioning only at the 80th percentile of the average scores attained by hearing students. According to Traxler, and an analysis by Qi and Mitchell (2007), 17- and 18-year-old deaf and hard-of-hearing students achieve approximately fifth or sixth grade–level (11–12 years of age) skills in mathematics on average, even on tests of computation skills. Although this is relatively higher than their achievement in reading, it is still significantly below what would be expected for their age and years of education. Blatto-Valle et al. (2007) documented a lack of significant growth in mathematical skills from middle school to college age in deaf and hard-of-hearing students, showing that achievement levels begin and remain below those of hearing students. Qi and Mitchell noted that this gap between performance of hearing and of deaf and hard-of-hearing students has stabilized over the past 30 years, although it is difficult to see this as a positive development.

A variety of reasons have been proposed to account for the above pattern of results. These include deficits in early experiences with quantitative concepts (Kritzer, 2009), delays in language development (Gregory, 1998), and teaching qualifications and practices in the area of mathematics (Marschark, Lang, & Albertini, 2002), as well as sensory- and language-based differences in the ways that persons with and without hearing loss process information (Marschark & Hauser, 2008). It should be noted, however, that just as with literacy, there are deaf and hard-of-hearing students who excel in mathematical achievement. Wood et al. (1983) reported that approximately 15% of deaf students (in the

United Kingdom) performed at or above the average for hearing students, even though, as a group they lag behind hearing peers when they leave school (Wood et al., 1986). It is of particular interest, therefore, to explore factors that can support such development.

Recommendations for deaf education (Dietz, 1995) as well as for general education in the United States (National Council of Teachers of Mathematics, 2000) have called for frequent use of problem-solving activities in the form of story problems in the earliest grades of school. However, Pagliaro and Ansell (2002) found that such activity rarely occurs in classes for deaf and hard-of-hearing children. Less than one-fifth of the 36 first- through third-grade teachers they surveyed (representing five schools, all of which used sign language to some extent) reported presenting story problems daily. Teachers apparently believed that story problems, whether presented in sign, voice and sign, or written form, are too difficult for children until they achieve basic math and reading skills. Deaf and hard-of-hearing children's experience with mathematical problem solving, therefore, continues to be limited during the early school years. Pagliaro and Ansell (2002), in contrast, suggested that story problems be used from the earliest grades to engage deaf children in mathematical thinking and problem-solving processes: "Teachers should not wait for students to 'get the basics down' before introducing story problems to them; rather, they should employ the story problems as tools to help build those 'basics'" (p. 116).

One final aspect of the Pagliaro and Ansell study also is of interest here. Their survey data showed that teachers who had at least one mathematics methods course in pre-service training presented story problems more frequently than those with only in-service training sessions. Pagliaro and Ansell therefore called for all deaf education teacher candidates to have a required course to assure that they know mathematics content, how students learn mathematical concepts, and how to teach mathematics effectively.

Students with hearing loss may continue to suffer from lack of equal opportunity to acquire mathematical concepts as they go through school. Opportunities that are provided to those students in grades 6–12 (ages 12 to 18 years) in the United States have been shown by Kelly, Lang, and Pagliaro (2003) to relate to the type of school and classroom placement in which students are enrolled, although there are many similarities across settings. The researchers obtained survey data about the teaching of mathematics word problems from 132 mathematics teachers of deaf and hard-of-hearing children. Sixty-eight taught in center or special schools, 29 taught deaf students in mainstream classes integrated with hearing students, and 35 taught special classes for deaf and hard-of-hearing students in the context of a mainstream school. There were no significant differences among these groups of teachers in the overall time spent on problem-solving activities nor in the degree of emphasis reported for various types of problems-solving strategies. These strategies included identifying goals and key information, planning, identifying separate operations required to solve a problem, estimating, evaluating the plan and the obtained result, using a trial and error approach, and generating and testing hypotheses. Teachers in all three environments also emphasized concrete visualization strategies for problem solving (e.g., diagrams, illustrations, hands-on activities, signing) over more analytically oriented strategies, although Ansell and Pagliaro (2006) and Blatto-Vallee et al. (2007) found that middle school- to college-aged students generally failed to use such strategies successfully.

The groups of teachers in the Kelly et al. (2003) study did not differ in the degree to which they assigned practice exercises (for which the procedures had already been taught) as compared to "true" problems (which focus more on problem solving). However, there were differences in the levels of math texts used, with grade-level texts more often used in integrated mainstreamed classes than in the other two types. There also were differences in teachers' preparation to teach mathematics, with teachers of integrated mainstream classes more likely to have specific background in math. Teachers with certification in mathematics and mathematics education were more likely than the others to use analytically oriented problem-solving strategies, including the use of analogies to understand word problems and relate them to currently known information. Thus, students in integrated mainstream classrooms were more likely to experience challenging and nuanced problem-solving approaches. Finally, teachers working with integrated mainstreamed students had higher perceptions of their students' problem-solving abilities. They were less likely to declare that students' English skills were the primary barrier to successful solving of word problems.

Pagliaro and Kritzer (2005) similarly noted that U.S. elementary and high school teachers of deaf and hard-of-hearing students tended to make infrequent use of currently recommended or "reform-based" activities during class time. Based on a survey with 290 respondents who were identified as being the "most effective mathematics teacher" by their school administrators, Pagliaro and Kritzer noted that little time was spent on "discrete" or real-life-based problem solving (perhaps partially explaining the Ansell & Pagliaro, 2006, and Blatto-Vallee et al., 2007, findings). They attributed this, at least in part, to the teachers' limited training in mathematics (see also Kluwin & Moores, 1989; Pagliaro, 1998).

None of the above differences is surprising, given that certification for teachers in the higher grades in regular (mainstream) schools requires content-specific degrees and, for those teaching in special classrooms or center schools for students with hearing loss, specialization in deaf education. However, as Kelly et al. (2003) pointed out: "in two of the three school settings deaf students are receiving mathematics instruction from teachers who are not qualified by education or certification to teach mathematics...In the (other) setting, students are being taught by teachers who have not been educated in the specific needs of deaf learners" (p. 115). They also noted that differences in teachers' perceptions of students' skills, as well as higher use of verbally mediated analytical approaches such as analogical reasoning, may reflect reality-based differences in students that led to placement decisions (Stinson & Kluwin, 2003). Those in integrated mainstream classes, if placement is appropriate, can be expected to have higher language skills and at-grade or close to at-grade abilities in other areas such as mathematics. However, as Kelly et al. (2003) concluded: "Teachers cannot expect deaf students to perform well at problem-solving tasks if they do not give them opportunities to be engaged in cognitively challenging word-problem situations" (p. 117).

Components of Mathematics Performance

In addition to having an effect on teacher expectations and strategies, language skills of deaf and hard-of-hearing students are associated with mathematical concepts and skills at a more basic level, with language delays limiting the appreciation of technical vocabulary and ability to understand in-person as well as written problem presentation and problem-solving approaches (Gregory, 1998). Hyde et al. (2003) reported that deaf and hard-of-hearing students in Australia had difficulty understanding English syntax as well as vocabulary in word problems, failing to understand phrases like "at the start" and being unable to relate two sentences in which the second referred back to information in the first. Sentence constructions that did not represent the exact order in which events referred to would have happened were especially difficult, as were problems asking students to compare two quantities and determine the difference between them. Hyde et al. (2003) concluded that the results of their study were essentially in agreement with performance of deaf students in the United Kingdom as described earlier by Wood et al. (1986).

Kelly and Gaustad (2006) compared scores on math achievement tests with scores on tests of reading and, specifically, on tests of knowledge about morphological units (or meaning units) in English words among deaf college students enrolled at the National Technical Institute for the Deaf (NTID). They found that both morphological knowledge and general reading skill significantly predicted performance on one of the math tests, the American College Test (ACT, 2000) required for students entering NTID, and associated positively with scores on the other (the NTID Mathematics Placement Test). Kelly and Gaustad proposed that the specialized vocabulary required for math can be acquired and manipulated more readily when morphological skills can be applied consistently and automatically. They noted that sign language interpreters often use a simpler word/sign to substitute for a more technical one, like those encountered often in discussions of math theory and practice, and they called for use of fingerspelling or more specific signs (as have been created for New Zealand Sign Language).

Kelly and Gaustad noted, however, that their study failed to include a measure of general nonverbal cognitive functioning—a variable that might have predicted variance in both language and math achievement (Convertino et al., 2009).

As suggested in the Kelly and Gaustad study (2006), deaf and hard-of-hearing students have difficulties with mathematics even in college. Dowaliby, Caccamise, Marschark, Albertini, and Lang (2000) reported that of 248 deaf students entering two-year, NTID associate degree programs, 79% scored below the 50th percentile on the ACT mathematics subtest. Blatto-Vallee et al. (2007) compared performance of deaf students and hearing students in middle school (n = 18 and 43, respectively), high school (n = 28 deaf, 51 hearing), and college programs (n = 39 deaf, 62 hearing) on a test of mathematical problems. A group of 64 deaf students at the associate degree level was also included, but without a comparable hearing group. The mathematics test was slightly modified (to represent American instead of British English terms) from one developed by Hegarty and Kozhevnikov (1999) and included 15 short word problems that emphasized logical problem solving. Student visuospatial abilities also were assessed using a test of visual form completion and another test requiring the students to envision the shape of a complete form when component parts were illustrated. In addition, "notes" or "shown work" of students while problem solving were collected and analyzed according to the types of representations they had created. When the work illustrated "relationships between objects and/or parts of an object described in the problem" (p. 438) it was coded as being "schematic." "Pictorial" visual representations were those that showed the objects mentioned in the problem but did not indicate any relationship or discerned pattern among them. Only schematic representations were assumed to illustrate actual reasoning or problem solving.

At all age levels, the groups of participating hearing students obtained higher scores than the deaf students on the math test and both visual-spatial tests. Developmental trends on the mathematics test differed for deaf and hearing students, with the hearing students' scores increasing at a faster rate than those of the deaf students. Thus the advantage for hearing students at the college level was even greater than at the middle school level, reflecting the cumulative nature of learning.

Except for the college bachelor's degree group, hearing students also obtained higher schematic representation scores than deaf students on the drawings or visual aids they produced while solving the problems. Schematic scores were determined in regression analyses to be the best predictor of scores on the mathematics tests for students at all levels, and production of simple pictorial representations negatively correlated with math scores. For deaf students, the visual-spatial measures added to the prediction of math test scores at middle school, associate degree, and bachelor's degree levels. The visual-spatial scores were significant predictors of hearing students' math scores only at the middle-school level, and even the schematic scores lost predictive power in regression analyses at the high school and bachelor's degree program levels. Blatto-Vallee et al. (2007) concluded that use of pictorial representations during problem solving indicated only a surface understanding of the problem and that schematic representations of relations between entities in the problems was a developmental phenomenon, disappearing when mathematics procedures became automatic (for hearing students) beyond the middle school level. The continued relative lack of utilizing this approach, along with the relative lack of increase in math scores with age, indicated that deaf students tended to stabilize in their general problem-solving strategies and skills, falling further and further behind hearing peers with age (see Traxler, 2000).

Blatto-Vallee et al. (2007) related their findings to Marschark's (2003, 2006) proposal that cognitive processes and learning differ between deaf and hard-of-hearing and hearing people. Deaf and hard-of-hearing children appear to be merely delayed on some mathematic skill development, such as representation of number, estimation, and general computational skills (Bull, 2008; Hitch, Arnold, & Phillips, 1983; Nunes & Moreno, 1997). No delay has been shown for representation and discrimination of number when quantities are represented spatially and simultaneously (Zarfaty et al., 2004). However, hearing children generally have been found to be advantaged compared to deaf and hard-of-hearing children when sequential memory is needed for problem solving, as when one piece of information has to be kept in mind while another operation or calculation is accomplished (see also Ottem, 1980). In fact, processing of temporal information is an area in which deaf and hard-of-hearing children are often reported to perform less well than hearing children (Bull, 2008; Todman & Seedhouse, 1994; but see Zarfaty et al., 2004). Furthermore, there are indications that children with hearing loss tend not to spontaneously relate or coordinate bits of information or steps in a process (Hauser et al., 2008; Marschark & Hauser, 2008).

Deaf and hard-of-hearing children also are less likely than hearing children to bring previous knowledge and experience to the task of acquiring mathematical skills (Marschark et al., 2008). Kelly and Mousley (2001), in a study of 33 deaf and 11 hearing college students, argued that reading skills provide only a partial explanation for the difficulty that deaf and hard-of-hearing students demonstrate on word problems in mathematics. They reported that the deaf students in their sample made many computational errors even when they applied correct procedures. Kelly and Mousley attributed this to a lack of sustained focus on the problems. Kelly and Mousley also reported motivational problems, with deaf students often making comments that showed a lack of confidence in their ability to solve word problems—followed by lack of completion of those problems. Kritzer (2009) suggested that when (younger) deaf children show such attentional problems, it likely reflects a lack of foundational mathematics skills and concepts.

Mathematics Interventions for Deaf and Hard-of-Hearing Students

Bull (2008) recommended that mathematics instruction for students with hearing loss recognize both their visual-spatial orientation and their relative lack of confidence in their abilities to solve mathematics problems. Nunes and Moreno (2002) developed a program based on the ideas of providing visual representation of the relations between elements in mathematics problems and of providing deaf students the opportunity to use their visual-spatial strengths to learn basic or core mathematical concepts typically understood by hearing children. The program was designed for deaf and hard-of-hearing children in school years 2–5 (ages 7–11 years). The program included visually based (nonverbal) representations for problems focused on additive composition (number and measurement concepts), additive reasoning (addition and subtraction as inverse operations), multiplicative reasoning (reasoning about multiplication/division operations and graphic displays), and fractions based on understanding of ratio. (Teachers later reported that the ratio concept was difficult both for them and for the students.) Concepts were explained to the teachers, who were encouraged to use their school's language system/modality and their own ways of explaining the concepts to the children. About 1 hour a week was expected to be devoted to the program.

The evaluation project used a quasi-experimental design. A "baseline" group of 65 deaf or hard-of-hearing students were tested on the NFER-Nelson mathematics test, as were the 23 children in the experimental group. At the beginning of the project, scaled scores of the experimental and baseline groups did not differ significantly. After a year, the experimental group was reassessed and again compared with the baseline group's original scores. The experimental group's scores now significantly exceeded that of the baseline group. Although it is not known if or how much the baseline group's scores would have improved without the intervention, additional support was provided for the program's efficacy by comparing the experimental group's progress with that predicted (in the NFER-Nelson test manual) from their original scores. The majority (68.2%) of the children had scores at the end of the project that exceeded the prediction. This is especially impressive in that the prediction was based upon expectations for hearing, not deaf or hard-of-hearing students.

Anecdotally, teachers reported that students greatly enjoyed the booklets and the activities provided in the curriculum and that they spontaneously began to generate diagrams and illustrations during problem solving when the curriculum was not formally in use. Nunes and Moreno (2002) concluded that the program was successful, although they could not determine exactly which aspects led to the successful results. They suggested that both cognitive and motivational factors were probably involved: use of drawings and visual representations to support children's intuitions about mathematical and number concepts, and increasing children's interest in and enjoyment of mathematics. These advantages also may have accrued as a result of teachers' behavior, through their training in the program and their being reinforced by children's interest. It also is important that the mathematical problems were all conceptual and required reasoning and problem solving, thus reflecting observations by Blatto-Vallee et al. (2007) that visual-spatial displays of mathematical problems that represent schematic (relational or problem-solving) aspects of the problem are more helpful and more predictive of success than simple pictorial displays. This program thus built upon the potential for deaf children's visual-spatial strengths but emphasized the development of relational problem-solving approaches.

After conducting an extensive literature review, Easterbrooks and Stephenson (2006) summarized evidence on 10 math (and science) practices in deaf education that are frequently referred to in research literature or are practices considered important by teachers and others in the field. One practice the authors mentioned, an approach that they concluded has a sparse but positive research base, is that of using visual/graphic organizers such as graphs, charts, and concept maps. They also concluded that teachers' ability to communicate well in the language or language system used by their students represented "best practice" in deaf education as well as general education settings. Taking an active problem-solving approach in which students analyze multiple methods and explain potential solutions has strong research support when older deaf and hard-of-hearing students are considered, but Easterbrooks and Stephenson concluded that more evidence is needed for young children. They described the research base as "developing" for use of case-based, collaborative problem-solving situations and activities emphasizing critical thinking skills. Still needed, they suggested, is more research about the usefulness of technology-based approaches to learning focusing on specialized vocabulary or terminology and the efficacy of modifying the reading level of texts used in content areas such as mathematics.

Development of Mathematics Concepts and Skills: Where Are We?

Summarizing what we know about mathematics achievement by deaf and hard-of-hearing students, we see that they demonstrate basic concepts about number and quantity during pre-school years. However, delays in language development, a relative lack of exposure (both incidentally and in classrooms) to life-based problem-solving activities, and frequently inadequate pre-service teacher preparation in the area of mathematics appear to lead to the overall lag noted in subsequent development of mathematics concepts and skills. Below-age language skills limit access to teacher-provided as well as text-based explanations, and the majority of deaf and hard-of-hearing students lack age-appropriate command of technical vocabulary in the area of mathematics.

Surveys of teachers as well as classroom observations show relatively little class time devoted to problem-solving activities, although teachers certified in mathematics use more analytically oriented approaches. Although deaf and hard-of-hearing students show special difficulties dealing with word or story problems, testing also indicates lower-than-expected performance on calculation and computation.

Deaf and hard-of-hearing students show relative strength in visual-spatial abilities, although they do not necessarily apply these skills when presented with mathematics problems, and many students face special difficulties when needing to relate multiple pieces of information and identify relationships. Specific training has been recommended in approaching problems through producing schematic illustrations, and an elementary-level curriculum emphasizing visual-spatial over verbal activities has been found to increase students' problem-solving skills (Nunes & Moreno, 2002). Given the documented advantage of deaf signers in generating and manipulating visuospatial representations (see chapter 7) and emerging evidence of strength in similar processes even during pre-school years, such strategies may better suit the learning styles of many deaf students. The increased motivation Nunes and Moreno noted in the students who participated in their curriculum study may have resulted from its emphasis on visuospatial representation of the mathematical problems.

Other investigators have found that older deaf and hard-of-hearing students approach word problems in mathematics with a lack of confidence in their ability to perform them and subsequently fail to seriously attempt their solution. It also has been suggested that deaf and hard-of-hearing students tend to lose attentional focus, especially when problems require relating multiple operations or logical steps. This may reflect a lack of foundational concepts and automatization in employing foundational or basic computation processes. Although it is not clear to what extent these characteristics are attributable to differences in learning styles or cognitive processing between students with and without hearing loss, it is clear that modifications in curricula and in teaching strategies are required if deaf and hard-of-hearing students are to develop to their potential in the important areas of mathematics achievement.

SCIENCE EDUCATION AND ACHIEVEMENT

Curriculum reforms during the 1970s in the teaching of science in U.S. schools were never fully implemented in classes or schools for deaf and hard-of-hearing students (Marschark et al., 2002), despite reports of successful outcomes for students with hearing loss who participated in process-oriented, activity-based programs with low verbal demands (Boyd & George, 1973; Grant, Rosenstein, & Knight, 1975).

Marschark and Hauser (2008) suggested that gaps in knowledge and experience between deaf and hard-of-hearing students may not be obvious in the early years. In fact, Roald and Mikalsen (2000) showed that young children held similar concepts related to scientific phenomena regardless of hearing status. However, significant differences in levels of knowledge and achievement were noted by high school age. This situation occurs in part because (a) literacy difficulties limit deaf and hard-of-hearing students' exposure to information in the sciences; (b) these students have decreased opportunities to learn incidentally from conversations occurring around them; (c) they lack an understanding of the vocabulary used in science; and (d) it is difficult for them to use vision for both watching communication (whether signed or spoken) and attending to activities and other visual learning material essential to science learning (Marschark & Hauser, 2008). In addition, interpreters for signing deaf students often simplify scientific terms and explanations (Harrington, 2000). Lang et al. (2006) pointed out that of the words deemed important from a science curriculum review, approximately 60% do not have sign representation. The researchers indicated a need to identify signs that are in use and pointed out difficulties both in attempting to create signs for these ideas and in students' experiencing different signs for similar concepts across classes. Yet there has been considerable reluctance in the United States to collaboratively create a vocabulary of science signs similar to that developed for mathematics in New Zealand Sign Language.

Fostering Science Learning by Deaf and Hard-of-Hearing Students

Despite continuing difficulties with literacy skills, researchers have suggested that writing can be a supportive component of a strong science curriculum for deaf and hard-of-hearing students. Yore (2000), for example, proposed that embedding structured writing activities within the science curriculum could provide a way to guide students' thinking and encourage active evaluation of their own knowledge. Although he recommended "do first and read and write later," with concrete, hands-on activities being the core of instruction, he proposed that writing activities can support the integration of ideas and help students address relationships they have discovered. According to the approach he proposed, which has seen some success with hearing students at various levels in school, teachers should react to the content and structure of brief written work and not focus on issues such as spelling and grammar when meaning is not disrupted. The approach includes occasional use of templates or provided structures and initial group work to identify information sources, as well as peer review of written products to help students ascertain and improve the degree to which their written work communicates to others. Yore suggested that this kind of approach can be of use to deaf students as well, but his proposals clearly assume effective teacher-student and student-student communication (cf. Marschark et al., 2007; Matthews & Reich, 1993). The approach that Yore proposed also points out the importance of cognitive and metacognitive skills for science learning and, undoubtedly, for learning in general. He explained that effective reading and writing in science requires "conceptual background; knowledge about science text and science reading; declarations, procedures, and conditions of reading strategies; and executive control to set purpose, monitor progress, and adjust actions" (p. 110).

Lang and Albertini (2001) employed a qualitative approach to analyze teacher reports on classroom and student activity in Grades 6–11 (ages 12–17 years) after providing teachers with a workshop on development of science and English literacy for deaf and hard-of-hearing students. The workshops stressed acquisition of knowledge and concepts in a social construction context, in which communication with others is seen to have a critical influence on learning. After the training, Lang and Albertini collected and analyzed 228 writing samples that had been elicited from students in one of four contexts: (a) creative pieces, often asking students to imagine themselves as being an entity or phenomenon, such as a cookie passing through the digestive system, a simple machine, or a chemical element; (b) guided free writing, in which students were to record predictions, observations, and conclusions related to a hands-on, "authentic" science activity; (c) end-of-class reflection, in which they were asked to write down important points or concepts they had learned; or (d) double entry, which asked students to summarize and react to text selections provided by the teacher.

Teachers and researchers judged creative pieces and guided free writing to be effective for both learning and assessment. Creative pieces routinely resulted in the longest and most detailed writing. Guided free writing gave teachers useful information about students' ability to think logically and construct meaning from an activity, that is, about students' science process skills. End-of-class reflections were of lesser usefulness, and double entry effectiveness required extensive effort by teachers to identify text excerpts to be used and to prepare effective prompts. Despite these difficulties, double entry writing was thought by the teachers and researchers to be especially productive. Overall, teachers thought that the writing activities, although lengthening the time required for each lesson, provided important insights about individual student's grasp of science information and processes.

Usefulness of all four types of embedded writing activities was dependent upon teachers' abilities to provide explicit guiding prompts and questions to focus the students' writing. Teachers' ability to identify and emphasize appropriate content appeared to relate to their training in science. In fact, their training and background in the field is positively related to student achievement in science and mathematics (Kluwin & Moores, 1985, 1989) and to students' opinions about teacher effectiveness (Lang, McKee, & Conner, 1993). In addition, familiarity with patterns of written English usage by deaf students allowed teachers to identify and understand students' thinking processes and concepts learned.

Lang and Albertini (2001) found that follow-up activities were judged to be especially important as a way to consolidate learning—for example, following up on development of definitions and understanding of science vocabulary or, in other cases, clarifying conceptual misunderstandings. They called for more research into the effectiveness of various methods for follow up, setting up initial context, and posing prompts or guides. Investigation of the effects of the embedded writing approach in developing science, literacy, and cognitive skills and of interactions among methods used and a priori student characteristics and skills is especially needed.

In an interesting and creative qualitative study, Roald (2002) conducted conversation-based interviews with five deaf teachers in Norway who had majored in physics at the university level and who had also been students in the secondary science classes that he had taught. These former students, now teachers, reflected on their own education as well as the education they were providing for their students. They concluded that a teacher's knowledge of subject matter is critical for successful teaching, but so is the teacher's ability to communicate fluently with the students. In this case, the teacher-informants were referring to fluency in Norwegian Sign Language. They also made other comments that can provide some guidance for programming in the sciences. First, they believed that collaborative learning, in which students communicated among themselves and participated fully in discussions with the teacher about science problems and topics, was especially helpful. For this to be productive, the teachers suggested that class sizes smaller than five to nine students overly limit collaboration potential. They strongly favored structured lessons in which discussion of problems and concepts preceded both laboratory activities and reading. Most of the teachers had found both the content and the language in the textbooks to be very difficult for them as students. However, they also noted that having to write laboratory reports and other notes helped them to organize and remember what they had learned. Finally, they now favored the use of drawings to illustrate "objects and relations" (p. 65) and assist science learning and problem solving, even though they remembered having resisted this approach when they were students and now received similar initial reactions from their own students. When they had been students themselves, the teachers apparently had felt that this approach reflected their own teachers' expectations that their language skills were too weak to provide sufficient support for problem solving, so their reluctance may have been defensive.

Barman and Stockton (2002) presented a qualitative evaluation of the Science, Observing, and Reporting-High School Curriculum (SOAR-High) that was implemented in three schools for deaf students in the United States. The curriculum is accessed online, and information presented is accurate and of high quality given that experts in each scientific area have developed the lessons (http://csc.gallaudet.edu/soarhigh). Structured lessons address earth science and energy topics.

Written material, guide questions, illustrations, and hands-on activity suggestions are included. Materials guide students in the science processes of observation, inference, prediction, communication, measurement, classification, interpreting data, forming hypotheses, and designing experiments. The program emphasizes use of technology in that, in addition to being accessed online, it involves many opportunities for students to gain experience working with Internet searches, videoconferencing, and developing web pages. Students keep an electronic portfolio of work that allows them to share their ideas with others in group work and also provides a means for teachers to evaluate student progress. It was the technology aspects of the curriculum that the students reported enjoying most, even though a few students complained that there was too much work on the computer and too little interaction with the teacher. Some thought that the reading level of the text-based materials was too difficult, and the evaluators noted that students continued to have problems generating hypotheses. The teachers were positive about effects of the program, however, and they believed the online nature of the program and the technology emphasis helped students develop independence.

Fulfilling the potential for use of computer technology in classrooms serving deaf and hard-of-hearing students depends upon teachers feeling competent to use the software and thus encouraging its use. Kluwin and Noretsky (2005) cited work in Australia (Morton, 1996) that indicated the use of technology by teachers in regular education classrooms was affected by issues of anxiety, self-confidence, and perceived relevance. Peer support, mentoring, and formal collaborative work as part of teacher training also has been identified as influencing teachers' use of technology (Gray & McNaught, 2001; Sherman, 1998). Kluwin and Noretsky reported on process and outcomes of an online training program developed for teachers of deaf and hard-of-hearing students. A total of 47 teachers from 42 schools in the United States participated, most from programs located in urban areas. Participants were provided one online course a semester, up to three courses. The coursework included modules on integrating computers into the classroom (basic skills related to use of software programs, review and evaluation of computer-assisted instruction software, educational application issues), accessing and using Internet resources, and contributing resources to Internet sites. Course participation was managed using a commercially available online course management system (Eduprise). Textbooks and additional readings were also provided, while e-mail was used for communication between participants and instructors. Project money was available for each school district to provide a local support person, but not all participating districts did so.

Using a mixed methods approach (questionnaires, content analysis of communications in discussion forums, direct observations), Kluwin and Noretsky (2005) found no significant effects on teachers' persistence in the program based on their initial anxiety, expertise, or general access to technology in the classroom.

However, availability and quality of local support was significantly related to teachers' likelihood of completing the available coursework. The researchers noted trends in the data for teachers who were initially anxious and non-expert in use of technology to report greater challenges and less classroom use. There also was a trend for initially more expert users to be more positive and to report greater classroom use by the end of the project. The researchers noted the limitations of their analyses due to the relatively small number of participants, but concluded that teachers' skills in use of technology in the classroom can be improved through a combination of online coursework and local, in-person support. Therefore, as in the study of student technology use reported by Barman and Stockton (2002), effective teacher technology use depended strongly on in-person communication and support.

SUMMARY: DISCOVERIES IN MATH AND SCIENCE

Only limited research is available addressing science and mathematics programming for students with hearing loss, but available findings are consistent across the two topics:

- Delays in literacy development and deficits in content-specific and general vocabulary negatively affect achievement in mathematics and science, limiting opportunities for incidental learning and usefulness of text-based material. These effects are amplified by the fact that signs do not exist for some of the important concepts and ideas that need to be efficiently expressed.
- The gap between children with and without hearing loss appears early, often prior to school entry. Differences in average performance are small at early ages but increase with years in school.
- Students' participation and development of problem-solving abilities in realistic scenarios are limited, affecting their performance in both domains. This situation seems to result, in part, from the relative absence of true problem-solving activities provided in the classroom, but there may be other factors at work. Teachers report that even with specific interventions, many upper level deaf and hard-of-hearing students are unable to generate effective scientific hypotheses.
- Successful teachers tend both to have training in the subject matter being taught and to be knowledgeable about the learning styles and patterns of students who are deaf or hard-of-hearing. However, limited numbers of teachers have this combination of abilities.

Less information is available about achievement in science as compared to achievement in math. However, the following are supported by at least emerging data:

- Embedding writing within science projects appears to promote and consolidate benefits from activities, even though students' writing skills are typically delayed. Creative writing focused on science concepts and ideas also appears to be helpful, emphasizing effective communication instead of the mechanics of grammar.
- Group discussion and direct communication with the teacher are especially valued as methods for acquiring science knowledge by deaf and hard-of-hearing students. When technology is used to transmit scientific information (and thereby to provide science expertise that many teachers' pre-service training has not given them), the addition of person-to-person communication seems to be an important support for successful learning.
- Whether presented online or in printed text, the language of science explanations and material can easily overwhelm students' knowledge and reading skills, thus limiting benefits. As with students, significant amounts of in-person support to teachers are required for online-based training programs to be effective.

Both science and mathematics are areas in which significantly more research and curriculum development are needed. Advances in these and related areas will require pre- and in-service training for teachers and other professionals in subject matter areas as well as the learning characteristics of deaf and hard-of-hearing students.

9 Educational Placement Decisions and Outcomes

Two general philosophies of educational placement are held across, and often within, countries. The first is that placement in the "mainstream" or within schools and classes where most students are hearing and non-disabled offers the best opportunities for deaf and hard-of-hearing children to acquire age-level academic and social skills. The second major philosophy is that specialized schools, where all resources are focused on serving children with hearing loss, can best meet and promote their developmental and academic progress. The latter philosophy is based on recognition of the special communication needs of deaf and many hard-of-hearing students as well as the fact that such a large proportion of the population has related delays in academic areas. Despite the strong emotions associated with this difference of opinion, looking ahead, there is little empirical evidence that either of these approaches generally is better for deaf and hard-of-hearing students.

Researchers and practitioners typically distinguish between two subtypes when discussing educational models involving the integration of students with hearing loss into regular classrooms with hearing students: "Mainstreaming," in which it is generally assumed that the student with hearing loss will adapt to the general education system, and "inclusion" in which the teacher and class are expected to adapt to the needs of the students with hearing loss (Antia, Stinson, & Gaustad, 2002; Hyde, Ohna, & Hjulstadt, 2005; Power & Hyde, 2002; Stinson & Antia, 1999). The difference is one of both semantics and attitude, if not always practice. In both situations, the reality typically is one or a few deaf and hard-of-hearing students participating in a class of mostly hearing students, although "mainstreaming" is also used to refer to a context in which deaf and sometimes hard-of-hearing children are educated in special classrooms located within local public schools.

Over the past two centuries, as education has become more widely available for students who are deaf or hard-of-hearing, the most prevalent types of placement have changed. During the 18th and early 19th centuries, special separate schools, based on either oral or signed communication, were the norm in both the United Kingdom and the United States (Lang, in press). Such programs traced their histories at least in part to the schools established in the 18th century by Heinicke in Germany (spoken communication) and L'Épée in France (signed communication). Regardless of the choice of primary communication modality in these schools, there was a shared assumption that students who were deaf required specialized instruction methods and approaches to language that differed significantly from those of hearing students. As the 20th century progressed, and the 21st century began, however the prevailing educational and legal philosophies changed to emphasize the importance of interactions between deaf and hard-of-hearing students and hearing students in schools and classrooms where learning opportunities were similar and, at least in theory, equivalent.

Currently, several models of educational placement are available. The first remains special schools. By the mid-1970s, over a third of all deaf children in the United States attended residential schools, and another third attended special school programs. Beginning in 1975, legislation emphasizing placement of children with disabilities in local schools and parents' preferences for keeping their children at home led to significant changes (Marschark, 2007). By 1998, about 20% of deaf students were attending special schools (National Center for Education Statistics, 1999), and that proportion has since dropped to approximately 15% (Mitchell & Karchmer, 2006). This trend is not limited to the United States.

Some of the special schools (e.g., the Central Institute for the Deaf in the United States, the Mary Hare Schools in the United Kingdom) continue to emphasize spoken communication to the exclusion of sign language. This is also the case for some private schools in Australia (e.g., the Cora Barclay Center for the Deaf and Hearing Impaired), as programs stressing auditory-verbal approaches have increased since early cochlear implantation has become more prevalent (Hyde et al., 2005; Power & Hyde, 1997, 2003). Other separate or special schools, including the (publicly funded) Clerc Center at Gallaudet University in Washington, D.C., and the (privately funded) Learning Center in Massachusetts, emphasize use of natural sign language while making varied levels of accommodation for support of spoken language development, especially for children who are hard of hearing or who use cochlear implants (Seal et al., 2005). Similarly, in Australia, there are some schools that emphasize use of sign language in a sign/bilingual educational approach (Hyde et al., 2005).

The larger proportion of students with hearing loss in England (Powers, 1996), Australia (Power & Hyde, 2002, 2003), Israel (Zandberg, 2005), and the United States (Mitchell & Karchmer, in press) now attend local schools in which they are grouped in special classrooms or, if primarily in classrooms for the general (hearing) population, typically receive part-time special services from a resource room teacher. Resource room teachers are often *itinerant* or *peripatetic*, meaning that they travel among several schools and provide a range of services from consultation with the general education teacher to direct, individualized academic support to deaf and hard of hearing students. Much of the direct teaching they provide is remedial in nature (Kluwin, Stewart, & Sammons, 1994; Stinson & Kluwin, in press), and this model seems to be especially prevalent in the United States (cf. Power & Hyde, 2002).

STUDENT CHARACTERISTICS, NEEDS, AND PLACEMENT PATTERNS

Demographic differences between students in special versus local schools and, within local schools, between those in special classes versus those primarily in classes with hearing peers, are striking and create significant difficulties for program comparisons. In many special classrooms and special schools in the United States, more than half of the students are from minority ethnic groups; the opposite is true for children in general education classrooms (Mitchell & Karchmer, in press). This may be because ethnic status is generally a proxy for general socioeconomic status in the United States and, unfortunately, continues to influence learning opportunities (Kluwin, 1993). Students who attend their local schools are also less likely to have any identified disabilities to complicate the effects of their hearing loss relative to those in special schools (Allen, 1992; see chapter 10). Practically, separate schools may be better equipped to handle the needs of children with multiple disabilities but, theoretically, comparisons of academic outcomes in the two settings are inherently invalid because the children who attend them are different.

Another difference between students in local versus special schools is level of hearing loss. Both in the United States (Antia et al., 2004; Mitchell & Karchmer, in press) and Australia (Power & Hyde, 2002), students in general education classrooms tend to have lesser degrees of hearing loss and therefore are more likely to be considered hard of hearing than deaf. This also means that more of the students in general classrooms use spoken language as their primary means of communication, although some require and are provided sign language interpreters (Antia, Kreimeyer, & Reed, 2010).

Some investigators have concluded that academic achievement is higher on average for students attending general education classrooms in local schools compared to those in special classrooms or special, separate schools (Holt, 1994; Kluwin, 1993; Kluwin & Stinson, 1993). Kluwin and Moores (1985, 1989) showed that more progress in mathematics was made by students in general education than those in special classes. However, what may at first seem to be an effect of placement has since been recognized as reflecting other variables, primary among them being students: Those who begin with higher skill levels tend also to make faster progress over a given amount of time.

Powers (1999) sought to predict performance of deaf and hard-of-hearing students on the General Certificate of Secondary Education examination (that is administered to students in England and Wales) from a number of background variables, including hearing thresholds (with hearing losses ranging from moderate, or about 40 dB, to profound, over 90 dB). Powers found that students in special schools for the deaf tended to perform less well than those who were in mainstream programs. After further investigation, however, he concluded that this was probably a result of placement decisions being made on the basis of initial skill levels and not due to characteristics of the educational placement itself. Regression equations accounted for only 20% of the differences in outcomes, with significant predictors including age of hearing loss onset (later onset predicted better academic performance), family socioeconomic status, presence or absence of additional disabilities, and having at least one deaf parent. This set of background variables has been found to associate with academic performance of deaf and hard-of-hearing students regardless of their type of placement (Marschark et al., 2002; Moores, 2001). Thus, in contrast with findings for students with cognitive or emotional disabilities (but without hearing loss), for whom achievement has been found to be better supported in mainstreamed or general education classes than in separate classes (Carlberg & Kavale, 1980), no functionally significant effect has been found for students with hearing loss.

Over a series of studies accounting for initial student and family characteristics, type of school placement for deaf and hard-of-hearing students has been found to account for only about 1% to 5% of the variance in academic outcome (Allen & Osbourne, 1984; Kluwin & Moores, 1985, 1989; Powers, 1999). A stronger and more significant predictor has been the presence of additional disabilities, but overall, an average of 75% of the variance in academic outcomes has remained unexplained. In their study of math achievement, Kluwin and

Moores (1989) attributed some of the previously unexplained variance to differences in teacher preparation and quality of teaching and suggested that future research should focus more on this aspect of the educational experience than on the makeup of the class itself. More than a decade later, however, teacher variables remain largely unexplored.

The shift toward educating more deaf and hard-of-hearing students in general educational classrooms early requires changes in teacher preparation for both general education teachers and those specializing in deaf education. Even if, for the reasons noted above, deaf and hard-of-hearing students in such settings show academic achievement somewhat higher than that of their peers in special classrooms or special schools (Antia et al., 2008), performance of students with hearing loss who are in general education classes continues to lag that of hearing student peers, generally falling in the "low-average" range (Antia et al., 2008; Blair, Peterson, & Viehweg, 1985; Most, 2006).

One reason for this continuing lag is undoubtedly that, as Antia et al. (2010) caution, students who are deaf or hard-of-hearing and use spoken language are often assumed to understand and to be processing more information than is actually the case. As discussed in more detail later in this chapter, Marschark and his colleagues (Marschark, Convertino, et al., 2007; Marschark, Leigh, et al., 2006; Marschark, Sapere, et al. 2005; Marschark, Sapere, et al., 2004) have found this to be true also of deaf adolescents and college students using both sign language and spoken language. Regardless of a specific placement choice, ongoing assistance and resource teaching will be needed from teachers knowledgeable about the characteristics of deaf and hard-of-hearing children. The need for such support can be expected to increase rather than decrease if early identification and intervention, as well as use of advanced hearing technologies, lead to an even greater proportion of deaf children being placed in general education classes.

Even if the potential impact of specific teacher variables remains unclear, the overall importance of teachers' understanding what deaf students know and how they think and learn should not be underestimated. Marschark et al. (2008), for example, found that when deaf and hearing college students were taught by experienced teachers of the deaf, the deaf students learned just as much as their hearing peers relative to their initial levels of content knowledge. This result contrasted with previous studies involving mainstream instructors which had shown deaf students to fall further behind in those settings. Marschark et al. therefore suggested that still-to-be-determined accommodations made by experienced teachers of the deaf can significantly enhance deaf students' learning, even when they come into the classroom lagging behind hearing classmates. To provide such support, teachers of deaf and hard-of-hearing students must be prepared to work closely with general education teachers, and this may well require that they be knowledgeable about curriculum approaches used in general education classrooms. Effective skills at consultation and collaboration are critical in addition to skills in supporting the use of varied technologies. Knowledge about the special learning needs and styles of students with hearing loss (e.g., Hauser, Lukomski, & Hillman, 2008; Marschark & Hauser, 2008) as well as communication methods will continue to be required. Finally, teachers supporting deaf and hard-of-hearing students need to be able to serve as advocates for their students and to facilitate the students' becoming advocates for themselves, as well as supporting students' developing positive self-esteem and social-emotional characteristics (Antia et al., 2010; Bullard, 2003; Smith, 1998).

SOCIAL-EMOTIONAL FUNCTIONING AND CO-ENROLLMENT PROGRAMS

Social-emotional aspects of deaf and hard-of-hearing students' participation in general education classrooms have been an area of special concern and much research. The literature is replete with reports of negative self-esteem, lack of friendships, and loneliness among students with hearing loss who are being educated in mainstream or general education settings (e.g., Stinson & Antia, 1999). In general, more opportunities for leadership, participation in extracurricular activities, and communicatively easy social interactions are available in special schools and in special classes within local schools compared to situations in which one or a few students with hearing loss are placed in a classroom with hearing students (Moores, 2001; Ramsey, 1997; Stinson & Foster, 2000; Stinson, Whitmire, & Kluwin, 1996; van Gurp, 2001). Among other reasons for this situation, hearing students have been reported to lack understanding of attention-getting signals and skills in clear speaking to assist speechreading. In addition, many are reported to evidence general unease in interacting with deaf and hard-of-hearing peers (Stinson & Liu, 1999).

A placement option referred to as "co-enrollment" has been reported to minimize negative social-emotional reactions while allowing more integration of deaf and hard-of-hearing students in local general education programs. The defining characteristic of this approach is that a "critical mass" of students with hearing loss, instead of an isolated child or two, attends class with hearing students (Banks, 1994; Kirchner, 1994, 1996). Although a 1:1 ratio of deaf or hard of hearing to hearing students might be ideal, the demographics of hearing loss generally do not allow such a ratio to be achieved, and Antia, Kreimeyer, Metz, and Spolsky (in press) suggested that such a program can be successful if students with hearing loss make up one-fourth to one-third of the class. Multi-age co-enrollment classrooms allow the combining of sufficient numbers of students with hearing loss and, because students continue together for more than 1 school year, allow time for students with and without hearing loss to develop significant friendships. Multi-age groupings also encourage individualization of instruction depending upon skill and developmental levels for all students (Dorta, 1995; Kreimeyer, Crooke, Drye, Egbert, & Klein, 2000) assuming that sufficient teacher resources are available.

Building on earlier reports of the TRIPOD co-enrollment program in California (Kirchner, 1994, 1996), Kluwin (1999; Kluwin, Gonsher, Silver, & Samuels, 1996) and Kreimeyer et al. (2000) described model co-enrollment programs that included co-teaching by a general- and deaf-education teacher team, sign language instruction for hearing students and the general education teacher, and signing aides or interpreters. In such a placement, both groups of students experience the same curriculum and expectations for learning. Results from these three programs revealed academic achievement that was, on average, higher than that typical for deaf and hard-of-hearing students, albeit still below that of typical hearing age-mates. They also indicated increased social interaction between students with and without hearing loss.

Wauters and Knoors (2008) suggested that peer acceptance in an inclusive or co-enrollment program has effects beyond the social arena and that frequent, friendly interactions also support cognitive development. Participants in their study were either in co-enrollment programs, where sign language was being learned and used by hearing peers, or had sufficient spoken language skills to support participation in an oral environment. Thus, communication abilities generally were shared between deaf and hearing children in the classrooms rather than being a barrier to interaction. Administering an attitude scale to deaf and hearing classmates, the researchers found no differences between deaf and hearing classmates on measures of how popular they were as playmates or on how positively or negatively they were perceived overall. The distribution of children across categories of popularity (popular/rejected/neglected/ controversial/ average) also failed to differ significantly by hearing status, although deaf children were, on average, rated lower by their classmates than hearing children on production of prosocial behaviors and were said to be more socially withdrawn. Wauters and Knoors noted, however, that evidence of overall positive social interaction may have reflected the selectivity with which Dutch students with hearing loss are placed in general education classrooms, because the Netherlands also has separate programs available for deaf and for hard-of-hearing students.

Knoors and Hermans (2010) summarized their ongoing empirical research on educating deaf children in the co-enrollment setting, emphasizing that the program and a separate school for deaf children have different strengths in providing qualitatively good education. They found that the school for the deaf excelled in adapting educational methods to the communicative and individual needs of their students, whereas the co-enrollment program significantly exceeded the separate program on measures tapping classroom management and instructional techniques. Their findings indicated that mainstream and special schools "face different challenges in providing deaf children with qualitatively good education."

PROGRAM PLACEMENT AND STUDENT OUTCOMES

Given the fact that student characteristics, not to mention the characteristics of teachers and hearing peers, co-vary with types of placement, it is not surprising that few data are available to provide valid group comparisons of outcomes. Perhaps a better sense of the way in which various placements can support (or fail to support) deaf and hard-of-hearing students' social and academic achievement can be provided by a review of selected program examples. This section of the chapter, therefore, provides information about three current programs representing different placement options: a co-enrollment program using signs, a mainstream approach for oral students, and programming based on a sign/bilingual approach.

A Co-Enrollment Model

An example of a co-enrollment program in which great efforts were made to assure communication skills between deaf and hard-of-hearing students and hearing students was described by Kreimeyer et al. (2000). This program was conducted in the southwestern United States, where there is a relatively large Hispanic and Native American population. The majority of participating students, 60%, were from low-income families. Students tended to stay in the same classroom, with the same teachers, for 3 successive academic years. Before the co-enrollment classroom was established, deaf and hard-of-hearing children attended a special class in the same school and had possibilities for interacting with hearing students for an hour a day in non-academic activities (accompanied by an interpreter). Kreimeyer et al. reported that during the period prior to establishing the co-enrollment classroom, both the hearing students and the teachers of the general education classes considered the attendance of the deaf and hard-of-hearing students to be negative and disruptive, and academic achievement of students with hearing loss was significantly below grade-level expectations in literacy and mathematics.

The co-enrollment program began in a combination second, third, and fourth grade class of 9 students with hearing loss and 19 hearing students. The students with hearing loss used a variety of communication methods, including sign only, sign plus speech, and primarily speech with a few signs. Two experienced teachers—one who was certified to teach deaf children and was fluent in sign language, the other an accomplished general education teacher—were provided support by a certified speech/language therapist. The goal of increasing students' interaction and communication was facilitated by provision of sign instruction for all students, designation of deaf and hard-of-hearing students as "sign specialists," and a 10- to 15-minute period each day when only non-vocal communication was allowed. This period often included games, and all varieties of non-vocal communication (including gesturing and pantomiming) were encouraged. By teacher report, hearing students signed half of the time during interactions with deaf and hard-of-hearing students by the end of the first year. Girls acquired signs more quickly than boys and tended to be more verbal and less physical. Hearing students became used to tapping on deaf and hard-of-hearing students or using other visual or tactile signals to get their attention and begin a conversation. The general education teacher also learned to sign and reported that she combined signing with speaking approximately 80% of the time by the end of the year and understood the students with hearing loss most of the time without support from the other teacher.

Noting that students tended to self-segregate by hearing status when the program began, Kreimeyer et al. (2000) employed a single-subject design to track changes in this pattern. They collected quantitative observational data on interactions of each of the deaf and hard-of-hearing students during the first week (to serve as a baseline) and then collected the same kind of information over time as the above-described procedures were implemented. Data indicated that interactions in the classroom between students with and without hearing loss increased over the course of the first year. This change was less pronounced during lunchtime than during classroom activities, and it was not as evident for one child who had multiple disabilities. Although this research design allowed comparison with a baseline, it did not provide any way to determine whether the observed trends would have occurred over time without the specific interventions that were implemented—that is, whether the changes were due to hearing students' acquiring signs or simply to the two groups of children having an extended time to get to know each other. Nevertheless, the data provide some support for the efficacy of the sign intervention activities and give no evidence of negative outcomes.

Reported academic outcomes for deaf and hard-of-hearing students from participating in this co-enrollment classroom were mixed. Scores on tests of academic skills were conducted near the end of the academic year, and scores of the deaf and hard-of-hearing students in this classroom were compared with normative scores provided for deaf peers and for hearing age-peers in the test manuals. Participating students scored above expectations compared to deaf and hard-of-hearing norms for reading comprehension but still below norms for hearing students. The deaf and hard-of-hearing students' performance on mathematics did not differ significantly from norms for students with hearing loss and, again, were below the average scores for hearing students. Thus, although use of this co-enrollment model of class organization and placement had apparent value in providing experiences for deaf and hard-of-hearing and hearing children to get to know each other, to interact, and to learn from each other, there was no consistent evidence of academic benefits. Gains in cognitive processes might be expected for both deaf and hard-of-hearing and hearing groups if experiences in language code-switching promote flexibility in perspective taking and problem solving. The possibility of such gains was not investigated, however, and there are no data to support this potential effect. Long-term consequences of the co-enrollment experience as well as potential benefits of beginning it earlier, at school entry, are yet to be determined.

Despite some advantages, potential benefits of a co-enrollment approach to class placement are limited in that the approach obviously requires considerable resources. Stinson and Kluwin (in press) noted that several experimental co-enrollment programs have been discontinued after a few years, and that continuation is dependent upon trained and motivated staff as well as a large enough body of students with hearing loss to provide a critical mass of deaf and hard-of-hearing students in the classroom. Kreimeyer et al. (2000) and Luckner (1999) emphasized that successful implementation of co-enrollment programming requires more work from staff due to time needed to plan and coordinate activities, relies upon designation of a clear team leader, and necessitates the definition of shared educational and social goals. Teachers need to be able to work well as a team, and it is advantageous for them to have made a conscious decision to participate in this kind of approach.

A Mainstreaming Approach for Students Using Spoken Language

In the co-enrollment program described above, a major effort was undertaken to assist hearing students and teachers to learn to use sign language to facilitate deaf and hard-of-hearing students' ability to interact and to learn in the general educational classroom. In mainstream settings where students with hearing loss used spoken language, communication barriers still may require significant resources if they are to be surmounted. Hadjikakou, Petridou, and Stylianou (2005) reported on the experience of deaf and hard-of-hearing students, their parents, and their teachers on the island of Cyprus, where mainstreaming has been common in the primary grades since the 1980s. All students use oral communication at school and almost 90% of secondary-level students with hearing loss have been integrated in general education classrooms since the 1990s. The move toward mainstreaming resulted in large part from parent demands that their children share equal access to educational services. Responses to questionnaires in the Hadjikakou et al. study indicated a fairly high level of satisfaction from parents and students, overall, with the services provided to deaf and hard-of-hearing students in the general education classrooms.

Greek Cyprus has set up an organized and resource-intensive service system for deaf and hard-of-hearing students, including one-on-one or small group pull-out classes focused on Greek language, history, and physics (for which general achievement testing is required) as well as for English as a second language. A significant function of these one-on-one/small group sessions is pre-teaching of lessons and materials that will then be covered in the general classroom, and more than half of the students reported that these pre-teaching sessions allowed them to understand the subsequent regular classroom lessons. However, although all of the 69 secondary students surveyed (100% of the target population) reported that they were able to understand material presented during the pull-out sessions, 20 of them said they remained unable to participate during the regular class, and a small number reported that they *never* understood lessons presented in the regular classroom.

In addition to the pre-teaching and focused one-on-one or small group work, a small number of "coordinator" teachers, who are trained teachers of the deaf, serve as itinerant consultants for the general classroom teachers and are responsible for monitoring student performance in accordance with goals set in IEPs. Despite the availability of trained counselors and psychologists in the schools, the deaf and hard-of-hearing students reported that they were most likely to talk about issues and problems at school with the coordinator teachers (and, at home, with their parents). Parents also reported more communication with these specialists than with other school personnel. Coordinator teachers also provide in-service training and demonstration "micro-lessons" for the general education teachers, 81% of whom reported that they found them to be helpful. However, students continue to report that many general education teachers do not modify lessons or approaches to them, and teachers themselves reported that the degree of adaptation varies.

Teachers, parents, and deaf students in Cyprus all indicated that there were educational needs not being optimally served in the current classroom environments. Students and parents requested fewer lessons, less homework, clearer and slower speech used by teachers during class, and modified written language in texts and on tests. Hadjikakou et al. (2005) referred to current integration procedures as "effective and adequate" (p. 211); however, they also argued that "alternative teaching methods and curricular modifications and adaptations should be developed to meet the needs of deaf children in an integrated environment" (p. 210). Although there were no data reported on the specific academic achievements or interactive patterns of the deaf and hard-of-hearing students surveyed, other aspects of the report suggest that their academic achievements on the whole lagged behind those of hearing peers and that teachers face additional challenges in the regular classrooms if they are to meet those educational needs.

Special Classrooms, Centers, or Schools: Sign/Bilingual Programming

Unlike Cyprus and some other countries, Norway has a long tradition of use of natural sign language (Norwegian Sign Language, NSL) among its deaf population. When legislation was passed to allow deaf and hard-of-hearing students to attend local general education schools, those students continued to have the right to be educated in NSL. The system of separate schools that had previously provided sign-based educational programs was modified to establish those schools as resource centers providing in-service training for general education teachers and instruction in NSL. They also provide support services for deaf students by consulting with the local schools while still also serving as a part- or full-time education setting for some of the deaf and hard-of-hearing students. In the 2001–2002 school year, one-third of Norway's students with hearing loss were being educated in general education classrooms, but two-thirds were in special classes either in the local schools or the resource centers. To better accommodate the needs of students with hearing loss, Norway made some modifications in its national curriculum to provide more appropriate options. These options include changing language-learning expectations by substituting sign language skills for spoken Norwegian and English and changing expectations for the music curriculum.

Additional teachers are provided so those students using NSL who are integrated into general education classrooms have a signing teacher in the classroom and, in some situations, pupil-teacher ratios have been reduced. Decisions about these arrangements tend to be made at the local school level. As Hyde et al. (2005) concluded, the move from separate schools to this more integrated system resulted in the education system in Norway becoming more complicated administratively for the students and for teacher preparation programs. Data on educational outcomes are not yet available.

Singleton and Morgan (2006) discussed perceived advantages of a sign/bilingual (ASL/written English) approach for deaf and hard-of-hearing children in the United States who are in special classrooms or schools. They pointed out the socioemotional and sociocultural identity benefits of being in classrooms with other deaf students and, much more often than in inclusive settings, with deaf teachers. Deaf teachers are not only typically more fluent in the natural sign first-language being learned by the students, but they are adept at managing the visual attention needs of students who are dependent primarily upon vision for classroom communication. In addition, deaf teachers working in this kind of placement have been reported in qualitative studies (e.g., Bailes, 2001; Evans, 2004) to engage in complex information-based conversations with deaf students, thereby at least potentially supporting cognitive development and general knowledge as well as academic skills. Such conversational interactions may be especially important for children whose parents are not fluent signers and therefore cannot engage them fully and fluently. Singleton and Morgan noted that hearing teachers "cannot, and should not, speak to what it is like *to be Deaf*" (p. 368, italics in original) and therefore deaf teachers fill a special role in deaf students' education. Unfortunately, to our knowledge there are few data available about the academic progress of students in sign/bilingual programs (but see Rydberg et al., 2009; Singleton et al., 2004) that might justify use of the approach in separate, special schools and classrooms.

CLASSROOM PHYSICAL SETTINGS AND ACOUSTIC CONCERNS

Beyond administration and teaching methods, there are additional considerations to be faced when deaf and hard-of-hearing students are to be educated in general education settings. Often overlooked is the appropriateness of the physical setting in which classes are taught, given that most children with hearing loss, including those using hearing aids and cochlear implants, have difficulty understanding spoken language in settings (like classrooms) with significant amounts of background noise (Moeller, Tomblin, et al., 2007). Crandall and Smaldino (2000) pointed out that typical classroom signal-to-noise ratios are not conducive to learning, especially for students with hearing loss, and Finitzo-Heiber and Tillman (1978) indicated that speech reception is significantly reduced with even moderate levels of classroom noise. For this reason, more than half of the educational programs in Cyprus have made physical modifications to classrooms to improve acoustical characteristics (Hadjikakou et al., 2005), and itinerant teachers in Canada have been known to collect used tennis balls to place on the legs of classroom chairs.

Wilkins and Ertmer (2002) evaluated the classroom needs of children with hearing loss in the United States who are using cochlear implants and are enrolled in integrated (or inclusion) settings. They concluded that preferential seating, use of personal and soundfield frequency modulated (FM) systems, and presentation of important material in writing followed by frequent checks of comprehension are needed when students with hearing loss (especially those depending upon spoken language) are integrated with hearing students. Wilkins and Ertmer cautioned that teachers in general education classrooms should not assume that deaf and hard-of-hearing students comprehend language as well as their hearing classmates, and teachers need to monitor students' understanding frequently (see also Marschark et al., 2004, 2005). Given these constraints, integration in general education classrooms can be difficult even for deaf and hard-of-hearing children with relatively strong speech and language skills.

The use of sign language does not eliminate concerns about acoustic proper-ties of the classroom in that many children in such settings utilize some auditory processing and auditory-based language skills. Questions also remain about optimal class size in sign-based programs. Both Roald (2002) and Evans (2004) suggested that larger class sizes promote better sharing and learning in a sign/bilingual environment while most others (e.g., Marschark et al., 2002; Moores, 2001) indicate that small class sizes more effectively support deaf and hard-of-hearing children's learning. Most likely, the effects of class size will depend on the heterogeneity and specific characteristics of the students involved (e.g., cogni-tively, academically, hearing level) as well as teacher skill and training.

CLASSROOM INTERPRETING AND REAL-TIME TEXT

Beyond improving acoustics in the classroom, access to instruction can be faciliated directly by the provision of real-time text and, for students who use sign language, sign language interpreting. Oral interpreting (also known as *oral transliteration*) has been used in post-secondary education, but rarely in K–12 settings.

Within integrated classrooms, real-time text (a form of captioning provided in real time) frequently is promoted as a relatively inexpensive means of provid-ing deaf and hard-of-hearing students access to instruction and discussion in the classroom.[1] Despite common assumptions, however, there is relatively little evi-dence that this assumption is true. Not surprisingly, real-time text can present a challenge for deaf and hard-of-hearing students because the speed of verbatim real-time captioning is likely to exceed their reading abilities. Even controlling for reading level, Lewis and Jackson (2001) found that deaf 9- to 11-year-olds learned less from captioning on videos than did their hearing peers, apparently because of differences in background knowledge and information-processing strategies (Strassman, 1997).

Stinson, Stuckless, Henderson, and Miller (1988) and Elliot, Stinson, McKee, Everhart, and Francis (2001) surveyed deaf and hard-of-hearing students about their use of real-time text and interpreting. Students in both studies assigned higher ratings of understanding to real-time text than to interpreting. No direct evidence of comprehension or learning was reported, however, nor did the researchers evaluate students' reading or sign language skills. The validity of stu-dent comprehension ratings is questionable, in any case, insofar as Marschark,

---

[1] This issue is distinct from claims that regular use of television captioning and TTYs minicoms would facilitate deaf children's literacy skills. No empirical evidence has been offered to support these latter claims.

Sapere, et al. (2004) showed that deaf students tend to overestimate their comprehension in the classroom. Steinfeld (1998) found that captioning improved working memory performance (relative to no captioning) for both deaf and hearing students; however, hearing students' memory performance still surpassed that of deaf students. The author concluded that provision of real-time captions improved deaf students' comprehension, although comprehension was not specifically examined.

Other studies have demonstrated advantages of captioning for hearing students who were second language learners or who had learning disabilities (e.g., Koskinen, Wilson, Gambrell, & Jensema, 1986; Neuman & Koskinen, 1992). Little evidence is available indicating benefits for deaf and hard-of-hearing students, however. Koskinen, Wilson, and Jensema (1986), for example, conducted a study in which deaf 13- to 15-year-olds saw 10 repetitions of a 30-minute captioned video and also received intensive vocabulary and reading practice. Subsequently, students' sight reading of the material was reported to increase by only 10%, and there was no mention of increases in comprehension or transfer to other materials.

Stinson, Elliot, Kelly, and Liu (2009) compared deaf secondary school and post-secondary students' comprehension and memory of a lecture supported by either sign language interpreting or real-time text. No significant differences were observed between conditions for the college students, but secondary school students showed significantly greater performance on a post-lecture test when they received real-time text or read a transcript of the class lecture than when they received interpreting (see also Marschark, Sapere, et al., 2009). Stinson et al. suggested that the secondary school students retained more information with real-time text than interpreting due to the completeness of the information, the longer visibility of captioning on a computer display, and the availability of a printed transcript (for studying) afterward. Deaf college students' greater experience in receiving information in a variety of formats was assumed to override any potential relative benefit of the particular form of support.

Marschark, Leigh, et al. (2006) also examined the utility of real-time text in supporting deaf students' learning in secondary and post-secondary classrooms. In one experiment, they compared the effects on learning of real-time text, sign language interpreting, and both. Real-time text alone led to significantly higher performance by deaf students than the other two conditions, but their performance in all conditions was significantly below that of hearing peers who saw lectures without any support services. The advantage of text was not replicated in a second experiment comparing interpreting and two forms of real-time text, at immediate testing and after a 1-week delay (with notes from a professional notetaker and transcripts, respectively). Similarly, no significant differences were found in either immediate or delayed testing when learning in geography lessons by 12- to 16-year-olds was compared under three conditions: (a) a deaf teacher signing in Auslan (Australian Sign Language), (b) the teacher signing in Auslan with simultaneous real-time text, and (c) real-time text alone (cf. Andrews et al., 1997). Marschark, Leigh, et al. also failed to find any significant differences between interpreting and interpreting plus real-time text in a fourth experiment examining the learning via television captioning. Taken together, these experiments led to the conclusion that neither sign language interpreting nor real-time text has any inherent, generalized advantage over the other in supporting deaf students in secondary or post-secondary settings. At the same time, both provide superior access relative to no communication support, even if they fail to fully eliminate learning differences between deaf and hearing students.

That latter qualification remains an important caveat to the above findings. In all of the studies described in this section, as well as in a series of other studies by Marschark and his colleagues (e.g., Marschark, Sapere, et al. 2004, 2005, 2009), any time hearing students have been included, they have outscored deaf students on post-instruction tests, regardless of whether the deaf students received real-time text, sign language interpreting, or direct instruction by teachers who signed for themselves. Those results have been attributed in part to the finding that deaf students consistently came into the classroom with less content knowledge than their hearing peers (as indicated by pretests), but even controlling for prior knowledge, they are outscored by hearing peers. Marschark, Sapere, et al. (2008), however, found that teachers' experience with deaf students had a positive effect on student learning. In that study, deaf college students learned just as much as hearing students from classroom lectures when they were taught by experienced teachers of the deaf, regardless of whether the instructors were hearing or deaf and whether they were signing for themselves or utilizing interpreters. Those findings have been replicated in ongoing research, but the issue has not yet been investigated with younger students.

SUMMARY: THE WHO, WHAT, AND WHERE OF GOING TO SCHOOL

It appears that there is a convergence of opinion at various governmental levels (although not in the conclusions of data-based research) that participation in general education settings is of value to students who are deaf or hard-of-hearing. It was suggested in early research that deaf and hard-of-hearing students would benefit from attending math and science classes, at least at the secondary level, in settings with teachers who are experts in those fields. To date, however, evaluations have failed to consistently indicate significant academic benefits from different placements. Nevertheless, some issues are clear:

- Effectively managing specialized learning and communication needs of students with hearing loss requires training of both general education teachers and special education teachers, as well as modification of the physical environment and class size. The model in which itinerant or visiting teachers consult with the regular classroom teacher and provide individual or small group tutoring or pre-learning activities is becoming prevalent, but frequently there is no time for consultation among the itinerant teachers, general education teachers, and other providers of student services, creating potential impediments to student progress. Teacher preparation programs need to assure that knowledge about the general curriculum and general educational practices, as well as specialized knowledge in communication methods and learning styles of deaf and hard-of-hearing children, are provided to specialist teachers.

• Although evidence is scarce, that which is available suggests that at a minimum, social benefits accrue from co-enrollment and integrated placements where a significant number of children with hearing loss become part of a class with two or more co-teachers, at least one of whom specializes in education of deaf and hard-of-hearing children. This kind of approach requires an investment of resources and both leadership and teaming abilities from teachers, but it is not yet clear to what extent benefits of this model generalize across situations. Co-enrollment appears to represent the concept of inclusion at its best in that it promotes modifications in the provision of educational services to meet the needs of students with hearing loss while preserving their opportunities to interact with the regular curriculum, other students with hearing loss, and the larger society of hearing students.

• Multilevel systems that provide options for separate full- and partial-day classes for deaf and hard-of-hearing students as well as placement in classes with a majority of hearing students also require significant administrative resources, but they permit placement decisions to be based on assessments of individual needs. Such individualized decision making is important because recent evidence indicates that the learning styles and needs of deaf and hard-of-hearing students differ somewhat from those of their hearing peers. Specialized programming and teaching methods therefore are required if children with hearing loss are to achieve their full potential, and teachers who understand the needs of students who are deaf or hard-of-hearing are needed regardless of placement options or models.

• Students with hearing loss will need communication accommodations regardless of the language modalities they use. Neither the use of spoken language nor provision of interpreters nor use of real-time text has been shown to assure equal access to information presented in the classroom.

To the extent that placement in general education classes (mainstreaming or inclusion) remains a societal or personal goal for students with hearing loss, more research is needed on methods of matching child needs with environmental accommodation and supports. Also in need of further investigation are methods and outcomes in the preparation of both general and special education teachers who will be needed to fulfill the responsibilities and roles required in any of the existing models of academic placement for deaf and hard-of-hearing students.

10 Programming for Children With Multiple Disabilities

A significant proportion of the population of deaf or hard-of-hearing children have one or more disabilities that are not caused by their hearing loss, even if they sometimes co-occur with it (Arnos & Pandya, in press). The Gallaudet Annual Survey of Deaf and Hard-of-Hearing Children and Youth (Holden-Pitt & Diaz, 1998; Mitchell & Karchmer, 2006) has indicated that at least 35% and perhaps over 50% of deaf and hard-of-hearing students in the United States have an additional, educationally significant condition or disability. Shallop (2008) reported equally high estimates of the proportion of deaf students using cochlear implants who have developmental conditions that complicate their progress. Despite the high prevalence of multiple disabilities combined with hearing loss, however, it remains difficult to locate either data-based studies of these children or carefully documented evidence regarding educational progress. On the basis of her review of the literature, Guardino (2008) went so far as to suggest that despite the increasing incidence of multiple disabilities among deaf and hard-of-hearing students, there appears to be a decrease over time in research on these students.

The lack of published research concerning children with multiple disabilities, especially at the group-comparison level, is in large part because their unique needs necessitate highly individualized programming that does not lend itself to generalization. Jones and Jones (2003) pointed out that the heterogeneity in both type and severity of developmental difficulties among deaf and hard-of-hearing children requires that decisions about appropriate educational placement and programming must be made on an individual basis. They stressed that interventions need to be family focused and to involve a team of specialists based on both child and family needs. Like Meadow-Orlans et al. (2003), Jones and Jones argued that it is crucial for a case manager to be available to coordinate services in such cases because the needs of these children are so complex. Programming for children with hearing loss and multiple disabilities can and should incorporate approaches and interventions that have shown evidence of success with other children with various types of disabilities. At the same time, it is critical that interventions be sensitive to and provide appropriate accommodations for hearing loss. Such support is required even in the earliest months of life, since early intervention shows positive effects for children with a wide range of disabilities.

VARIABILITY AMONG DEAF AND HARD-OF-HEARING CHILDREN WITH MULTIPLE DISABILITIES

Meadow-Orlans and her colleagues (Meadow-Orlans, Smith-Gray, & Dyssegaard, 1995; Meadow-Orlans et al., 2004) studied a small group of five infants with hearing loss plus a physical, cognitive, or emotional condition that was diagnosed during infancy. Etiology of the identified disabilities included cytomegalovirus (CMV) and birth trauma. There were three comparison groups: one consisting of infants with hearing loss who were identified as being "at risk" for but were not yet identified as having multiple disabilities, a second group of infants with hearing loss who were not considered to be at risk for any additional disability, and a group of hearing infants. Both the infants already identified as having multiple disabilities and those considered at risk had significantly lower birth weights than the hearing children and the children with hearing loss who were not deemed to be at risk.

Meadow-Orlans et al. (1995, 2004) were particularly interested in the levels of stress reported by the hearing mothers of the children identified as having multiple disabilities. Assessments of family stress and child behaviors were conducted using standardized parent-response instruments, the Parenting Stress Index (PSI, Abidin, 1986) and the Stress of Life Events (Holmes & Rahe, 1967) when children were 9 months old, and the Family Support Scale (Dunst,

Jenkins, & Trivette, 1984) and the Parenting Events Inventory (Crnic & Greenberg, 1990) when the children were 15 months of age. The results showed a bimodal distribution of stress ratings, with individual ratings falling either at the highest stress level or at a level lower than that typical for hearing parents of hearing infants. The low ratings fell in the area defined by the test as "suspect denial of stress," and the researchers suggested that such denial was taking place. They noted that a similar bimodal pattern of reported stress was obtained from the group of parents whose children were currently "at risk" but not identified as having multiple disabilities.

Although parents' ratings of stress varied, all five children in the Meadow-Orlans et al. (1995) study with confirmed multiple disabilities showed clear developmental delays by 12 months of age. Each child's profile of functioning was unique, but three of the five were described as uninterested in interacting with others and showed aberrant patterns of visual attention to people and objects. Two were reported to have extremely short attention spans. In contrast, over 70% of the children in the group identified as being at risk for but not identified with multiple disabilities showed no evidence of developmental delays or difficulties by 12 months of age. Meadow-Orlans et al., suggested that the early identification of hearing loss together with early intervention services had helped to prevent more instances of delays in this group. Other investigators also have reported varying developmental patterns in at-risk groups, including variability in the vocal behaviors achieved by children with moderate-to-severe hearing loss who have multiple disabilities (Nathani, Oller, & Neal, 2007). Although early intervention can provide positive developmental and family support, it cannot eliminate most organically based difficulties and delays.

In a study focused on older deaf and hard-of-hearing children, Meadow-Orlans et al. (2003) surveyed parents of 6- and 7-year-old children with hearing loss, some of whom had significant additional conditions affecting their development. The initial survey (n = 404) was followed by phone interviews with randomly selected parents (n = 62) and several face-to-face interviews. All of the children were enrolled in programs for deaf and hard-of-hearing students, but 32% of the respondents indicated that their children had educationally significant conditions in addition to hearing loss. Of the children reported to have additional complicating conditions, the largest specific group involved 12% of the sample, who were identified as having intellectual or cognitive delays. Significant proportions of those children also were reported to have vision loss, learning disability, attention deficit disorder, emotional or behavioral problems, cerebral palsy, or motor disabilities. Another 29% of the children with additional complicating conditions were reported to be in an "other" category, including children with brain damage, epilepsy, and health conditions. Clearly, this was a very heterogeneous group, and in that respect it is representative of children with hearing loss and additional developmentally relevant conditions.

Parents of children with multiple disabilities who responded to the survey and telephone interviews reported early experiences with their children as being highly stressful (see also Powers, Elliott, Patterson, Shaw, & Taylor, 1995), but they also expressed pride in their children's ability to overcome challenges. A number of parents reported significant problems identifying appropriate services for their children, a difficulty echoed by reports from other researchers (e.g., Ewing & Jones, Guardino, 2008). Finally, it is noteworthy that the hearing losses of those children in the study who had multiple disabilities were identified later than those of children without other disabilities. In some cases, it appeared that the other condition initially had "masked" evidence that the child had a significant hearing loss.

CHILDREN WITH COGNITIVE OR INTELLECTUAL DISABILITIES

Although estimates vary widely, it appears that a significant proportion of deaf and hard-of-hearing children with multiple disabilities have conditions that result in cognitive delays or learning disabilities. The 2005 Gallaudet Annual Survey (see also Holden-Pitt & Diaz, 1998) found that just over 8% of children who were included had "mental retardation" or cognitive delays. Looked at from the opposite direction, Guardino (2008) estimated that over 9% of children who have cognitive delays also have a hearing loss. In her review of the research, Guardino found that many of the data-based reports available about children with hearing loss plus cognitive challenges had been conducted in the 1980s. She suggested that the subsequent decrease in research involving this population resulted from the aging of the children who were affected by maternal rubella and, to some degree, by the non-categorical approach to education that has occurred since then. Whatever the cause, there remains a significant need for research into educational and family interventions oriented toward this combination of developmental challenges.

Knoors and Vervloed (in press) noted that of the children who have diagnosed cognitive delays in addition to hearing loss, approximately 30% have unknown etiologies. Of those with known etiologies, the majority has histories of pre- or perinatal CMV, rubella (German measles), kernicterus (severe jaundice/bilirubin encophalopathy) or, particularly in the case of later onset of learning difficulty, infections such as meningitis. These etiologies typically have multiple developmental sequelae, and Knoors and Vervloed argued that while assessment and educational programming need to vary according to the profile of cognitive abilities, they also have to take into account the needs of children with hearing loss. In some cases, these children may be able to use spoken language, while for others a natural sign language or a total communication approach may be more appropriate (van Dijk, van Helvoort, Aan den Toorn, & Bos, 1998, cited in Knoors & Vervloed, in press; van Dijk, Nelson, Postma, & van Dijk, in press). Van Dijk et al. (1998) found that a group of five deaf adults with moderate cognitive/intellectual disabilities living in a residential group home were able to learn and use signs that were taught during school time. Although sign-supported speech (using Signed Dutch) was the officially preferred mode of communication at school, van Dijk et al., noted that the participants spontaneously developed some sign structures that were like those in Sign Language of the Netherlands (NGT). Van Dijk et al. posited that more interaction with signing caregivers and other professionals who were fluent signers would have accelerated the participants' signed communication abilities. Depending upon their level of cognitive functioning, some students may require instruction in using a selected and simplified set of signs or even picture- or symbol-based augmentative and alternative communication systems. These systems can involve communication boards on which symbols are manipulated, or they may be electronic, employing sometimes sophisticated software (see www.asha.org for information about augmentative and alternative systems).

Cochlear Implants, Cognitive Delays, and Language Development

Cochlear implants are sometimes provided to children who are deaf and have cognitive or related disabilities, but the effectiveness of the implants typically decreases compared with that of children who are only deaf. Parents therefore need to be informed that results cannot be expected to match those of children without cognitive disabilities (Pyman, Blamey, Lacy, Clark, & Dowell, 2000; Spencer, 2004). Pyman et al. found that basic auditory awareness and discrimination of vowels and consonants increased for children with motor and/or cognitive disabilities after 4 years of cochlear implant use. Nevertheless, only about 60% of the children could identify spoken words in sentences, while 80% of children in their study without cognitive disabilities could do so. Waltzman, Scalchunes, and Cohen (2000) similarly found increases in awareness of sound and increased evidence of being "connected" or "in touch" with their environment in a group of children with diverse multiple disabilities who received cochlear implants. Increases in language abilities were highly variable within the group, however, and children with greater cognitive disability were unable to complete the series of tests that were administered. A similarly wide range of functioning after cochlear implantation was shown in a German study by Hamzavi et al. (2000), in which 5 of the 10 participating children did not acquire spoken word reception or production skills after 3 years of using the implant, although 4 of the 5 lower functioning children gave evidence of some awareness of sound using the implants. Fukuda et al. (2003) presented single-case data on a child with moderate developmental delay who had a sizable sign language vocabulary prior to cochlear implantation and who developed spoken language skills after implantation.

The type and severity of additional disabilities may be the determining factor for spoken language progress using cochlear implants. Holt and Kirk (2005) assessed the speech and spoken language development of 19 children with mild cognitive delays compared to 50 children without cognitive or any other identified disabilities; all had cochlear implants. Using a standardized parent report instrument completed at 6-month intervals, auditory skills at the awareness and word identification levels were found to advance for both groups, although children in the group with cognitive delays showed slower average progress and greater variability. Consistent with results of Pyman et al. (2000), children with cognitive disabilities required longer experience with their implants to achieve multiword/sentence understanding. Differences with the Waltzman et al. (2000) study were presumed to result from differences in type and severity of additional disabilities in the groups.

A final note: None of the investigators whose work is summarized above were able to identify specific predictors of outcomes of cochlear implantation for children with multiple disabilities, including mild cognitive delay and hearing loss. All called for further investigation of both predictors and methods for providing supportive therapy.

LEARNING DISABILITIES AND ATTENTION DEFICIT DISORDER

The term "learning disabilities" comprises a group of learning problems such as dyslexia, auditory processing disorder, visual perception difficulties, memory or executive function disorder, specific language impairment that is not due to hearing loss, and general cognitive or experiential deficits (Edwards, 2010). Learning disabilities so defined, regardless of whether children have a hearing loss, are considered to be of an organic origin, and medical testing typically indicates some central nervous system dysfunction. In an early electroencephalogram (EEG) study of 286 children in a special school for deaf children, Zwiercki, Stansberry, Porter, and Hayes (1976) found that 35 had obvious signs of neurological dysfunction and 21 had signs of minimal brain dysfunction. This finding suggested that a high proportion of children have learning disabilities not directly resulting from their hearing loss. Pisoni, Conway, Kronenberger, Henning, and Anaya (2010) reached a similar conclusion from studies of children with cochlear implants, suggesting that many have dysfunctions or delays in basic neurocognitive functioning underlying information processing. Hawker et al. (2008) suggested that the language delays of some children using cochlear implants have the same basis as specific language impairments in hearing children and do not require an explanation based on auditory experience. At this time, however, clear diagnostic guidelines for identification of specific language and learning disabilities in children with hearing loss continue to evade understanding, perhaps in part due to lack of sufficient descriptions of children's performance and learning in varied contexts.

Laughton (1989, p. 74) proposed that children who are deaf or hard of hearing and also have learning disabilities will have "significant difficulty with the acquisition, integration, and use of language and/or nonlinguistic abilities" relative to peers with hearing loss only. Given the complexities associated with these processes in deaf children at large (see chapter 7), diagnosing learning disabilities remains a process of clinical judgment and problem solving on the part of clinicians who are conducting the assessment (see van Dijk et al., 2010). Perhaps as a result, both learning disabilities and attention dysfunctions appear to be overdiagnosed among those children (see Parasnis, Samar, & Berent, 2001). To some extent, this situation undoubtedly results from the overlap of behaviors symptomatic of learning disabilities in hearing children and behaviors due to late and inconsistent experience with language and resultant communication disabilities in children with hearing loss (Morgan & Vernon, 1994; Samar, Parasnis, & Berent, 1998).

On the other hand, Calderon (1998) suggested that learning disabilities tend to co-occur with hearing loss at a high rate due to shared etiologies, and this phenomenon may be one source of the cognitive differences between students with and without hearing loss summarized previously in this book (see, especially, chapter 7). Mauk and Mauk (1998) noted that estimates of the prevalence of learning disabilities in the population of deaf and hard-of-hearing children are highly variable, ranging from 3% to 60%. Samar et al. (1998) posited that relative lack of auditory input cannot explain the high rate of phonological and reading difficulties in the population of children with hearing loss, implying that this rate reflects learning disabilities. Given that learning disabilities are said to occur in 3% to 10% of hearing children, at least that rate could be expected for those with hearing loss (Edwards, 2010; Edwards & Crocker, 2008).

Deaf and hard-of-hearing children suspected of having learning disabilities are most often placed in classes for children with hearing loss. However, their special difficulties with integration of information in addition to delays in language development (regardless of modality of input) are likely to require a more highly structured educational environment for optimal academic development (Stewart & Kluwin, 2001). Their greater problems with memory, sequencing, and attention, relative to hearing children, as well as inconsistent performance over times and contexts also may require special educational supports beyond those effective for other deaf children. Importantly, those difficulties generally are found to characterize the learning behaviors of many deaf children (e.g., Marschark & Hauser, 2008), and it is important to determine the extent to which such findings are affected by the inclusion in research studies of students who actually have concomitant learning disabilities.

Reliable and valid assessment of learning disability in a deaf or hard-of-hearing child presents special difficulties and must employ varied methods and measures. Morgan and Vernon (1994) recommended a specific battery of tests including a case history (noting especially medical conditions and family history of reading or learning disabilities); two standardized measures of nonverbal cognitive functioning (to rule out overall cognitive delay); a measure of academic achievement; neuropsychological screening (to look for signs of dysfunction typically found in hearing, learning disabled children); and an evaluation of adaptive behaviors or daily function skills; plus testing of hearing, language, and communication skills using formal assessment tools (see also Hauser et al., 2008).

One of the signs of learning disability is a gap between potential—as indicated by a nonverbal cognitive or intelligence test—and achievement. However, virtually all of the relevant tests have norms and instructions appropriate only for the hearing student population, and this can lead to invalid and misleading test interpretation. Edwards (2010) therefore suggested using more than one test when assessing a specific psychological function in a child with hearing loss. The use of multiple tests and testing procedures, in fact, generally is recommended for all educational and developmental assessments.

Effective programming for children with hearing loss plus learning disabilities is complicated by the above-described lack of specific diagnostic approaches. The situation is made more complex by the necessity of cooperation among professionals in several different fields and the need for specialists who understand the particular effects of hearing loss (Laughton, 1989; Mauk & Mauk, 1998). Intervention-focused research in this area could be of much benefit, but additional work first is needed on identifying children with a combination of hearing loss and learning disabilities. Mauk and Mauk noted that simply using interventions designed for hearing children is neither sufficient nor appropriate, but there is a general lack of research in the area that might help to change the situation (Guardino, 2008).

Attention Disorders

Although they often co-occur, attention disorders (characterized by inattentiveness, hyperactivity, and/or impulsivity) can be present even when other learning disabilities are not. Like learning disabilities, the diagnosis of attention disorders in children with hearing loss is complex and remains more art than science. The communication histories of many children with hearing loss make it difficult to distinguish between those with organic attention and activity difficulties as opposed to patterns typical of deaf and hard-of hearing children in general.

For example, we noted in the discussion of cognitive performance and cognitive styles (chapter 7) that selective and sustained attention is often attenuated for children with hearing loss compared to hearing children (e.g., Kritzer, 2009; Quittner et al., 1994), and many deaf or hard-of-hearing children appear to fit a category designated as "hyperactive."

Kelly, Forney, Parker-Fisher, and Jones (1993) and Samar et al. (1998) found a greatly increased prevalence of attention and activity-level disorders in deaf and hard-of-hearing children with acquired hearing loss compared to those with an identified hereditary etiology. This suggests that some of the non-genetic causes of hearing loss during pre-, peri-, or post-natal periods (such as viral infections, prematurity, or meningitis) can have effects on the nervous system beyond auditory functioning. Kelly et al. (1993) suggested that interventions for children with hearing loss and attention disorders should be similar to those already used in practice with hearing children who have attention disorders: Classrooms should be designed so that visual distractions are minimized, basic study routines and techniques for organization should be explicitly taught, and visual organizers such as charts should be used whenever possible in the curriculum. Unfortunately, we were not able to find outcome data based on experimental manipulation of these or other intervention techniques for children with both hearing loss and attention disorders beyond occasional case studies. Because of the apparent prevalence of their co-occurrence, there is an urgent need for research and the development of assessment tools in this area.

AUTISM SPECTRUM DISORDERS

Diagnoses of childhood Autism-Spectrum Disorders (ASD) have increased over the past few decades. This disability can and does co-occur at a fairly high rate with hearing loss (Bailly, de Chouly de Lenclave, & Lauwerier, 2003; Rosenhall, Nordin, Sandstrom, Ahlsen, & Gillberg, 1999). The behaviors characteristic of deaf or hearing children with ASD differ significantly from those of children who are only deaf or hard of hearing, however, so they cannot be entirely explained by hearing loss itself (Gravel, Dunn, Lee, & Ellis, 2006). ASD generally is characterized by severe impairment of social interaction abilities, disruptions in eye contact with others, production of repetitive stereotyped movements, language delay and disorders, and cognitive impairment or uneven profiles of cognitive skills (Edwards & Crocker, 2008; Kanner, 1943, summarized in Vernon & Rhodes, 2009). Hyperactivity, attention span disorders, and aggression toward self or others also may be present although, as with other disorders, the presence and the severity of characteristics vary across individuals. (For more details, see Diagnostic and Statistical Manual of Mental Disorders-IV-RT of the American

Psychiatric Association, 2000.) For example, one of the subtypes currently considered to be within the spectrum of autism is Asperger Syndrome. Children with "Asberger's" typically pass language milestones at the expected ages and show average or even much higher levels of most aspects of cognition along with varied degrees of impairment of social behaviors (Volkmar, Klin, Schultz, Rubin, & Bronen, 2000). A diagnosis of ASD thus can represent a wide range of functioning skills and potential.

Autism Spectrum Disorders were once thought (incorrectly) to result from poor early interactive experiences, but they are now known to have organic, neurological, or physiological origins (Vernon & Rhodes, 2009), even if the exact mechanisms remain unknown (Rutter, 2005). Using generally accepted criteria for the identification of ASD, Jure, Rapin, and Tuchman (1991) concluded that about 4% to 5% of a population of 1,150 children with hearing loss also had autism. The etiology of the children so identified varied widely, however, and hearing loss and ASD can be associated with the same or similar etiologies (e.g., meningitis, epilepsy, congenital rubella syndrome, CHARGE;[1] van Dijk et al.,2010). Deafblindness (see below) can lead to disrupted communicative behaviors and repetitive, stereotyped actions like those produced by many children with ASD, but Hoevenaars-van den Boom, Antonissen, Knoors, and Vervloed (2009) reported that deaf children with autism can be differentiated from deafblind children based on the quality of their social interactions.

Because children who are deaf or hard of hearing and have ASD vary greatly in their individual behaviors and abilities, treatment and educational interventions cannot be generalized for all children with the diagnosis. Nevertheless, Vernon and Rhodes (2009) indicated that there is consensus about the importance of early and intensive interventions, including treatments for both behavioral and communication aspects. Some interventions for autism alone employ signed language or other forms of visual communication (Bonvillian, Nelson, & Rhyne, 1981) and thus may be especially appropriate for children with autism plus hearing loss. Augmentative/alternative communication devices such as the Picture Exchange Communication System (PECS) also are used with some children who have severe ASD and might be appropriate for some children who also have hearing loss. In a recent review, however, Ostryn (2008) noted that there are few empirical studies of its effects, even with the general ASD population.

Lovaas (1987) developed a treatment approach referred to as Applied Behavior Analysis (ABA) in which negative and positive reinforcements are used to

---

[1] CHARGE takes its name from the related symptomology: **C**oloboma (a keyhole type opening in iris and retina), **H**eart defect, **A**tresia of the choanae (blockage of the passages between the nasal cavity and the naso-pharynx), **R**etarded growth and/or development, **G**enital hypoplasia, and **E**ar anomalies/ deafness.

modify the behaviors of children with ASD. This approach is labor intensive, highly structured, and greatly extended over time. Treatment involves parents, therapists, aides, and teachers working to improve a child's functioning in carefully defined, small steps. It is expensive to implement, but Lovaas reported data that showed some success with hearing children. Zacher, Ben-Itzchak, Rabinovich, and Lahat (2007) reported that 20 young children with ASD made more progress over a year's time in an ABA intervention program than 19 children of the same age and diagnosis who participated in a more developmentally oriented, eclectic program. This finding is consistent with other reports indicating that a highly structured program is necessary for children with ASD, especially if learning is to transfer beyond the teaching situation. Unfortunately, there appear to be no scientific studies available on the outcomes of interventions specifically with children with ASD and hearing loss beyond an occasional case study or personal report (Edwards & Crocker, 2008). An evidence base for practice is lacking.

DEAFBLINDNESS

There is a long history of programming and research involving children who have a combination of hearing and visual impairment, now referred to as deafblindness (van Dijk et al., 2010). Although total loss of either sense is rare, van Dijk et al. noted that the condition is characterized by enough loss in each area to preclude using it to compensate for loss in the other. Deafblindness can occur congenitally or at an early stage of life and, if so, has much more severe effects than if acquired later. Nevertheless the well-known stories of Helen Keller (who became deafblind at 19 months) and Laura Bridgeman (who became deafblind at 24 months) demonstrate the difficulty of communication development even when a child initially has sight and hearing.

Jan van Dijk and his colleagues developed a curriculum that is used in many countries to facilitate development of deafblind students. The curriculum stresses building relationships between the child and caregivers, gradually building awareness in the child of others, and supporting transition of communication behaviors from the concrete to the symbolic level. Chen, Klein, and Haney (2007) and van den Tillaart and Janssen (2006) developed curricula based on van Dijk's ideas, and a single subject, multiple baseline study conducted with four deafblind children indicated effectiveness of the approach. At least one comprehensive instrument for assessing behaviors of deafblind children with multiple difficulties, the Callier-Azusa Scales (Stillman, 1978; Stillman & Battle, 1986), also has been developed based on van Dijk's work.

Congenital Rubella Syndrome

Deafblindness can result from many of the same etiologies listed above for other disabilities, including a variety of pre-, peri-, and post-natal illnesses. Deafblindness can be, but is not always, associated with cognitive delays or deficits or with autism. Individuals who are deafblind due to rubella contracted during the early gestational period are particularly likely to also have a number of developmental difficulties, including intellectual deficits, behavioral difficulties, and repetitive stereotypical or obsessive movements like those found in children with autism (Munroe, 1999).

The incidence of congenital rubella syndrome (CRS) has decreased with the rise of vaccine use worldwide, but it is still an etiology that occurs in some parts of the world, and persons born during previous epidemics, although now adults, are still in need of special programming. There is some evidence that vision and hearing losses of deafblind persons with CRS worsen with age (Kingma, Schoenmaker, Damen, & Nunen, 1997; Munroe, 1999; van Dijk, 1999), so continuing individualization and modification of interventions are necessary.

Genetic/Chromosomal Syndromes

A number of genetic/chromosomal syndromes are associated with deafblindness (see Arnos & Pandya, in press). These include but are not limited to CHARGE and Usher syndromes. CHARGE syndrome is the most prevalent etiology for deafblind people in the United States (Killoran, 2007). It can include "keyhole" openings in the irises and retinas of the eyes causing vision loss, blockage of passages between nasal cavity and nasopharynx, structural ear anomalies and hearing loss, balance problems, genital anomalies, hypotonia (low muscle strength), feeding and swallowing problems, and asymmetric facial palsy. Children with CHARGE can be medically fragile and require multiple surgeries early in life. Related behavior problems are common, characterized by a lack of impulse control. As with other conditions described above, severity of these impairments and the number of symptoms differ across children. Blake (2005) reported that the majority of a group of 30 individuals he studied required medications for behavior control and that two-thirds required substantial supervision and support. Van Dijk et al. (2010) noted that education and management of CHARGE children is particularly difficult and can be further complicated if supportive early interaction experiences are disrupted due to parental stress. Clearly, children with this syndrome, and their families, require consistent and specialized support.

Usher syndrome is another prevalent genetic cause of deafblindness, occurring in around 4% of children with hearing loss. There are several different subtypes of Usher syndrome, and different characteristics suggest different emphases in educational interventions (Knoors & Vervloed, in press; van Dijk et al., 2010). Persons with Usher type 1 typically have significant hearing loss at or soon after birth, with visual loss occurring later. They usually are supported educationally through programs serving deaf children and with essentially the same methods—and arguments about language methods—as other children with hearing loss. Individuals with Usher type 2 tend to have lesser hearing losses (in the hard-of-hearing range), with vision loss typically occurring in adolescence. Persons with Usher type 3 have both hearing and vision functioning for a number of years before experiencing deterioration in both senses.

There is no intellectual disability associated with Usher syndrome, and van Dijk et al. (2010) indicated that clinical practice has suggested considerable emotional strength in students with this diagnosis. Vermeulen and van Dijk (1994) administered a personality assessment instrument to 16 adolescents with Usher syndrome and reported that these individuals showed strong ego functioning, social competence, and self-esteem. They noted that the group's scores indicated a relative lack of assertiveness, however, which they attributed to probable overprotection from parents and educators. Damon, Krabbe, Kilsby, and Mylanus (2005) surveyed 67 persons from six European Union countries who had a diagnosis of Usher syndrome and found that the respondents had generally positive attitudes and strived to maintain their independence. Respondents were particularly interested in methods and technologies that would support their socialization and independence.

Cochlear implants are considered to be a viable option for children with Usher syndrome or other children who have hearing loss in association with visual impairment. Yoshinaga-Itano (2003) reported on one child with profound hearing loss and progressive vision loss who began receiving intervention services at 6 weeks of age. Her hearing family used ASL along with some pidgin signed English for communication with her, and when she was 20 months old, she scored at the 99th percentile on the MacArthur Communicative Development Inventory Words and Sentences form (Fenson et al., 1993, 1994), using signs but compared to hearing norms. At that time she produced no spoken language. After cochlear implantation at 21 months of age, however, she began to use more vocal behaviors and to build auditory awareness. By 51 months of age, she had become primarily a spoken language user, a particularly fortunate transition due to deteriorating vision which seriously interfered with her reception of sign language. Yoshinaga-Itano presented this case as an example of the way that sign language can support emerging spoken language development when auditory reception is improved via use of a cochlear implant. This case also indicates that children who are eventually identified as deafblind do not necessarily experience significantly delayed early development.

A BROADER VIEW

The information in this chapter is limited in that it focuses on only some of the disabilities that can co-occur with hearing loss. One area that was not reviewed, for example, was the co-occurrence of motor/physical disabilities such as cerebral palsy with hearing loss. Meadow-Orlans et al. (2003) included comments from several parents of children with this combination of challenges, and it was clearly difficult for them to find appropriate programming and support. When motor disabilities complicate both expressive signing and speech, communication options are more limited and augmentative alternative methods must be considered.

Another area that was not discussed in this chapter was that of general emotional and behavioral disorders (Edwards & Crocker, 2008). These long have been evident as a potential problem area for deaf and hard-of-hearing children (e.g., Glenn, 1988; Meadow & Trybus, 1985), but such a wide variety of descriptors have been given across research reports (including, for example, inattentiveness, aggressiveness, anxiety, and even academic disorders) that it is not clear to what extent emotional/behavioral disorders form a discrete category. In addition, some emotional/behavioral problems of deaf and hard-of-hearing children have been posited to arise from basic communication and language delays, with concomitant disruption in the ability to communicate with parents and caregivers rather than indicating an organically based "disability."

Despite the organization of this chapter by type of disability, current educational philosophies emphasize individual differences instead of such categorization. Evidence presented in each of the categories above illustrated a range of functional skills and needs, so that placement decisions cannot validly be based on etiology or labeling of the disability associated with the hearing loss. Accordingly, Ewing and Jones (2003) argued for a transdisciplinary approach to assessment and programming for multiply disabled deaf and hard-of-hearing children, which they described as characterized by indirect instead of direct service. This approach is highly collaborative, with around 10 specialists (including at least one knowledgeable with regard to deaf children) potentially needed to program sufficiently for a single child. Only one or two professionals are primary service deliverers or facilitators, however, so that communication with parents, therapists, and other educators can be more coherent and consistent. Such an approach would be responsive to parents' complaints that they often have had to deal with too many professionals, some of whom give divergent recommendations and are seemingly unaware of recommendations from other specialists (Giangreco, Edelman, MacFarland, & Luiselli, 1997; Meadow-Orlans et al., 2003).

Ewing and Jones (2003) also recommended the use of person-centered instead of category-centered programming and offered the McGill Action Planning

System (Forest & Pearpoint, 1992) as one example. A person-centered approach is based on identifying the strengths and learning abilities of a student, motivating factors, environments and contexts in which learning is facilitated, and specific instructional procedures that best promote learning. The process of identifying these components should include family, child, and professionals and would follow best from actual teaching-learning trials instead of use of standardized tests or procedures. Although this would be an ideal approach with all students, it may be a necessity for students with hearing loss plus additional disabilities. Furthermore, because there are few curriculum materials designed for specific combinations of disabilities, teachers need to be knowledgeable about a wide range of disabilities, even when they have the advantage of working with a supportive team.

SUMMARY: SERVING CHILDREN WITH MULTIPLE CHALLENGES

The presence of additional disabilities in the population of students with hearing loss continues and appears to be growing, as children who are born prematurely, have severe birth complications, or survive serious illness are increasingly likely to survive. As with other deaf and hard-of-hearing children, generalizations cannot be made about these children's academic and functional capabilities based on their etiologies, but it is clear that the effect of disabilities multiplies as they increase in severity and number.

- With one-third to as much as one-half of students with hearing loss being diagnosed as having some additional disability, educational planning must provide for handling a diversity of needs. Service provision for those children requires multiple specialists and, typically, more intensive service delivery than that for children with hearing loss alone. Collaboration across disciplines and among teachers and other service providers is critical.
- As with other students with hearing loss, those with multiple disabilities will vary in their abilities to acquire language skills, and options ranging from oral approaches to sign-only and augmentative or picture/computer-based approaches may be appropriate for specific individuals and must be available.
- In many cases, the additional difficulties shown by children identified as having multiple disabilities may be only mild cognitive delays or learning problems similar to those recognized as learning disabilities in the hearing population. The options for such children will differ

significantly from those for children with more severe learning challenges and educational placement decisions should differ accordingly.

- Ongoing assessment of developmental progress is critical, so that placement and service decisions can be modified as needed if those initially chosen prove ineffective.

Approaches that focus on individual children and carefully track their progress over time and with different interventions are necessary to effectively support the development of most children who have multiple disabilities. Even interventions specific to an individual child can produce useful research-based information, however, if they are carefully designed, conducted using rigorous single-subject methods, and well documented. Such studies, as well as comparison studies when they are possible, will be increasingly necessary if programming efforts are to meet the needs of the majority of deaf and hard-of-hearing students.

11 Issues and Trends in Best Practice

We began this volume by stressing two realities: First, hearing loss in childhood is a low incidence condition but has great impact on a child's development unless (and often even when) appropriate educational support is provided. Second, programming for children with hearing loss has proceeded historically without reference to a strong evidence base, a situation created in part by the low incidence of childhood hearing loss and the great variability of characteristics and experiences in the population. Reflecting upon the evidence from studies summarized in this book, there are several emerging realities with regard to deaf and hard-of-hearing children that need to be considered if further progress is to be made in understanding the factors contributing to their development and in improving their academic outcomes. These generalizations are not mutually exclusive but highlight several convergences we have identified in what we know, what we do not know, and what we only thought we knew in several areas.

- *Early identification of hearing loss and immediate provision of effective intervention services for both child and family can raise the general levels of language skills attained by deaf and hard-of-hearing children with subsequent benefit to academic achievement.*

Effective early intervention usually is characterized by a family-centered approach, with educators and therapists serving as consultants to parents or caregivers. Support for family emotional needs as well as information about hearing loss and intervention approaches should be available, and the family's degree of involvement with the child's development and education must be encouraged. That involvement is consistently identified as a predictive factor of developmental and academic success. Early access to positive interactions and accessible language must be assured if optimal development is to be promoted. The language approach chosen should be based on child and family factors, not on pre-determined educator bias or administrative expedience. Decisions once made can and should be changed if circumstances and assessment data indicate a need. There is a large body of converging evidence indicating benefits to development following early identification and intervention, but the lag between achievement levels of children with and without hearing loss has only been decreased, not eliminated.

- *A variety of approaches to supporting language development in deaf and hard-of-hearing children continue to be available. Research has indicated each to be effective in some cases, but no one approach is appropriate for all.*

Natural sign languages are learned readily and develop at a pace typical of hearing children's spoken language, but only when fluent sign models are available. In addition, the transition from using a natural sign language for communication and a written code for a spoken language for literacy purposes is not automatic. Total communication programming, including sign, speech, and their simultaneous combination, does not typically provide a complete model of either a signed language or a spoken language. However, children have been shown to be capable of integrating auditory information with sign when it can be accessed along with visual information from phonological and syntactic systems. Such integration has been shown to occur regardless of whether the visual input is provided via sign, via cued speech, or via instructional approaches such as Visual Phonics. Despite claims to the contrary, the addition of signs or the use of cues to disambiguate spoken language has never been found to interfere with the process of developing spoken language. At the same time, when sufficient auditory awareness is available, development of spoken language may be well supported by intensive experience listening to and using speech as provided in oral and auditory-verbal programs.

- *It remains difficult to predict an individual child's language development or academic achievement, and most factors predictive of success are shared among the various communication and early intervention approaches.*
Predictors include absence of disabilities in addition to hearing loss, higher levels of nonverbal cognitive ability, family support for the child and for education, consistent exposure to fluent language models accessible within the child's sensory processing capabilities, and adaptive behaviors such as attention skills that reinforce interaction experiences and promote learning in general. Degree of hearing loss associates with some, although not all, aspects of language learning in auditory and oral modalities. Thus, increasing the amount that a child can hear (and discriminate) tends to improve his or her spoken language skills. In contrast, hearing thresholds have not been consistently found to associate with varying levels of academic achievement. There is increasing recognition of the need for research that focuses on identifying methods of promoting successful language development across language approaches rather than continuing fruitless attempts to compare outcomes from one approach with those of another in order to claim that one is superior.

- *Advanced hearing aid technology and use of cochlear implants have provided increased access to auditory information and spoken language for many children with hearing loss, and spoken language achievements for many deaf children are significantly more probable than in the past.*
Cochlear implants, in particular, support spoken language across a variety of language approaches, and positive effects tend to increase with early first use, consistent with the predictors of language development that were listed above. Although reports of striking improvements in early spoken language accomplishments are emerging for children with implants obtained prior to 2 years of age, it is not clear whether that rate of development will continue with age; some children, especially those with additional disabilities, show significantly less positive outcomes. Use of sign language together with cochlear implants continues to be controversial, but there is no evidence indicating that its use interferes with spoken language acquisition. In fact, the evidence suggests that sign language potentially provides support for developing language and cognitive abilities as well as academic achievement. The amount of spoken language exposure needed for its acquisition seems to vary widely across children, but few studies have investigated this variable.

- *An evidence base is beginning to accrue related to educational approaches to promote literacy skills regardless of the modes or approaches used for language development.*

  There is a convergence of data indicating that direct instruction in literacy must be provided in meaningful and interactive contexts to support deaf and hard-of-hearing students' acquisition of vocabulary as well as syntactic and phonological knowledge. Increases in these skills, along with programming that explicitly supports reading comprehension and use of metacognitive strategies, have been shown in a small number of studies using various populations and designs to have positive effects on reading and writing abilities. The current data, however, do not provide clear guidance on exactly how that instruction should best proceed. Limited evidence is available that literacy skills of students with hearing loss can be enhanced by early shared reading and writing experiences, incorporation of literacy activities in content subject lessons and activities, and directed reading comprehension experiences in which "thinking aloud" and other metacognitive strategies are actively promoted.

- *Researchers have long been seemingly obsessed with the literacy challenges of deaf and hard-of-hearing children, but academic challenges are seen across the curriculum.*

  Students with hearing loss frequently show delays and deficits in the areas of mathematics and science; similar delays appear to occur in other content areas, but those have not been documented. Such difficulties have been attributed to a variety of factors including underuse of metacognitive strategies, decreased visual attention to information provided in classrooms, lack of language skills for understanding written texts and information presented during class, lack of background content and world knowledge, and relatively infrequent exposure to problem-solving activities in formal and informal educational settings. Achievement tends to be higher when teachers are subject-matter specialists but are also knowledgeable about the special learning needs of students with hearing loss. Few data are available that directly address programming characteristics and outcomes, but approaches that emphasize visual modeling and visual presentation of mathematical and science concepts appear to have promise. In addition, embedding writing activities into science and related classes appears to have a mutually positive effect on concept development and literacy skills. Much more research is needed to guide programming efforts in academic content areas, which are becoming of increasing importance in a continually more technologically oriented and interdependent world.

- *Although a social and political consensus seems to have occurred supporting integration of students with and without hearing loss in classes, specific placement options have been found to have little independent effect on academic outcomes.*

  A variety of approaches to academic integration (mainstreaming) can be found. Some models allow for placement options based on individual need; in others, such as co-enrollment models and congregated settings, a "critical mass" of children with hearing loss is placed within a somewhat larger group of hearing classmates. All of these appear to produce positive social-emotional effects but minimal differences in academic achievement. Because deaf and hard-of-hearing students tend to have special learning needs in addition to potential communication barriers, teachers or teaching teams need to have a mix of expertise and strong collaboration skills. Ultimately, greater social comfort of deaf and hard-of-hearing students in mainstream settings and a greater understanding of their academic strengths and needs on the part of teachers may improve students' academic outcomes. To date, however, there is no evidence that either mainstream or separate education is inherently superior for deaf and hard-of-hearing students' academic achievement. Comparison studies are difficult to interpret because both student characteristics that led to the initial placement decision and characteristics of the program operate and influence outcomes, independently and in interaction.

- *Research involving students with hearing loss, especially those in upper grades, frequently indicates patterns of cognitive skills, problem-solving approaches, and learning strategies that do not match practices in most educational environments.*

  Specific differences between students with and without hearing loss have been identified in a variety of cognitive areas including sequencing skills, integration of information across sources and time, focus on detail versus conceptual conclusions, selective and sustained visual attention, prior content knowledge, and creative problem solving. Structured interventions have shown some success in promoting better metacognitive abilities and their use in learning contexts, but cognitive differences can interfere with learning across the curriculum, especially when teachers are unaware of them (e.g., in mainstream settings). It is not clear to what degree these differences reflect sensory as opposed to communication experience differences, but effects may vary across skill areas. Research is critically needed, particularly with regard to assessing outcomes of varied interventions as they interact with individual differences.

- *Children with significant disabilities beyond hearing loss present even more varied needs than those with hearing loss alone and make up an increasing proportion of the population of deaf and hard-of-hearing students.*

  Children with severe challenges in social interaction, communication, or cognition may require highly specialized settings and curricula. The majority of children identified with multiple disabilities, however, present with a combination of mild to moderate conditions that, together, magnify the challenges that would be presented by hearing loss alone. Given the great individual variability among these children, there is little well-defined evidence on which to guide instructional practice or the design of educational interventions. Use of single-subject designs to test effectiveness of specific interventions for individual children may provide helpful guides for individual children and, with appropriate aggregation of records over time, begin to suggest patterns of more general, successful approaches. Although it sometimes has been helpful for researchers to exclude children with multiple disabilities from their research in order to identify more specifically outcomes related only to hearing loss, continuing to do so ignores a significant segment of the students served by programs for deaf and hard-of-hearing children.

Although information about levels of hearing loss has not been a focus in this review, almost every section has included some mention of their potential effects. Children who have been referred to as "hard of hearing" and who have access to varied amounts and quality of auditory information comprise the largest segment of the population of children with hearing loss. This is a segment of the population for which development of an evidence base is especially important now that many children who would have functioned as profoundly deaf in the past can access more auditory information with the use of technology. There has been increasing recognition and research interest in students who are hard of hearing or have minimal hearing loss since the turn of the century, and we expect that more specific information on their needs and educational outcomes will be forthcoming.

In this and other areas, the convergence of data across the topics and areas reviewed in the preceding chapters indicates that there is much need for teachers who are trained and knowledgeable about specific social and learning characteristics of deaf and hard-of-hearing children. Teachers also need to be well prepared in their respective content areas (e.g., math, science, social studies), to understand the dynamics and outcomes of varied placement options, to have the ability to collaborate in various settings with other teachers and support personnel, to be current on emerging knowledge about and promoting of enhanced cognitive and learning profiles and abilities of students with hearing loss, and to be aware of the wide variety of disabilities in motor, social, and other areas that frequently co-occur with hearing loss. Of course, training also needs to be provided in an array of the communication approaches that will be used by deaf and hard-of-hearing students, in emerging approaches to supporting literacy development, and in methods of evaluating student progress. These needs place a heavy burden on teacher-training programs and also may lead to varied staffing models in schools in order to obtain the needed mix of expertise in teaching staff. Data continue to indicate, however, that specially trained teachers (and other professionals) for deaf and hard-of-hearing students are critical to supporting the students' development.

Despite the unanswered questions and continuing needs that have been emphasized in this book, we believe that the overall picture is both more positive and more hopeful than at any time in the past. Conducting this review gave ample evidence that there is a large and varied amount of information available from research and practice with deaf and hard-of-hearing students, and that more and more sophisticated studies continue to take place. Dissemination of such data is critical if the field is to continue to move forward, and there are increasing avenues in which this is occurring. In many cases, developments in teaching methods, understanding of learning styles and abilities of deaf and hard-of-hearing children, and influences of new technologies and practices are leading to discarding, or at least decreasing the hold, of paradigms that have not promoted overall successful development. Newer and more divergent approaches to education are being at least considered and, increasingly often, evaluated with scientifically appropriate procedures.

Existing reports from standardized testing involving students with significant hearing losses remain discouraging, but it is clear that opportunities for language and academic development of children with hearing loss are increasing and, with continuing progress, those reports will become more positive. The wide range of achievement levels in the existing population of deaf and hard-of-hearing students may be vexing to researchers attempting to conduct nicely controlled studies. At the same time, those individual differences remind us that many students with hearing loss, with guidance from parents and teachers and other professionals, are reaching ever higher levels of accomplishment. Our job as professionals who care about these students is to continue to look past what we *used* to think we knew, consider the great body of information available, and use that to develop ever stronger supports that will allow all children to reach their potential.

REFERENCES

Abidin, R. (1986). *Parenting Stress Index—Manual (PSI)*. Charlottesville, VA: Pediatric Psychology Press.

Abrahamsen, A., Cavallo, M., & McCluer, J. (1985). Is the sign advantage a robust phenomenon? From gesture to language in two modalities. *Merrill-Palmer Quarterly, 31,* 177–209.

Ackley, R. S., & Decker, T. N. (2006). Audiological advancement and the acquisition of spoken language in deaf children. In P. Spencer & M. Marschark (Eds.), *Advances in spoken language development of deaf and hard-of-hearing children* (pp. 64–84). New York: Oxford University Press.

Akamatsu, C. T., Mayer, C., Hardy-Braz, S. (2008). Why considerations of verbal aptitude are important in educating deaf and hard-of-hearing students. In M. Marschark & P. Hauser (Eds.), *Deaf cognition: Foundations and outcomes* (pp. 131–169). New York: Oxford University Press.

Akamatsu, C. T., & Stewart, D. (1998). Constructing Simultaneous C and ommunication: The contributions of natural sign language. *Journal of Deaf Studies and Deaf Education, 3,* 302–319.

Alegria, J., & Lechat, J. (2005). Phonological processing in deaf children: When lipreading and cues are incongruent. *Journal of Deaf Studies and Deaf Education, 10,* 122–133.

Al-Hilawani, Y., Easterbrooks, S., & Marchant, G. (2002). Metacognitive ability from a theory-of-mind perspective: A cross-cultural study of students with and without hearing loss. *American Annals of the Deaf, 147,* 38–47.

Allen, T. (1986). Pattern of academic achievement among hearing impaired students: 1974 and 1983. In A. Schildroth & M. Karchmer (Eds.), *Deaf children in America* (pp. 161–206). San Diego, CA: College-Hill Press.

Allen, T. (1992). Subgroup differences in educational placement for deaf and hard-of-hearing students. *American Annals of the Deaf, 137*, 381–388.

Allen, T. (1995). Demographics and national achievement levels for deaf and hard of hearing students: Implications for mathematics reform. In C. H. Dietz (Ed.), *Moving toward the standards: A national action plan for mathematics education reform for the deaf* (pp. 41–49). Washington, DC: Pre-College Programs, Gallaudet University.

Allen, T., & Osbourne, T. (1984). Academic integration of hearing-impaired students: Demographic, handicapping, and achievement factors. *American Annals of the Deaf, 129*, 100–113.

American College Test. (2000). *ACT assessment: User handbook* 2000–2001. Iowa City, IA: ACT National Office.

American Psychiatric Association (2000). *Diagnostic and Statistical Manual of Mental Disorders*, 4th Edition, Text Revision. Washington, DC: American Psychiatric Association.

Anderson, A. (1997). Families and mathematics: A study of parent-child interactions. *Journal for Research in Mathematics Education, 28*, 484–511.

Anderson, D. (2006). Lexical development of deaf children acquiring signed languages. In B. Schick, M. Marschark, & P. Spencer (Eds.), *Advances in sign language development of deaf children* (pp. 135–160). New York: Oxford University Press.

Anderson, D., & Reilly, J. (2002). The MacArthur Communicative Development Inventory: Normative data for American Sign Language. *Journal of Deaf Studies and Deaf Education, 7*, 83–106.

Andrews, J., Ferguson, C., Roberts, S., & Hodges, P. (1997). What's up, Billy Jo? Deaf children and bilingual-bicultural instruction in east-central Texas. *American Annals of the Deaf, 142*, 16–25.

Andrews, J., & Mason, J. (1986a). Childhood deafness and the acquisition of print concepts. In D. Yaden & S. Templeton (Eds.), *Metalinguistic awareness and beginning literacy: Conceptualizing what it means to read and write* (pp. 277–290). Portsmouth, NH: Heinemann.

Andrews, J., & Mason, J. (1986b). How do deaf children learn about pre-reading?. *American Annals of the Deaf, 131*, 210–217.

Ansari, M. S. (2004). Screening programme for hearing impairment in newborns: A challenge during rehabilitation for all. *Asia Pacific Disability Rehabilitation Journal, 15*(1), 83–89.

Ansell, E., & Pagliaro, C. M. (2006). The relative difficulty of signed arithmetic story problems for primary level deaf and hard-of-hearing students. *Journal of Deaf Studies and Deaf Education, 11*, 153–170.

Anthony, D. (Ed.). (1971). *Seeing essential English* (2 vols.). Anaheim, CA: Educational Services Division, Anaheim Union High School District.

Antia, S., Jones, P., Reed, S., & Kreimeyer, K. (2009). Academic status and progress of deaf and hard-of-hearing students in general education classrooms. *Journal of Deaf Studies and Deaf Education, 14*, 293–311.

Antia, S., Jones, P., Reed, S., Kreimeyer, K., Luckner, H., & Johnson, C. (2008). *Longitudinal study of deaf and hard of hearing students attending general education classrooms in public schools.* Final report submitted to Office of Special Education Programs for grant H324C010142. Tucson: University of Arizona.

Antia, S., & Kreimeyer, K. (2003). Peer interactions of deaf and hard-of-hearing children. In M. Marschark & P. Spencer (Eds.), *The Oxford handbook of deaf studies, language, and education* (pp. 164–176). New York: Oxford University Press.

Antia, S., Kreimeyer, K., & Reed, S. (2010). Supporting students in general education classrooms. In M. Marschark & P. Spencer (Eds.), *The Oxford handbook of deaf studies, language, and education (vol. 2)* (pp. 72–92). New York: Oxford University Press.

Antia, S., Reed, S., & Kreimeyer, K. (2005). Written language of deaf and hard-of-hearing students in public schools. *Journal of Deaf Studies and Deaf Education, 10*, 244–255.

Antia, S., Reed, S., Kreimeyer, K., & Johnson, C. (2004). *Deaf and hard of hearing students in public schools: Who are they and how are they doing?* Paper presented at the Colorado Symposium on Language and Deafness, Colorado Springs, CO.

Antia, S., Stinson, M., & Gaustad, M. (2002). Developing membership in the education of deaf and hard of hearing students in inclusive settings. *Journal of Deaf Studies and Deaf Education, 7*, 214–229.

Aram, D., Most, T., & Mayafit, H. (2006). Contributions of mother-child storybook telling and joint writing to literacy development in kindergartners with hearing loss. *Language, Speech, and Hearing Services in Schools, 37*, 209–223.

Arnos, K. S., & Pandya, A. (in press). Advances in the genetics of deafness. In M. Marschark & P. Spencer (Eds.), *The Oxford handbook of deaf studies, language, and education*, Vol. 1, second edition. New York: Oxford University Press.

Bailes, C. (2001). Integrative ASL-English language arts: Bridging paths to literacy. *Sign Language Studies, 1*, 147–174.

Bailly, D., De Chouly de Lenclave, M., & Lauwerier, L. (2003). Deficience auditive et trubles psychopathologiques chez l'enfant et l'adolescent. *L'Encephale, 29*, 329–337.

Bandurski, M., & Galkowski, T. (2004). The development of analogical reasoning in deaf children and their parents' communication mode. *Journal of Deaf Studies and Deaf Education, 9*, 153–175.

Banks, J. (1994). *All of us together: The story of inclusion at the Kinzie School.* Washington, DC: Gallaudet University Press.

Banks, J., Gray, C., & Fyfe, R. (1990). The written recall of printed stories by severely deaf children. *British Journal of Educational Psychology, 60*, 192–206.

Barker, L. (2003). Computer-assisted vocabulary acquisition: The CSLU vocabulary tutor in oral-deaf education. *Journal of Deaf Studies and Deaf Education, 8*, 187–198.

Barman, C., & Stockton, J. (2002). An evaluation of the SOAR-High project: A web-based science program for deaf students. *American Annals of the Deaf, 147*, 5–10.

Bat-Chava, Y. (1993). Antecedents of self-esteem in deaf people: A meta-analytic review. *Rehabilitation Psychology, 38,* 221–234.

Bat-Chava, Y. (2000). Diversity of deaf identities. *American Annals of the Deaf, 145,* 420–428.

Beattie, R. (2006). The oral methods and spoken language acquisition. In P. Spencer & M. Marschark (Eds.), *Advances in the spoken language development of deaf and hard-of-hearing children* (pp. 103–135). New York: Oxford University Press.

Bebko, J. (1998). Learning, language, memory, and reading: The role of language automatization and its impact on complex cognitive activities. *Journal of Deaf Studies and Deaf Education, 3,* 4–14.

Becket, C., Maughan, G., Rutter, M., Castle, J., Colvert, E., Groothues, C., Kreppner, J., Stevens, S., O'Connor, T. G., & Sonuga-Barke, E. J. S. (2006). Do the effects of early severe deprivation on cognition persist into early adolescence? Findings from the English and Romanian adoptees study. *Child Development, 77,* 696–711.

Bellugi, U., O'Grady, L., Lillo-Martin, D., O'Grady, M., van Hoek, K., & Corina, D. (1990). Enhancement of spatial cognition in deaf children. In V. Volterra and C. Erting (Eds.), *From gesture to language in hearing and deaf children* (pp. 278–298). New York: Springer-Verlag.

Bess, F., Dodd-Murphy, J., & Parker, R. (1998). Children with minimal sensorineural hearing loss: Prevalence, educational performance, and functional status. *Ear & Hearing, 19,* 339–354.

Bess, F., & Paradise, J. (1994). Universal screening for infant hearing impairment: Not simple, not risk-free, not necessarily beneficial, and not presently justified. *Pediatrics, 98,* 330–334.

Blair, H., Peterson, M., & Viehweg, S. (1985). The effects of mild sensorineural hearing loss on academic performance of young school-age children. *Volta Review, 96,* 207–236.

Blake, K. (2005). Adolescent and adult issues in CHARGE syndrome. *Clinical Pediatrics, 44,* 151–159.

Blamey, P., & Sarant, J. (in press). Development of spoken language by deaf children. In M. Marschark & P. Spencer (Eds.), *The Oxford handbook of deaf studies, language, and education, vol. 1, second edition.* New York: Oxford University Press.

Blamey, P., Sarant, J., Paatsch, L., Barry, J., Bow, C., Wales, R., Wright, M., Psarros, C., Rattigan, K., & Tooher, R. (2001). Relationships among speech perception, production, language, hearing loss, and age in children with impaired hearing. *Journal of Speech, Language, and Hearing Research, 44,* 264–285.

Blatto-Vallee, Kelly, R., Gaustad, M., Porter, J., & Fonzi, J. (2007). Visual-spatial representation in mathematical problem solving by deaf and hearing students. *Journal of Deaf Studies and Deaf Education, 12,* 432–448.

Bodner-Johnson, B., & Sass-Lehrer, M. (Eds.). (2003). *The young deaf or hard of hearing child. A family-centered approach to early education.* Baltimore, MD: Paul H. Brookes.

Bogdan, R., & Biklen, S. (2003). *Qualitative research for education* (4th ed.). New York: Pearson Education Group.

Bonvillian, J., Nelson, K., & Rhyne, J. (1981). Sign Language and autism. *Journal of Autism and Developmental Disorders, 11,* 125–137.

Bonvillian, J., Orlansky, M., & Folven, R. (1990/1994). Early sign language acquisition: Implications for theories of language acquisition. In V. Volterra & C. Erting (Eds.), *From gesture to language in hearing and deaf children* (pp. 219–232). Berlin/Washington, DC: Springer-Verlag/Gallaudet University Press.

Boothroyd, A., & Eran, O. (1994). Auditory speech perception capacity of child implant users expressed as equivalent hearing loss. *Volta Review, 96*, 151–169.

Boothroyd, A., Geers, A., & Moog, J. (1991). Practical implications of cochlear implants in children. *Ear & Hearing, 12*(Suppl.), 81–89.

Bornstein, H. (1990). Signed English. In H. Bornstein (Ed.), *Manual communication: Implications for education* (pp. 128–138). Washington, DC: Gallaudet University Press.

Bornstein, H., Saulnier, K., & Hamilton, L. (1980). Signed English: A first evaluation. *American Annals of the Deaf, 125*, 467–481.

Bornstein, M., Selmi, A., Haynes, O., Painter, K., & Marx, E. (1999). Representational abilities and the hearing status of child/mother dyads. *Child Development, 70*, 833–852.

Bowey, J., & Francis, J. (1991). Phonological analysis as a function of age and exposure to reading instruction. *Applied Psycholinguistics, 12*, 91–121.

Boyd, E., & George, K. (1973). The effect of science inquiry on the abstract categorization behavior of deaf children. *Journal of Research in Science Teaching, 10*, 91–99.

Braden, J. (1994). *Deafness, deprivation, and IQ.* New York: Plenum Press.

Brantlinger, E., Jimenez, R., Klingner, J., Pugach, M., & Richardson, V. (2005). Qualitative studies in special education. *Exceptional Children, 71*, 195–207.

Brown, P. M., & Nott, P. (2006). Family-centered practice in early intervention for oral language development: Philosophy, methods, and results. In P. E. Spencer & M. Marschark (Eds.), *Advances in the spoken language development of deaf and hard-of-hearing children* (pp. 136–165). New York: Oxford University Press.

Brown, P. M., Rickards, F., & Bortoli, A. (2001). Structures underpinning pretend play and word production in young hearing children and children with hearing loss. *Journal of Deaf Studies and Deaf Education, 6*, 15–31.

Bu, X. (2004, May). *Universal newborn hearing screening programs in China.* Paper presented at NHS 2004 International Conference on Newborn Screening, Diagnosis and Intervention, Milan, Italy.

Bull, R. (2008). Deafness, numerical cognition, and mathematics. In M. Marschark & P. Hauser (Eds.), *Deaf cognition. Foundations and outcomes* (pp. 170–200). New York: Oxford University Press.

Bullard, C. (2003). *The itinerant teachers' handbook.* Hillsboro, OR: Butte Publications.

Burman, D., Nunes, T., & Evans, D. (2006). Writing profiles of deaf children taught through British Sign Language. *Deafness & Education International, 9*, 2–23.

Bus, A. (2003). Social-emotional requisites for learning to read. In A. van Keeck, S. Stahl, & E. Bauer (Eds.), *On reading books to children* (pp. 3–15). Mahwah, NJ: Lawrence Erlbaum.

Bus, A., van Ijzendoorn, M., & Pelligrini, A. (1995). Joint book reading makes for success in learning to read. A meta-analysis on intergenerational transmission of literacy. *Review of Educational Research, 65*, 1–21.

Butterworth, B. (2005). The development of arithmetical abilities. *Journal of Child Psychology and Psychiatry, 46*, 3–18.

Calderon, R. (1998). Learning disability, neuropsychology, and deaf youth: Theory, research, and practice. *Journal of Deaf Studies and Deaf Education, 3*, 1–3.

Calderon, R. (2000). Parent involvement in deaf children's education programs as a predictor of a child's language, early reading, and social-emotional development. *Journal of Deaf Studies and Deaf Education, 5*, 140–155.

Calderon, R., & Greenberg, M. (2003). Social and emotional development of deaf children. In M. Marschark & P. Spencer (Eds.), *The Oxford handbook of deaf studies, language, and education* (pp. 177–189). New York: Oxford University Press.

Calderon, R., & Naidu, S. (1999). Further support of the benefits of early identification and intervention with children with hearing loss. *Volta Review, 100*, 53–84.

Campbell, D., & Stanley, J. (1966). *Experimental and quasi-experimental designs for research*. Boston, MA: Houghton Mifflin.

Campbell, R., & Wright, H. (1988). Deafness, spelling and rhyme: How spelling supports written words and picture rhyming skills in deaf subjects. *Quarterly Journal of Experimental Psychology, 40A*, 771–788.

Carlberg, C., & Kavale, K. (1980). The efficacy of special versus regular class placement for exceptional children. *Journal of Special Education, 14*, 295–309.

Carney, A., & Moeller, M. P. (1998). Treatment efficacy: Hearing loss in children. *Journal of Speech Language and Hearing Research, 41*, S61–S84.

Chen, D., Klein, M., & Haney, M. (2007). Promoting interaction with infants who have complex multiple disabilities. *Infants and Young Children, 20*, 149–262.

Cheung, H., Hsuan-Chih, C., Creed, N., Ng, L., Wang, S. P., & Mo, L. (2004). Relative roles of general and complementation language in theory-of-mind development: Evidence from Cantonese and English. *Child Development, 75*, 1155–1170.

Chin, S., Tsai, P., & Gao, S. (2003). Connected speech intelligibility of children with cochlear implants and children with normal hearing. *American Journal of Speech-Language Pathology, 12*, 440–451.

Ching, T., Dillon, H., Day, J., & Crowe, K. (2008). The NAL study on longitudinal outcomes of hearing-impaired children: Interim findings on language of early and later-identified children at 6 months after hearing aid fitting. In R. Seewald & J. Bamford (Eds.), *A sound foundation through early amplification: Proceedings of the Fourth International Conference*. Stafa, Switzerland: PhonakAG.

Clemens, C., Davis, S., & Bailey, A. (2000). The false positive in universal newborn hearing screening. *Pediatrics, 106*, e7.

Cochard, N. (2003). Impact du LPC sur l'evolution des enfants implantes. *Actes des Journees d'etudes Nantes, 40*, 65–77.

Colin, S., Magnan, A., Ecalle, J., & Leybaert, J. (2007). Relation between deaf children's phonological skills in kindergarten and word recognition performance in first grade. *Journal of Child Psychology and Psychiatry, 48*, 139–146.

Cone, B. (in press). Screening and assessment of hearing loss in infants. In M. Marschark & P. Spencer (Eds.), *The Oxford handbook on deaf studies, language, and education*. Vol. 1, second edition. New York: Oxford University Press.

Connor, C., Hieber, S., Arts, H. A., & Zwolan, T. (2000). Speech, vocabulary, and the education of children using cochlear implants: Oral or total communication? *Journal of Speech, Language, and Hearing Research, 43*, 1185–1204.

Connor, C., & Zwolan, T. (2004). Examining multiple sources of influence on the reading comprehension skills of children who use cochlear implants. *Journal of Speech, Language, and Hearing Research, 47*, 509–526.

Convertino, C. M., Marschark, M., Sapere, P., Sarchet, T., & Zupan, M. (2009). Predicting academic success among deaf college students. *Journal of Deaf Studies and Deaf Education, 14*, 324–343.

Conway, D. (1985). Children (re)creating writing: A preliminary look at the purposes of free-choice writing of hearing-impaired kindergarteners. *Volta Review, 87*, 91–107.

Cornett, O. (1967). Cued speech. *American Annals of the Deaf, 112*, 3–13.

Cornett, O. (1973). Comments on the Nash case study. *Sign Language Studies, 3*, 93–98.

Cornett, O. (1994). Adapting cued speech to additional languages. *Cued Speech Journal, 5*, 19–29.

Court, J. H., & Raven, J. (1995). *Manual for Raven's Progressive Matrices and Vocabulary Scales.* Section 7: Research and References: Summaries of Normative, Reliability, and Validity Studies and References to All Sections. San Antonio, TX: Harcourt Assessment.

Courtin, C. (2000). The impact of sign language on the cognitive development of deaf children: The case of theories of mind. *Journal of Deaf Studies and Deaf Education, 5*, 266–276.

Courtin, C., & Melot, A. (1998). Development of theories of mind in deaf children. In M. Marschark & D. Clark (Eds.), *Psychological perspectives on deafness* (Vol. 2, pp. 79–102). Mahwah, NJ: Lawrence Erlbaum.

Crain-Thoreson, C., & Dale, P. (1999). Enhancing linguistic performance: Parents and teachers as book reading partners for children with language delays. *Topics in Early Childhood Special Education, 19*, 28–39.

Crandall, C., & Smaldino, J. (2000). Classroom acoustics for children with normal hearing and with hearing impairment. *Language, Speech, and Hearing Services in Schools, 31*, 362–370.

Crowe, T. (2003). Self-esteem scores among deaf college students: An examination of gender and parents' hearing status and signing ability. *Journal of Deaf Studies and Deaf Education, 8*, 199–206.

Crnic, K., & Greenberg, M. (1990). Minor parenting stresses with young children. *Child Development, 61*, 1628–1637.

Culpepper, B. (2003). Identification of permanent childhood hearing loss through universal newborn hearing screening programs. In B. Bodner-Johnson and M. Sass-Lehrer (Eds.), *The young deaf or hard of hearing child* (pp. 99–126). Baltimore, MD: Paul H. Brookes.

Cummins, J. (1989). A theoretical framework of bilingual special education. *Exceptional Children, 56*, 111–119.

Cummins, J. (1991). Interdependence in first- and second-language proficiency in bilingual children. In E. Bialystok (Ed.), *Language processing in bilingual children.* Cambridge: Cambridge University Press.

Damon, G., Krabbe, P., Kilsby, M., & Mylanus, E. (2005). The Usher lifestyle survey: Maintaining independence: A multi-centre study. *International Journal of Rehabilitation Research, 28*, 309–320.

Davey, B., & King, S. (1990). Acquisition of word meanings from context by deaf readers. *American Annals of the Deaf, 135*, 227–234.

Day [Spencer], P. (1986). Deaf children's expressions of communicative intentions. *Journal of Communication Disorders, 19*, 367–385.

DeBruin-Parecki, A. (1999). *Assessing adult-child storybook reading practices.* CIERA Report 2-004. Ann Arbor: University of Michigan, Center for the Improvement of Early Reading Achievement.

DeFord, D. (2001). *Dominie Reading and Writing Assessment portfolio* (3rd ed.). Carlsbad, CA: Dominie Press.

DeLana, M., Gentry, M., & Andrews, J. (2007). The efficacy of ASL/English bilingual education: Considering public schools. *American Annals of the Deaf, 152*, 73–87.

Delk, L., & Weidekamp, L. (2001). *Shared Reading Project: Evaluating implementation processes and family outcomes.* Washington, DC: Gallaudet University, Laurent Clerc National Deaf Education Center.

Descourtieux, C. (2003). Seize ans d'experience practique a CODADI: Evaluation—evolutions. *Actes des Journees d'etudes Nantes, 40*, 77–88.

DesJardin, J. (2006). Family empowerment: Supporting language development in young childen who are deaf or hard of hearing. *Volta Review, 106*, 275–298.

Dettman, S., Pinder, D., Briggs, R., et al. (2007). Communication development in children who receive the cochlear implant younger than 12 months: Risks versus benefits. *Ear & Hearing, 28*(suppl), 11S–18S.

deVilliers, P. (1991). English literacy development in deaf children: Directions for research and intervention. In J. Miller (Ed.), *Research on child language disorders: A decade of progress* (pp. 277–284). Austin TX: Pro-Ed.

deVilliers, P., & Pomerantz, S. (1992). Hearing-impaired students' learning new words from written context. *Applied Psycholinguistics, 13*, 409–431.

Dietz, C. (1995). *Moving toward the standards: A national action plan for mathematics education reform for the deaf.* Washington, DC: Gallaudet University, Pre-College Programs.

Dodd, B., & Hermelin, B. (1977). Phonological coding by the prelinguistically deaf. *Perception and Psychophysics, 21*, 413–417.

Donovan, M., & Cross C. (Eds.). (2002). *Minority students in special education and gifted education.* Washington, DC: National Academy Press.

Dorta, P. (1995). Moving into multiage. In A. Bingham, P. Dorta, M. McClaskey, & J. O'Keefe (Eds.), *Exploring the multiage classroom* (pp. 193–202). York, ME: Stenhouse Publishers.

Dowaliby, F., Caccamise, F., Marschark, M., Albertini, J., & Lang, H. (2000). NTID admissions and placement research strand, FY2000 report. Rochester, NY: Rochester Institute of Technology, Internal Report of the National Technical Institute for the Deaf.

Dromi, E. (1987). *Early lexical development.* New York: Cambridge University Press.

Duchesne, L., Sutton, A., & Bergeron, F. (2009). Language achievement in children who received cochlear implants between 1 and 2 years of age: Group and individual patterns. *Journal of Deaf Studies and Deaf Education, 14,* 465–485.

Duncan, J. (1999). Conversational skills with hearing loss and children with normal hearing in an integrated setting. *Volta Review, 101,* 193–211.

Duncan, J., & Rochecouste, J. (1999). Length and complexity of utterances produced by kindergarten children with impaired hearing and their hearing peers. *Australian Journal of Education of the Deaf, 5,* 63–69.

Dunn, L., & Dunn, L. (1997). *Peabody Picture Vocabulary Test-Third Edition.* Circle Pines, MN: American Guidance Service.

Dunst, C., Jenkins, V., & Trivette, C. (1984). The Family Support Scale: Reliability and validity. *Journal of Individual, Family, and Community Wellness, 1,* 45–52.

Dye, P., Hauser, P., & Bavelier, D. (2008). Visual attention in deaf children and adults: Implications for learning environments. In M. Marschark & P. Hauser, *Deaf Cognition* (pp. 250–263). New York: Oxford University Press.

Easterbrooks, S., & Baker, S. (2002). *Language learning in children who are deaf and hard of hearing: Multiple pathways.* Boston: Allyn & Bacon.

Easterbrooks, S., & Handley, C. M. (2005/2006). Behavior change in a student with dual diagnosis of deafness and Pervasive Developmental Disorder: A case study. *American Annals of the Deaf, 150,* 401–407.

Easterbrooks, S., & O'Rourke, C. (2001). Gender differences in response to auditory-verbal intervention in children who are deaf or hard of hearing. *American Annals of the Deaf, 146,* 309–319.

Easterbrooks, S., & Stephenson, B. (2006). An examination of twenty literacy, science, and mathematics practices used to educate students who are deaf or hard of hearing. *American Annals of the Deaf, 151,* 385–399.

Edwards, L. (2010). Learning disabilities in deaf and hard-of-hearing children. In M. Marschark & P. Spencer (Eds.). *The Oxford handbook of deaf studies, language, and education, vol. 2* (pp. 425–438). New York: Oxford University Press.

Edwards, L., & Crocker, S. (2008). *Psychological processes in deaf children with complex needs: An evidence-based practical guide.* London: Jessica Kingsley.

El-Hakim, H., Papsin, B., Mount, R. J., Levasseur, J., Panesar, J., Stevens, D., & Harrison, R. V. (2001). Vocabulary acquisition rate after pediatric cochlear implantation and the impact of age of implantation. *International Journal of Pediatric Otorhinolaryngology, 59,* 187–194.

Elahi, M. M., Elahi, F., Elahi, A., & Elahi, S. B. (1998). Paediatric hearing loss in rural Pakistan. *Journal of Otolaryngology, 27*(6), 348–353.

Elfenbein, J., Hardin-Jones, M., & Davis, J. (1994). Oral communication skills of children who are hard of hearing. *Journal of Speech and Hearing Research, 37,* 216–226.

Elliott, L. B., Stinson, M. S., McKee, B. G., Everhart, V. S., & Francis, P. J. (2001). College students' perceptions of the C-Print speech-to-text transcription system. *Journal of Deaf Studies and Deaf Education, 6,* 286–298.

Emmorey, K. (2002). *Language, cognition, and the brain: Insights from sign language research.* Mahwah, NJ: Lawrence Erlbaum.

Engen, E., & Engen, T. (1983). *Rhode Island Test of Language Structure*. Baltimore: University Park Press.

Englemann, S., & Brunner, E. (1995). *Reading Mastery I*. Columbus, OH: Science Research Associates.

Eriks-Brophy, A. (2004). Outcomes of Auditory-Verbal Therapy: A review of the evidence and a call for action. *Volta Review, 104*, 21–35.

Estabrooks, W. (1994). *Auditory-verbal therapy*. Washington, DC: A. G. Bell Association.

Estabrooks, W. (1998). *Cochlear implants for kids*. Washington, DC: A. G. Bell Association.

Evans, C. (2004). Literacy development in deaf students: Case studies in bilingual teaching and learning. *American Annals of the Deaf, 149*, 17–26.

Ewing, K., & Jones, T. (2003). An educational rationale for deaf students with multiple disabilities. *American Annals of the Deaf, 148*, 267–271.

Ewoldt, C. (1981). A psycholinguistic description of selected deaf children reading in sign language. *Reading Research Quarterly, 17*, 58–89.

Ewoldt, C. (1985). A descriptive study of the developing literacy of young hearing impaired children. *Volta Review, 87*, 109–126.

Ewoldt, C., & Saulnier, K. (1992). *Beginning in literacy: A longitudinal study with three to seven year old deaf participants*. Washington, DC: Gallaudet University, Center for Studies in Education and Human Development.

Fenson, L., Dale, P., Reznick, J., Bates, E., Thal, D., & Pethick, S. (1994). Variability in early communicative development. *Monographs of the Society for Research in Child Development, 59*, 1–173.

Fenson, L., Dale, P., Reznick, J., Thal, D., Bates, E., Hartung, J., Pethick, W., & Reilly, J. (1993). *The MacArthur Communicative Development Inventories: User's guide and technical manual*. San Diego, CA: Singular.

Feuerstein, R. (1980). *Instrumental enrichment*. Baltimore, MD: University Park Press.

Finitzo-Heiber, T., & Tillman, T. (1978). Room acoustics' effects on word discrimination ability for normal and hearing impaired children. *Journal of Speech and Hearing Research, 21*, 440–458.

Fischer, S. (1998). Critical periods for language acquisition: Consequences for deaf education. In A. Weisel (Ed.), *Issues unresolved: New perspectives on language and deaf education* (pp. 9–26). Washington, DC: Gallaudet University Press.

Fitzpatrick, E., Angus, D., Durieux-Smith, A., Graham, I., & Coyle, D. (2008). Parents' needs following identification of childhood hearing loss. *American Journal of Audiology, 17*, 38–49.

Forest, M., & Pearpoint, J. (1992). MAPS: Action planning. In J. Pearpoint, M. Forest, & J. Snow (Eds.), *The inclusion papers: Strategies to make inclusion work* (pp. 52–56). Toronto, Canada: Inclusion Press.

Fortnum, H., Stacey, P., Barton, G., & Summerfield, A. Q. (2007). National evaluation of support options for deaf and hearing-impaired children: Relevance to education services. *Deafness & Education International, 9*, 120–130.

Fortnum, H., Summerfield, A., Marshall, D., Davis, A., & Bamford, J. (2001). Prevalence of permanent childhood hearing impairment in the United Kingdom and implications for universal neonatal hearing screening: Questionnaire-based ascertainment study. *British Medical Journal, 323,* 1–6.

Fryauf-Bertschy, J., Tyler, R., Kelsay, D., et al. (1997). Cochlear implant use by prelingually deafened children: The influences of age at implant and length of device use. *Journal of Speech Language and Hearing Research, 40,* 183–199.

Fukuda, S., Fukushima, K., Maeda, Y., Tsukamura, K., Nagayasu, R., Toida, N., Kibayashi, N., Kasai, N., Sugata, A., & Nishizake, K. (2003). Language development of a multiply handicapped child after cochlear implantation. *International Journal of Pediatric Otorhinolaryngology, 67,* 627–633.

Fung, P., Chow, B., & McBride-Chang. (2005). The impact of a Dialogic Reading Program on deaf and hear-of-hearing kindergarten and early primary school-aged students in Hong Kong. *Journal of Deaf Studies and Deaf Education, 10,* 82–95.

Gardner, H. (1984). *Frames of mind.* Cambridge, MA: Harvard University Press.

Gaustad, M., & Kelly, R. (2004). The relationship between reading achievement and morphological word analysis in deaf and hearing students matched for reading level. *Journal of Deaf Studies and Deaf Education, 9,* 269–285.

Geers, A. (2002). Factors affecting the development of speech, language, and literacy in children with early cochlear implantation. *Language, Speech, and Hearing Services in the School, 33,* 172–183.

Geers, A. (2005, April 7–10). *Factors associated with academic achievement by children who received a cochlear implant by 5 years of age.* Presentation at pre-conference workshop, Development of Children with Cochlear Implants, at biennial meetings of the Society for Research in Child Development, Atlanta, GA.

Geers, A. (2006). Spoken language in children with cochlear implants. In P. Spencer & M. Marschark (Eds.), *Advances in the spoken language development of deaf and hard-of-hearing children* (pp. 244–270). New York: Oxford University Press.

Geers, A., & Moog, J. (1989). Factors predictive of the development of literacy in profoundly hearing-impaired adolescents. *Volta Review, 91,* 69–86.

Geers, A., & Moog, J. (1992). Speech perception and production skills of students with impaired hearing from oral and total communication education settings. *Journal of Speech and Hearing Research, 35,* 1384–1393.

Geers, A., & Moog, J. (1994). Spoken language results: Vocabulary, syntax and communication. *Volta Review, 96,* 131–150.

Geers, A., Moog, J., & Schick, B. (1984). Acquisition of spoken and signed English by profoundly deaf children. *Journal of Speech and Hearing Disorders, 49,* 378–388.

Geers, A., Tobey, E., Moog, J., & Brenner, C. (2008). Long-term outcomes of cochlear implantation in the pre-school years: From elementary grades to high school. *International Journal of Audiology, 47,* Suppl 2, S21–30.

Gersten, R., Fuchs, L., Compton, D., Coyne, M., Greenwood, C., & Innocenti, M. (2005). Quality indicators for group experimental and quasi-experimental research in special education. *Exceptional Children, 71,* 149–164.

Giangreco, M., Edelman, S., MacFarland, S., & Luiselli, T. (1997). Attitudes about educational and related service provision for students with deaf-blindness and multiple disabilities. *Exceptional Children, 36,* 56–60.

Ginsburg, H., & Baroody, A. (2003). *Test of Early Mathematics Ability*. Austin TX: Pro-Ed.

Gioia, B. (2001). The emergent language and literacy experiences of three deaf pre-schoolers. *International Journal of Disability, Development, and Education, 48,* 411–428.

Glenn, S. (1988). A deaf re-education program: A model for deaf students with emotional and behavioral problems. In H. Prickett & E. Duncan (Eds.), *Coping with the multi-handicapped hearing impaired* (pp. 7–18). Springfield, IL: Charles C. Thomas.

Goldberg, L. R., & Richburg, C. M. (2004). Minimal hearing impairment: Major myths with more than minimal implications. *Communication Disorders Quarterly, 25,* 152–160.

Goldfield, B., & Reznick, J. (1990). Early lexical acquisition: Rate, content, and the vocabulary spurt. *Journal of Child Language, 17,* 171–183.

Goldin-Meadow, S., & Mayberry, R. (2001). How do profoundly deaf children learn to read?. *Learning Disabilities Research and practice, 16,* 222–229.

Grandori, F., & Lutman, M., (1999). The European Consensus Development Conference on Neonatal Hearing Screening (Milan, May 15–16, 1998). *American Journal of Audiology, 8,* 19–20.

Grant, W., Rosenstein, J., & Knight, D. (1975). A project to determine the feasibility of BSCS's Me Now for hearing impaired students. *American Annals of the Deaf, 120,* 63–69.

Gravel, J., Dunn, M., Lee, W., & Ellis, M. (2006). Peripheral audition of children on the autistic spectrum. *Ear & Hearing, 27,* 299–312.

Gray, K., & McNaught, C. (2001, December). *Evaluation of achievements from collaboration in a learning technology mentoring program: Meeting at the crossroads.* Paper presented at the annual conference of the Australasian Society for Computers in Learning in Tertiary Education, Melbourne, Australia.

Greenberg, M., Calderon, R., & Kusché, C. (1984). Early intervention using simultaneous communication with deaf infants: The effect on communication development. *Child Development, 55,* 607–616.

Greenberg, M., & Kusché, C. (1998). Preventive intervention for school-age deaf children: The PATHS curriculum. *Journal of Deaf Studies and Deaf Education, 3,* 49–63.

Gregory, S. (1998). Mathematics and deaf children. In S. Gregory, P. Knight, W. McCracken, S. Powers, & L. Watson (Eds.), *Issues in deaf education.* London: David Fulton.

Gregory, S. (1999). *Cochlear implantation and the under 2's: Psychological and social implications.* Paper presented to the Nottingham Paediatric Implant Program International Conference, Cochlear Implantation in the under 2's: Research into Clinical Practice, Nottingham, UK.

Gregory, S. (2001, September). *Consensus on auditory implants.* Paper presented to the Ethical Aspects and Counseling Conference, Padova, Italy.

Griswold, L., & Commings, J. (1974). The expressive vocabulary of pre-school deaf children. *American Annals of the Deaf, 119,* 16–29.

Groht, M. (1958). *Natural language for deaf children.* Washington, DC: Alexander Graham Bell Association for the Deaf and Hard of Hearing.

Guardino, C. (2008). Identification and placement for deaf students with multiple disabilities: Choosing the path less followed. *American Annals of the Deaf, 153*, 55–64.

Gustason, G., Pfetzing, D., & Zawolkow, E. (1980). *Signing exact English.* Los Alamitos, CA: Modern Sign Press.

Hadjikakou, K., Petridou, L., & Stylianou, C. (2005). Evaluation of the support services provided to deaf children attending secondary general schools in Cyprus. *Journal of Deaf Studies and Deaf Education, 10*, 204–211.

Hage, C., Alegria, J., & Perier, O. (1991). Cued speech and language acquisition: The case of grammatical gender morpho-phonology. In D. Martin (Ed.), *Advances in cognition, education and deafness* (pp. 395–399). Washington, DC: Gallaudet University Press.

Hage, C., & Leybaert, J. (2006). The effect of cued speech on the development of spoken language. In P. Spencer & M. Marschark (Eds.), *Advances in the spoken language development of deaf and hard-of-hearing children* (pp. 193–211). New York: Oxford University Press.

Hall, M., & Bavelier, D. (2010). Working memory, deafness and sign language. In M. Marschark & P. E. Spencer (Eds.), *The Oxford handbook of deaf studies, language, and education, vol. 2* (pp. 458–472). New York: Oxford University Press.

Hammill, D., & Larsen, S. (1996). *Test of Written Language* (3rd ed.). Austin TX: Pro-Ed.

Hamzavi, J., Baumgartner, W., Egelierler, B., Franz, P., Schenk, B., & Gstoettner, W. (2000). Follow up of cochlear implanted handicapped children. *International Journal of Pediatric Otorhinolaryngology, 56*, 169–174.

Harcourt Educational Management. (1996). *Stanford Achievement Test Series, Ninth Edition.* San Antonio: Harcourt Educational Management.

Hargrave, A., & Senechal, M. (2000). A book reading intervention with preschool children who have limited vocabularies: The benefits of regular reading and dialogic reading. *Early Childhood Research Quarterly, 15*, 75–90.

Harrington, F. (2000). Sign language interpreters and access for deaf students to university curricula: The ideal and the reality. In R. P. Roberts, S. E. Carr, D. Abraham, & A. Dufour (Eds.), *The critical link 2: Interpreters in the community* (pp. 219–273). Amsterdam: John Benjamins.

Harris, M. (2001). It's all a matter of timing: Sign visibility and sign reference in deaf and hearing mothers of 18-month-old children. *Journal of Deaf Studies and Deaf Education, 6*, 177–185.

Harris, M., & Beech, J. (1998). Implicit phonological awareness and early reading development in pre-lingually deaf children. *Journal of Deaf Studies and Deaf Education, 3*, 205–216.

Harris, M., & Chasin, J. (2005). Visual attention in deaf and hearing infants: The role of auditory cues. *Journal of Child Psychology and Psychiatry, 46*, 1116–1123.

Harris, M., & Mohay, H. (1997). Learning to look in the right place: A comparison of attentional behavior in deaf children with deaf and hearing mothers. *Journal of Deaf Studies and Deaf Education, 2*, 96–102.

Harris, M., & Moreno, C. (2006). Speech reading and learning to read: A comparison of 8-year-old profoundly deaf children with good and poor reading ability. *Journal of Deaf Studies and Deaf Education, 11*, 189–201.

Hart, B., & Risley, T. (1995). *Meaningful differences in the everyday experience of young American children*. Baltimore, MD: Paul H. Brookes.

Hauser, P. C., Lukomski, J., & Hillman, T. (2008). Development of deaf and hard-of-hearing students' executive function. In M. Marschark & P. C. Hauser (Eds.), *Deaf cognition: Foundations and outcomes* (pp. 286–308). New York: Oxford University Press.

Hauser, P., & Marschark, M. (2008). What we know and what we don't know about cognition and deaf learners. In M. Marschark & P. C. Hauser (Eds.), *Deaf cognition: Foundations and outcomes* (pp. 439–458). New York: Oxford University Press.

Hawker, K., Ramirez-Inscoe, J., Bishop, D., Twomey, T., O'Donoghue, G., & Moore, D. (2008). Disproportionate language impairment in children using cochlear implants. *Ear & Hearing, 29*, 467–471.

Hegarty, M., & Kozhevnikov, M. (1999). Types of visual-spatial representation and mathematical problem solving. *Journal of Educational Psychology, 91*, 684–689.

Hermans, D., Knoors, H., Ormel, E., & Verhoeven, L. (2008a). Modeling reading vocabulary learning in deaf children in bilingual education programs. *Journal of Deaf Studies and Deaf Education, 13*, 155–174.

Hermans, D., Knoors, H., Ormel, E., & Verhoeven, L. (2008b). The relationship between the reading and signing skills of deaf children in bilingual education programs. *Journal of Deaf Studies and Deaf Education, 13*, 518–530.

Hernandez, R. S., Montreal, S., & Orza, J. (2003). The role of cued speech in the development of Spanish prepositions. *American Annals of the Deaf, 148*, 323–327.

Hitch, G., Arnold, P., & Phillips, L. (1983). Counting processes in deaf children's arithmetic. *British Journal of Psychology, 74*, 429–437.

Hoevenaars-van den Boom, M., Antonissen, A., Knoors, H., & Vervloed, M. (2009). Differentiating characteristics of deafblindness and autism in people with congenital deafblindness and profound intellectual disability. *Journal of Disability Research, 53*, 548–558.

Hoffmeister, R. (2000). A piece of the puzzle: ASL and reading comprehension in deaf children. In C. Chamberlain, J. Morford, & R. Mayberry (Eds.), *Language acquisition by eye* (pp. 143–163). Mahwah, NJ: Lawrence Erlbaum.

Hoffmeister, R., Philip, M., Costello, P., & Grass, W. (1997). Evaluating American Sign Language in deaf children: ASL influences on reading with a focus on classifiers, plurals, verbs of motion and location. In J. Mann (Ed.), *Proceedings of Deaf Studies V Conference*. Washington, DC: Gallaudet University Press.

Hogan, A., Stokes, J., White, C., Tyszkiewicz, E., & Woolgar, A. (2008). An evaluation of Auditory Verbal Therapy using the rate of early language development as an outcome measure. *Deafness & Education International, 10*, 143–167.

Hoiting, N. (2006). Deaf children are verb attenders: Early sign vocabulary department in Dutch toddlers. In B. Schick, M. Marschark, & P. Spencer (Eds.), *Advances in the sign language development of deaf children* (pp. 161–188). New York: Oxford University Press.

Holcomb, R. (1970). The total approach. *Proceedings of International Conference on Education of the Deaf* (pp. 104–107), Stockholm, Sweden.

Holden-Pitt, L., & Diaz, J. (1998). Thirty years of the Annual Survey of Deaf and Hard-of-Hearing Children and Youth: A glance over the decades. *American Annals of the Deaf, 142*, 72–76.

Holmes, T., & Rahe, R. (1967). The Social Readjustment Rating Scale. *Journal of Psychosomatic Research, 11*, 213–218.

Holt, J. (1994). Classroom attributes and achievement test scores for deaf and hard of hearing students. *American Annals of the Deaf, 139*, 430–437.

Holt, J., Traxler, C., & Allen, T. (1997). *Interpreting the scores: A user's guide to the 9th Edition Stanford Achievement Test for educators of deaf and hard-of-hearing students (Technical Report 97-1)*. Washington, DC: Gallaudet University, Gallaudet Research Institute.

Holt, R., & Kirk, K. (2005). Speech and language development in cognitively delayed children with cochlear implants. *Ear & Hearing, 26*, 132–148.

Holt, R., & Svirsky, M. (2008). An exploratory look at pediatric cochlear implantation: Is earliest always best?. *Ear & Hearing, 29*, 492–511.

Horner, R., Carr, E., Halle, J., McGee, G., Odom, S., & Wolery, M. (2005). The use of single-subject design research to identify evidence-based practice in special education. *Exceptional Children, 71*, 165–179.

Hyde, M., Ohna, S. E., & Hjulstadt, O. (2005). Education of the deaf in Australia and Norway: A comparative study of the interpretations and applications of inclusion. *American Annals of the Deaf, 150*, 415–426.

Hyde, M. B., & Power, D. J. (1992). The receptive communication abilities of deaf students under oral, manual and combined methods. *American Annals of the Deaf, 137*, 389–398.

Hyde, M., Power, D., & Leigh, G. (1996). Characteristics of the speech of teachers of the deaf to hearing students and deaf students under oral-only and Simultaneous Communication conditions. *Australian Journal of Education of the Deaf, 1*, 5–9.

Hyde, M., Zevenbergen, R., & Power, D. (2003). Deaf and hard of hearing students' performance on arithmetic word problems. *American Annals of the Deaf, 148*, 56–64.

International Communications Learning Institute. (1996). *See the Sound. Visual Phonics.* Webster, WI: International Communications Learning Institute.

Israelite, N., Ower, J., & Goldstein, G. (2002). Hard-of-hearing adolescents and identity construction: Influences of school experiences, peers, and teachers. *Journal of Deaf Studies and Deaf Education, 7*, 134–148.

Izzo, A. (2002). Phonemic awareness and reading ability: An investigation with young readers who are deaf. *American Annals of the Deaf, 147*, 18–28.

Jacob, A., Rupa, V., Job, A., & Joseph, A. (1997). Hearing impairment and otitis media in rural primary school in south India. *International Journal of Pediatric Otorhinolaryngology, 39*(2), 133–138.

James, D., Rajput, K., Brinton, J., & Goswami, U. (2008). Phonological awareness, vocabulary, and word reading in children who use cochlear implants: Does age of implantation explain individual variability in performance outcomes and growth?. *Journal of Deaf Studies and Deaf Education, 13*, 117–137.

Jimenez, T., Filippini, A., & Gerber, M. (2006). Shared reading within Latino families: An analysis of reading interactions and language use. *Bilingual Research Journal, 30,* 431–452.

Johnson, R., Liddell, S., & Erting, C. (1989). *Unlocking the curriculum: Principles for achieving access in deaf education.* Gallaudet Research Institute Working Paper 89-3. Washington, DC: Gallaudet University.

Johnston, T. (2003). W(h)ither the deaf community? Population, genetics, and the future of Australian Sign Language. *American Annals of the Deaf, 148,* 358–377.

Jones, T., & Jones, J. (2003). Educating young deaf children with multiple disabilities. In B. Bodner-Johnson & M. Sass-Lehrer (Eds.), *The young deaf and hard-of-hearing child* (p. 297–332). Baltimore, MD: Paul H. Brookes Publishing Co.

Jure, R., Rapin, I., & Tuchman, R. (1991). Hearing impaired autistic children. *Developmental Medicine and Child Neurology, 33,* 1062–1072.

Justice, L., & Ezell, H. (2002). Use of storybook reading to increase print awareness in at-risk children. *American Journal of Speech-Language Pathology, 11,* 17–29.

Kanner, I. (1943). Autistic disturbances of affective contact. *Nervous Child, 2,* 217–250.

Kelly, D., Forney, G., Parker-Fisher, S., & Jones, M. (1993). The challenge of attention deficit disorder in children who are deaf or hard of hearing. *American Annals of the Deaf, 38,* 343–348.

Kelly, L. (1996). The interaction of syntactic competence and vocabulary during reading by deaf students. *Journal of Deaf Studies and Deaf Education, 1,* 75–90.

Kelly, L. (1998). Using silent motion pictures to teach complex syntax to adult deaf readers. *Journal of Deaf Studies and Deaf Education, 3,* 217–230.

Kelly, L. (2003a). Considerations for designing practice for deaf readers. *Journal of Deaf Studies and Deaf Education, 8,* 171–186.

Kelly, L. (2003b). The importance of processing automaticity and temporary storage capacity to the differences in comprehension between skilled and less skilled college-age deaf readers. *Journal of Deaf Studies and Deaf Education, 8,* 230–249.

Kelly, R., & Gaustad, M. (2006). Deaf college students' mathematical skills relative to morphological knowledge, reading level, and language proficiency. *Journal of Deaf Studies and Deaf Education, 12,* 25–37.

Kelly, R., Lang, H., Mousley, K., & Davis, S. (2003). Deaf college students' comprehension of relational language in arithmetic compare problems. *Journal of Deaf Studies and Deaf Education, 8,* 120–132.

Kelly, R., Lang, H., & Pagliaro, C. (2003). Mathematics word problem solving for deaf students: A survey of practices in grades 6–12. *Journal of Deaf Studies and Deaf Education, 8,* 104–119.

Kelly, R., & Mousley, K. (2001). Solving word problems: More than reading issues for deaf students. *American Annals of the Deaf, 146,* 251–262.

Kennedy, C., McCann, D., Campbell, M., Law, C., Mullee, M., Petrou, S., et al. (2006). Language ability after early detection of permanent child hearing impairment. *New England Journal of Medicine, 354,* 2131–2141.

Killoran, J. (2007). *The national deaf-blind child count: 1998–2005. Review.* Monmouth: Western Oregon University, Teaching Research Institute.

King, C., & Quigley, S. (1985). *Reading and deafness.* San Diego, CA: College-Hill Press.

Kingma, J., Schoenmaker, A., Damen, S., & Nunen, T. (1997). Late manifestations of congenital rubella. www.nud.dk. Retrieved June 12, 2009.

Kipila, B. (1985). Analysis of an oral language sample from a prelingually deaf child's cued speech: A case study. *Cued Speech Annals, 1,* 46–59.

Kirchner, C. (1994). Co-enrollment as an inclusion model. *American Annals of the Deaf, 139,* 163–164.

Kirshner, C. (1996, October). *Full inclusion: An educational model for the 21st century.* Paper presented at the conference on Issues in Language and Deafness, Omaha, NE.

Kirk, K. (2000). Challenges in the clinical investigation of cochlear implant outcomes. In J. Niparko, K. Iler-Kirk, N. Mellon, A. Robbins, D. Tucci, & B. Wilson (Eds.), *Cochlear implants: Principles and practices* (pp. 225–265). Philadelphia: Lippincott, Williams, & Wilkins.

Kluwin, T. (1981). The grammaticality of manual representations of English in classroom settings. *American Annals of the Deaf, 127,* 417–421.

Kluwin, T. (1993). Cumulative effects of mainstreaming on the achievement of deaf adolescents. *Exceptional Children, 60,* 73–81.

Kluwin, T. (1999). Co-teaching deaf and hearing students. Research on social integration. *American Annals of the Deaf, 144,* 339–344.

Kluwin, T., Gonsher, W., Silver, K., & Samuels, J. (1996). Team teaching students with hearing impairments and students with normal hearing together. *Teaching Exceptional Children, 29,* 11–15.

Kluwin, T., & Moores, D. (1985). The effect of integration on the achievement of hearing-impaired adolescents. *Exceptional Children, 52,* 153–160.

Kluwin, T., & Moores, D. (1989). Mathematics achievement of hearing impaired adolescents in different placements. *Exceptional Children, 55,* 327–335.

Kluwin, T., & Noretsky, M. (2005). A mixed-methods study of teachers of the deaf learning to integrate computers into their teaching. *American Annals of the Deaf, 150,* 350–357.

Kluwin, T., Stewart, D., & Sammons, A. (1994). The isolation of teachers of the deaf and hard of hearing in local public school programs. *ACEHI Journal/La Revue ACEDA, 20,* 16–30.

Kluwin, T., & Stinson, M. (1993). *Deaf students in local public high schools: Backgrounds, experiences, and outcomes.* Springfield, IL: Charles C. Thomas.

Knoors, H., & Hermans, D. (2010). Effective instruction for deaf and hard-of-hearing students: Teaching strategies, school settings, and student characteristics. In M. Marschark & P. E. Spencer (Eds.), *The Oxford handbook of deaf studies, language, and education Vol. 2* (pp. 57–71). New York: Oxford University Press.

Knoors, H., & Vervloed, M. (in press). Educational programming for deaf children with multiple disabilities. In M. Marschark & P. Spencer (Eds.), *The Oxford handbook of deaf studies, language, and education, vol. 1, second edition.* New York: Oxford University Press.

Koskinen, P., Wilson, R. M., Gambrell, L. B., & Jensema, C. (1986). using closed captioned television to enhance reading skills of learning disabled students. *National Reading Conference Yearbook, 35,* 61–65.

Koskinen, P. S., Wilson, R. M., & Jensema, C. J. (1986). Using closed-captioned television in the teaching of reading to deaf students. *American Annals of the Deaf, 131,* 43–46.

Kreimeyer, K., Crooke, P., Drye, C., Egbert, V., & Klein, B. (2000). Academic benefits of co-enrollment model of inclusive education of deaf and hard-of-hearing children. *Journal of Deaf Studies and Deaf Education, 5,* 174–185.

Kritzer, K. (2008). Family mediation of mathematically based concepts while engaged in a problem-solving activity with their young deaf children. *Journal of Deaf Studies and Deaf Education, 13,* 503–517.

Kritzer, K. L. (2009). Barely started and already left behind: A descriptive analysis of the mathematics ability demonstrated by young deaf children. *Journal of Deaf Studies and Deaf Education, 14,* 409-421.

Kyle, F., & Harris, M. (2006). Concurrent correlates and predictors of reading and spelling achievement in deaf and hearing school children. *Journal of Deaf Studies and Deaf Education, 11,* 273–288.

Lang, H. (in press). Perspectives on the history of deaf education. In M. Marschark & P. Spencer, (Eds.), *The Oxford handbook of deaf studies, language, and education, vol. 1, second edition* (pp. 9–20). New York: Oxford University Press.

Lang, H., & Albertini, J. (2001). Construction of meaning in the authentic science writing of deaf students. *Journal of Deaf Studies and Deaf Education, 6,* 258–284.

Lang, H., Hupper, M., Monte, D., Brown, S., Babb, I., & Scheifele, P. (2006). A study of technical signs in science: Implications for lexical database development. *Journal of Deaf Studies and Deaf Education, 12,* 65–79.

Lang, H., McKee, B., & Conner, K. (1993). Characteristics of effective teachers: A descriptive study of perception of faculty and deaf college students. *American Annals of the Deaf, 138,* 252–259.

Lartz, M., & Lestina, L. (1995). Strategies deaf mothers use when reading to their young deaf or hard of hearing children. *American Annals of the Deaf, 14,* 358–362.

LaSasso, C., Crain, K., & Leybaert, J. (2003). Rhyme generation in deaf students: The effect of exposure to cued speech. *Journal of Deaf Studies and Deaf Education, 8,* 250–270.

LaSasso, C., & Davey, B. (1987). The relationship between lexical knowledge and reading comprehension for prelingual profoundly hearing-impaired students. *Volta Review, 89,* 211–220.

LaSasso, C., & Metzger, M. (1998). An alternate route for preparing deaf children for BiBi programs: The home language as L1 and cued speech for conveying traditionally-spoken languages. *Journal of Deaf Studies and Deaf Education, 3,* 265–289.

Laughton, J. (1989). The learning disabled, hearing impaired students: Reality, myth, or overextension?. *Topics in Language Disorders, 9,* 70–79.

Lederberg, A., & Beal-Alvarez, A. (in press). Expressing meaning: From prelinguistic communication to building vocabulary. In M. Marschark & P. Spencer (Eds.), *The Oxford handbook of deaf studies, language, and education, vol. 1, second edition.* New York: Oxford University Press.

Lederberg, A., & Prezbindowski, A. (2000). Impact of child deafness on mother-toddler interaction: Strengths and weaknesses. In P. Spencer, C. Erting, & M. Marschark (Eds.), *The deaf child in the family and at school* (pp. 73–92). Mahwah NJ: Lawrence Erlbaum.

Lederberg, A., Prezbindowski, A., & Spencer, P. (2000). Word learning skills of deaf preschoolers: The development of novel mapping and rapid word learning strategies. *Child Development, 71,* 1571–1585.

Lederberg, A., & Spencer, P. (2001). Vocabulary development of deaf and hard of hearing children. In M. Marschark, M. Clark, & M. Karchmer (Eds.), *Context, cognition and deafness* (pp. 88–112). Washington, DC: Gallaudet University Press.

Lederberg, A., & Spencer, P. (2005). Critical periods in the acquisition of lexical skills: Evidence from deaf individuals. In, P. Fletcher and J. Miller (Eds.), *Developmental theory and language disorders* (pp. 121–145). Philadelphia: John Benjamins.

Lederberg, A., & Spencer, P. (2009). Word-learning abilities in deaf and hard-of-hearing preschoolers: Effect of lexicon size and language modality. *Journal of Deaf Studies and Deaf Education, 14,* 44–62.

Leigh, G., Newall, J. P., & Newall, A. T. (2010). Newborn screening and earlier intervention with deaf children: Issues for the developing world. In M. Marschark & P. Spencer (Eds.), *The Oxford handbook of deaf studies, language, and education, vol. 2* (pp. 345–359). New York: Oxford University Press.

Levitt, H., McGarr, N., & Geffner, D. (1987). *Development of language and communication skills in hearing-impaired children,. Monographs of the American Speech, Language and Hearing Association, No.* 26.

Lewis, S. (1996). The reading achievement of a group of severely and profoundly hearing-impaired school leavers educated within a natural aural approach. *Journal of the British Association of Teachers of the Deaf, 20,* 1–7.

Lewis, M. S. J, & Jackson, D.W. (2001). Television literacy: Comprehension of program content using closed-captions for the deaf. *Journal of Deaf Studies and Deaf Education, 6,* 43–53.

Leybaert, J. (1993). Reading in the deaf: The roles of phonological codes. In M. Marschark & M. D. Clark (Eds.), *Psychological perspectives on deafness* (pp. 269–310). Mahwah, N.J.: LEA.

Leybaert, J., & Alegria, J. (in press). The role of cued speech in language development of deaf children. In M. Marschark & P. Spencer (Eds.), *The Oxford handbook of deaf studies, language, and education, vol. 1, second edition.* New York: Oxford University Press.

Leybaert, J., & Charlier, B. (1996). Visual speech in the head: The effect of cued-speech on rhyming, remembering, and spelling. *Journal of Deaf Studies and Deaf Education, 1,* 234–248.

Leybaert, J., & Van Cutsem, M. (2002). Counting in sign language. *Journal of Experimental Child Psychology, 81*, 482–501.

Liben, L. (1979). Free recall by deaf and hearing children: Semantic clustering and recall in trained and untrained groups. *Journal of Experimental Child Psychology, 24*, 60–73.

Lichtert, G., & Loncke, F. (2006). The development of proto-performative utterances in deaf toddlers. *Journal of Speech, Language, and Hearing Research, 49*, 486–499.

Lillo-Martin, D. (1988). Children's new sign creations. In M. Strong (Ed.), *Language learning and deafness* (pp. 162–183). Cambridge: Cambridge University Press.

Lillo-Martin, D. (1991). *Universal grammar and American Sign Language.* Dordrecht: Kluwer.

Lillo-Martin, D., Hanson, V., & Smith, S. (1992). Deaf readers' comprehension of relative clause structures. *Applied Psycholinguistics, 13*, 13–30.

Lindert, R. (2001). Hearing families with deaf children: Linguistic and communicative aspects of American Sign Language development. *Dissertation Abstracts International, 2002, 63*–1066-B.

Lovaas, O. (1987). Behavioral treatment and normal educational and intellectual functioning in young autistic children. *Consulting Clinical Psychology, 55*, 3–9.

Lucas, C., & Valli, C. (1992). *Contact language in the American deaf community.* San Diego, CA: Academic Press.

Luckner, J. (1999). An examination of two co-teaching classrooms. *American Annals of the Deaf, 144*, 24–34.

Luckner, J., & Handley, C. M. (2008). A summary of the reading comprehension research undertaken with students who are deaf or hard of hearing. *American Annals of the Deaf, 153*, 6–36.

Luckner, J., & Isaacson, S. (1990). A method of assessing the written language of hearing-impaired students. *Journal of Communication Disorders, 23*, 219–233.

Luetke-Stahlman, B. (1988). The benefit of oral English-only as compared with signed input to hearing-impaired students. *Volta Review, 90*, 349–361.

Luetke-Stahlman, B., & Nielsen, D. (2003). The contribution of phonological awareness and receptive and expressive English to the reading ability of deaf students with varying degrees of exposure to accurate English. *Journal of Deaf Studies and Deaf Education, 8*, 464–484.

Lundy, J. (2002). Age and language skills of deaf children in relation to theory of mind development. *Journal of Deaf Studies and Deaf Education, 7*, 41–56.

Madriz, J. (2000). Hearing impairment in Latin America: An inventory of limited options and resources. *Audiology, 39*, 212–220.

Mahoney, T., & Eichwald, J. (1987). The ups and "Downs" of high-risk hearing screening: The Utah statewide program. *Seminars in Hearing, 8*, 155–163.

Maller, S. & Braden, J. P. (in press). Intellectual assessment of deaf people: A critical review of core concepts and issues. In M. Marschark & P. Spencer (Eds.), *The Oxford handbook of deaf studies, language, and education, vol. 1, second edition.* New York: Oxford University Press.

Maller, S., & Braden, J. (1993). The construct and criterion-related validity of the WISC-III with deaf adolescents. *Journal of Psychoeducational Assessment, WICS-III Monograph Series: WISC-III*, 105–113.

Maller, S., Singleton, J., Supalla, S., & Wix, T. (1999). The development and psychometric properties of the American Sign Language Proficiency Assessment (ASL-PA). *Journal of Deaf Studies and Deaf Education, 4*, 249–269.

Markwardt, F. (1970). *Peabody Individual Achievement Test*. Circle Pines, MN: American Guidance Service.

Marmor, G., & Pettito, L. (1979). Simltaneous Communication in the classroom: How well is English grammar represented?. *Sign Language Studies, 23*, 99–136.

Marschark, M. & Wauters, L. (in press). Cognitive functioning in deaf adults and children. In M. Marschark & P. Spencer (Eds.), *The Oxford handbook of deaf studies, language, and education, vol. 1, second edition*. New York: Oxford University Press.

Marschark, M. (2006). Intellectual functioning of deaf adults and children: Answers and questions. *European Journal of Cognitive Psychology, 18*, 70–89.

Marschark, M. (2007). *Raising and educating a deaf child* (2nd ed.). New York: Oxford University Press.

Marschark, M., Convertino, C., & LaRock, D. (2006). Assessing cognition, communication, and learning by deaf students. In C. Hage, B. Charlier, & J. Leybaert (Eds.), *L'evaluation de la personne sourd* (pp. 26–53). Brussels: Mardaga.

Marschark, M., Convertino, G., Macias, G., Monikowski, C., Sapere, P., & Seewagen, R. (2007). Understanding communication among deaf students who sign and speak: A trivial pursuit?. *American Annals of the Deaf, 152*, 415–424.

Marschark, M., Convertino, C., McEvoy, C., & Masteller, A. (2004). Organization and use of the mental lexicon by deaf and hearing individuals. *American Annals of the Deaf, 149*, 51–61.

Marschark, M., De Beni, R., Polazzo, M., & Cornoldi, C. (1993). Deaf and hearing-impaired adolescents' memory for concrete and abstract prose: Effects of relational and distinctive information. *American Annals of the Deaf, 138*, 31–39.

Marschark, M., & Everhart, V. (1999). Problem solving by deaf and hearing children: Twenty questions. *Deafness & Education International, 1*, 63–79.

Marschark, M., Green, V., Hindmarsh, G., & Walker, S. (2000). Understanding theory of mind in children who are deaf. *Journal of Child Psychology and Psychiatry, 41*, 1067–1074.

Marschark, M., & Hauser, P. (2008). Cognitive underpinnings of learning by deaf and hard-of-hearing students: Differences, diversity, and directions. In M. Marschark & P. Hauser (Eds.), *Deaf cognition: Foundations and outcomes* (pp. 3–23). New York: Oxford University Press.

Marschark, M., Lang, H., & Albertini, J. (2002). *Educating deaf students. From research to practice*. New York: Oxford University Press.

Marschark, M., Leigh, G., Sapere, P., Burnham, D., Convertino, C., Stinson, M., Knoors, H., Vervloed, M., & Noble, W. (2006). Benefits of sign language interpreting and text alternatives for deaf students' classroom learning. *Journal of Deaf Studies and Deaf Education, 11*, 421–437.

Marschark, M., Mouradian, V., & Hallas, M. (1994). Discourse rules in the language productions of deaf and hearing children. *Journal of Experimental Psychology, 57,* 89–107.

Marschark, M., Rhoten, C., & Fabich, M. (2007). Effects of cochlear implants on children's reading and academic achievement. *Journal of Deaf Studies and Deaf Education, 12,* 269–282.

Marschark, M., Sapere, P., Convertino, C., Mayer, C., Wauters, L., & Sarchet, T. (2009). Are deaf students' reading challenges really about reading? *American Annals of the Deaf, 154,* 357–370.

Marschark, M., Sapere, P., Convertino, C. M., & Pelz, J. (2008). Learning via direct and mediated instruction by deaf students. *Journal of Deaf Studies and Deaf Education, 13,* 446–461.

Marschark, M., Sapere, P., Convertino, C., & Seewagen, R. (2005). Access to post-secondary education through sign language interpreting. *Journal of Deaf Studies and Deaf Education, 10,* 38–50.

Marschark, M., Sapere, P., Convertino, C., Seewagen, R., & Maltzen, H. (2004). Comprehension of sign language interpreting: Deciphering a complex task situation. *Sign Language Studies, 4,* 345–368.

Marschark, M., Sarchet, T., Rhoten, C., & Zupan, M. (2010). Will cochlear implants close the reading achievement gap for deaf students? In M. Marschark & P. E. Spencer (Eds.)., *Oxford handbook of deaf studies, language, and education, vol.2.* NewYork: Oxford University Press.

Marschark, M., & Wauters, L. (2008). Language comprehension and learning by deaf students. In M. Marschark & P. Hauser (Eds.), *Deaf cognition: Foundations and outcomes* (pp. 309–350). New York: Oxford University Press.

Martin, D., Craft, A., & Sheng, Z. N. (2001). The impact of cognitive strategy instruction on deaf learners: An international comparative study. *American Annals of the Deaf, 146,* 366–378.

Martin, D., & Jonas, B. (1986). *Cognitive modifiability in the deaf adolescent.* Washington, DC: Gallaudet University. (ERIC Document Reproduction Service No. ED 276 159)

Massaro, D. (2006). A computer-animated tutor for language learning: Research and applications. In P. Spencer & M. Marschark (Eds.), *Advances in the spoken language development of deaf and hard-of-hearing children* (pp. 212–234). New York: Oxford University Press.

Matthews, T., & Reich, C. (1993). Constraints on communication in classrooms for the deaf. *American Annals of the Deaf, 138,* 14–18.

Mauk, G., & Mauk, P. (1998). Considerations, conceptualizations, and challenges in the study of concomitant learning disabilities among children and adolescents who are deaf or hard of hearing. *Journal of Deaf Studies and Deaf Education, 3,* 15–34.

Mauk, G., White, K., Mortensen, L., & Behrens, T. (1991). The effectiveness of screening programs based on high-risk characteristics in early identification of hearing impairment. *Ear & Hearing, 12,* 312–319.

Maxwell, M. (1984). A deaf child's natural development of literacy. *Sign Language Studies, 44,* 195–223.

Maxwell, M., & Bernstein, M. (1985). The synergy of sign and speech in Simultaneous Communication. *Applied Psycholinguistics, 6*, 63–81.

Maxwell, M., & Falick, T. (1992). Cohesion and quality in deaf and hearing children's written English. *Sign Language Studies, 77*, 345–371.

Mayer, C. (1999). Shaping at the point of utterance: An investigation of the composing processes of the deaf student writer. *Journal of Deaf Studies and Deaf Education, 4*, 37–49.

Mayer, C. (2010). The demands of writing and the deaf writer. In M. Marschark & P. Spencer (Eds.), *Oxford handbook of deaf studies, language, and education, vol. 2* (pp. 144–155). New York: Oxford University Press.

Mayer, C., & Akamatsu, C. T. (1999). Bilingual-bicultural models of literacy education for deaf students: Considering the claims. *Journal of Deaf Studies and Deaf Education, 4*, 1–8.

Mayer, C., & Wells, G. (1996). Can the linguistic interdependence theory support a bilingual-bicultural model of literacy education for deaf students?. *Journal of Deaf Studies and Deaf Education, 1*, 93–107.

Mayer, R. E., & Morena, R. (1998). A split-attention effect in multimedia learning: Evidence for dual processing systems in working memory. *Journal of Educational Psychology, 90*, 312–320.

Mayne, A., Yoshinaga-Itano, C., & Sedey, A. (2000a). Receptive vocabulary development of infants and toddlers who are deaf or hard of hearing. *Volta Review, 100*, 29–52.

Mayne, A., Yoshinaga-Itano, C., Sedey, A., & Carey, A. (2000b). Expressive vocabulary development of infants and toddlers who are deaf or hard of hearing. *Volta Review, 100*, 1–28.

McAnally, P., Rose, S., & Quigley, S. (1987). *Language learning practices with deaf children.* Boston: College-Hill Press.

McCall, R. (2009). Evidence-based programming in the context of practice and policy. *Social Policy Report, 23*, 3–11, 15–18.

McEvoy, C., Marschark, M., & Nelson, D. L. (1999). Comparing the mental lexicons of deaf and hearing individuals. *Journal of Educational Psychology, 91*, 1–9.

McGill-Franzen, A., & Gormley, K. (1980). The influence of context on deaf readers' understanding of passive sentences. *American Annals of the Deaf, 125*, 937–942.

McGowan, R., Nittrouer, S., & Chenausky, K. (2008). Speech production in 12-month-old children with and without hearing loss. *Journal of Speech, Language, and Hearing Research, 51*, 879–888.

McIntosh, R. A., Sulzen, L., Reeder, K., & Kidd, D. (1994). Making science accessible to deaf students: The need for science literacy and conceptual teaching. *American Annals of the Deaf, 139*, 480–484.

Meadow, K. (1980). *Deafness and child development.* Berkeley: University of California Press.

Meadow, K., & Trybus, J. (1985). Behavorial and emotional problems of deaf children: An overview. In L. Bradford & W. Hardy (Eds.), *Hearing and hearing impairment* (pp. 395–415). New York: Grune & Stratton.

Meadow-Orlans, K. (1997). Effects of mother and infant hearing status on interactions at twelve and eighteen months. *Journal of Deaf Studies and Deaf Education, 2*, 26–36.

Meadow-Orlans, K., Mertens, D., & Sass-Lehrer, M. (2003). *Parents and their deaf children. The early years.* Washington, DC: Gallaudet University Press.

Meadow-Orlans, K., Smith-Gray, S., & Dyssegaard, B. (1995). Infants who are deaf or hard of hearing, with and without physical/cognitive disabilities. *American Annals of the Deaf, 140,* 279–286.

Meadow-Orlans, K., & Spencer, P. (1996). Maternal sensitivity and the visual attentiveness of children who are deaf. *Early Development and Parenting, 5,* 213–223.

Meadow-Orlans, K., Spencer, P., & Koester, L. (2004). *The world of deaf infants: A longitudinal study.* New York: Oxford University Press.

Mehl, A., & Thomson, V. (2002). The Colorado newborn hearing screening project, 1992–1999: On the threshold of effective population-based universal newborn hearing screening. *Pediatrics, 109,* E7.

Meier, R., & Newport, E. (1990). Out of the hands of babes: On a possible sign advantage in language acquisition. *Language, 66,* 1–23.

Miller, P. (2000). Syntactic and semantic processing in Hebrew readers with prelingual deafness. *American Annals of the Deaf, 145,* 436–451.

Mitchell, R. (2004). National profile of deaf and hard of hearing students in special education from weighted survey results. *American Annals of the Deaf, 149,* 336–349.

Mitchell, R., & Karchmer, M. (2004). Chasing the mythical ten percent: Parental hearing status of deaf and hard of hearing students in the United States. *Sign Language Studies, 4,* 138–163.

Mitchell, R., & Karchmer, M. (2006). Demographics of deaf education: More students in more places. *American Annals of the Deaf, 151,* 95–104.

Mitchell, R., & Karchmer, M. (in press). Demographic and achievement characteristics of deaf and hard-of-hearing students. In M. Marschark & P. Spencer (Eds.), *The Oxford handbook of deaf studies, language, and education, vol. 1, second edition.* New York: Oxford University Press.

Mitchell, R., & Quittner, A. (1996). Multimethod study of attention and behavior problems in hearing-impaired children. *Journal of Clinical Child Psychology, 25,* 83–96.

Mix, K. S., Huttenlocher, J., & Levine, S. C. (2002). *Quantitative development in infancy and early childhood.* New York: Oxford University Press.

Moeller, M. P. (2000). Intervention and language development in children who are deaf and hard of hearing. *Pediatrics, 106,* E43.

Moeller, M. P., Hoover, B., Putman, C., Arbataitis, K., Bohnenkamp, G., Peterson, B., et al. (2007a). Vocalizations of infants with hearing loss compared with infants with normal hearing: Part I—Phonetic development. *Ear & Hearing, 28,* 605–627.

Moeller, M. P., Hoover, B., Putman, C., Arbataitis, K., Bohenenkamp, G., Peterson, B., et al. (2007b). Vocalizations of infants with hearing loss compared with infants with normal hearing: Part II—Transition to words. *Ear & Hearing, 28,* 628–642.

Moeller, M. P., Osberger, M., & Eccarius, M. (1986). Language and learning skills of hearing-impaired students. *ASHA Monographs, 23,* 41–54.

Moeller, M. P., & Schick, B. (2006). Relations between maternal input and theory of mind understanding in deaf children. *Child Development, 77,* 751–766.

Moeller, M. P., Tomblin, J. B., Yoshinaga-Itano, C., Connor, C., & Jerger, S. (2007). Current state of knowledge: Language and literacy of children with hearing impairment. *Ear & Hearing, 28*, 740–753.

Mohay, H. (1983). The effects of Cued Speech on the language development of three deaf children. *Sign Language Studies, 38*, 25–49.

Mohay, H., Milton, L., Hindmarsh, G., & Ganley, K. (1998). Deaf mothers as communication models for hearing families with deaf children. In A. Weisel (Ed.), *Issues unresolved: New perspectives on language and deaf education*. Washington, DC: Gallaudet University Press.

Moog, J., & Geers, A. (1985). EPIC: A program to accelerate academic progress in profoundly hearing-impaired children. *Volta Review, 87*, 259–277.

Mollink, H., Hermans, D., & Knoors, H. (2008). Vocabulary training of spoken words in hard-of-hearing children. *Deafness & Education International, 10*, 80–92.

Moores, D. (2001). *Educating the deaf* (5th ed.). Boston: Houghton Mifflin.

Moores, D. (2008). Research on Bi-Bi instruction. *American Annals of the Deaf, 153*, 3–4.

Moores, D., & Sweet, C. (1990). Factors predictive of school achievement. In D. Moores & K. Meadow-Orlans (Eds.), *Educational and developmental aspects of deafness* (pp. 154–201). Washington DC: Gallaudet University Press.

Morgan, A., & Vernon, M. (1994). A guide to the diagnosis of learning disabilities in deaf and hard-of-hearing children and adults. *American Annals of the Deaf, 139*, 358–370.

Morgan, G., & Woll, B. (2002). The development of complex sentences in British Sign Language. In G. Morgan & B. Woll (Eds.), *Directions in sign language acquisition* (pp. 255–275). Amsterdam: John Benjamin.

Morton, A. (1996). Factors affecting the integration of computers in Western Sydney secondary schools. In J. Hefberg J. Steele, & S. McNamara (Eds.), *Learning technologies: Prospects and pathways* (pp. 107–14). Canberra, Australia: AJET Publications.

Most, T. (2006). Assessment of school functioning among Israeli Arab children with hearing loss in the primary grades. *American Annals of the Deaf, 151*, 327–335.

Moseley, M., Scott-Williams, B., & Anthony, C. (1991, November). *Language expressed through Cued Speech: A preschool case study*. Paper presented at the American Speech and Hearing Association Conference, Atlanta, GA.

Mosteller, F., & Boruch, R. (Eds.). (2002). *Evidence matters: Randomized trials in educational research*. Washington, DC: Brookings Institution.

Mousley, K., & Kelly, R. (1998). Problem-solving strategies for teaching mathematics to deaf students. *American Annals of the Deaf, 143*, 325–336.

Mung'ala-Odera, V., Meehan, R., Njuguna, P., Mturi, N., Alcock, K., & Newton, C. (2006). Prevalence and risk factors of neurological disability and impairment in children living in rural Kenya. *International Journal of Epidemiology, 35*, 683–688.

Munroe, S. (1999). *A summary of late emerging manifestation of congenital rubella in Canada*. Ontario: Canadian Deafblind and Rubella Association.

Musselman, C. (2000). How do children who can't hear learn to read an alphabetic script? A review of the literature on reading and deafness. *Journal of Deaf Studies and Deaf Education, 5*, 9–31.

Musselman, C., & Szanto, G. (1998). The written language of deaf adolescents: Patterns of performance. *Journal of Deaf Studies and Deaf Education, 3,* 245–257.

Napier, J., & Barker, R. (2004). Access to university interpreting: Expectations and preferences of deaf students. *Journal of Deaf Studies and Deaf Education, 9,* 228–238.

Nash, J. (1973). Cues or signs: A case study in language acquisition. *Sign Language Studies, 3,* 80–91.

Nathani, S., Oller, D. K., & Neal. A. R. (2007). On the robustness of vocal development: An examination of infants with moderate-to-severe hearing loss and additional factors. *Journal of Speech, Language, and Hearing Research, 50,* 1425–1444.

National Center for Education Statistics (1999). Integrated postsecondary education data system, *Fall Enrollment Data File, Fall 1997.* http://nces.ed.gov/Ipeds/ef9798/, accessed 12 July 2001.

National Council of Teachers of Mathematics. (2000). *Principles and standards for school mathematics.* Reston, VA: NCTM.

National Reading Panel. (2000). *Report of the National Reading Panel: Teaching children to read—An evidence-based assessment of the scientific research literature on reading and its implications for reading instruction.* Jessup, MD: National Institute for Literacy.

Neuman, S. B., & Koskinen, P. (1992). Captioned television as comprehensible input: Effects of incidental word learning from context for language minority students. *Reading Research Quarterly, 27,* 95–106.

Neville, H., & Lawson, D. (1987a). Attention to central and peripheral visual space in a movement detection task: An event-related potential and behavioral study. II. Congenitally deaf adults. *Brain Research, 405,* 268–283.

Neville, H., & Lawson, D. (1987b). Attention to central and peripheral visual space in a movement decision task. III. Separate effects of auditory deprivation and acquisition of a visual language. *Brain Research, 405,* 284–294.

Newell, W. (1978). A study of the ability of day-class deaf adolescents to compare factual information using four communication modalities. *American Annals of the Deaf, 123,* 558–562.

Nicholas, J. (1994). Sensory aid use and the development of communicative function. *Volta Review Monograph, 96,* 181–198.

Nicholas, J., & Geers, A. (1997). Communication of oral deaf and normally hearing children at 36 months of age. *Journal of Speech and Hearing Research, 40,* 1314–1327.

Nicholas, J., & Geers, A. (2007). Will they catch up? The role of cochlear implantation in the spoken language development of children with severe to profound hearing loss. *Journal of Speech Language and Hearing Research, 50,* 1048–1062.

Nicholas, J., & Geers, A. (2008). Expected test scores for preschoolers with a cochlear implant who use spoken language. *American Journal of Speech-Language Pathology, 17,* 121–138.

Nicholls, C., & Ling, D. (1982). Cued Speech and the reception of spoken language. *Journal of Speech and Hearing Research, 25,* 262–269.

Nikolopoulos, T., Dyar, D., Archbold, S., & O'Donoghue, G. (2004). Development of spoken language grammar following cochlear implantation in prelingually deaf children. *Archives of Otolaryngology Head and Neck Surgery, 130,* 629–633.

Nolen, S., & Wilbur, R. (1985). The effects of context on deaf students' comprehension of difficult sentences. *American Annals of the Deaf, 130*(3), 231–35.

Nunes, T., & Moreno, C. (1997). Solving word problems with different ways of representing the task. *Mathematics and Special Educational Needs, 3*, 15–17.

Nunes, T., & Moreno, C. (2002). A intervention program for promoting deaf pupils' achievement in mathematics. *Journal of Deaf Studies and Deaf Education, 7*, 120–133.

O'Connor, N., & Hermelin, B. M. (1973). The spatial or temporal organization of short-term memory. *Quarterly Journal of Experimental Psychology, 25*, 335–343.

Odom, P. B., Blanton, R. I., & Laukhuf, C. (1973). Facial expressions and interpretation of emotion-arousing situations in deaf and hearing children. *Journal of Abnormal Child Psychology, 1*, 139–151.

Odom, S., Brantlinger, E., Gersten, R., Horner, R., Thompson, B., & Harris, K. (2005). Research in special education: Scientific methods and evidence-based practices. *Exceptional Children, 71*, 137–148.

Oller, D. K. (2000). *The emergence of the speech capacity.* Mahwah, NJ: Lawrence Erlbaum.

Oller, D. K. (2006). Vocal language development in deaf infants: New challenges. In P. Spencer & M. Marschark (Eds.), *Advances in the spoken language development of deaf and hard-of-hearing children* (pp. 22–41). New York: Oxford University Press.

Olusanya, B. O., Luxon, L. M., & Wirz, S. L. (2005). Screening for early childhood hearing loss in Nigeria. *Journal of Medical Screening, 12*, 115–118.

Olusanya, B. O., & Newton, V. E. (2007). Global burden of childhood hearing impairment and disease control priorities. *Lancet, 369*, 1314–1317.

Olusanya, B., & Okolo, A. (2006). Revisiting the ten questions questionnaire for developing countries. (Letter to the editor). *International Journal of Epidemiology, 35*, 1103.

Ostryn, C. (2008). A review and analysis of the Picture Exchange Program (PECS) for individuals with Autistic Spectrum Disorder using a paradigm of communicative competence. *Research and Practice for Persons with Severe Disability, 33*, 13–24.

Ottem, E. (1980). An analysis of cognitive studies with deaf subjects. *American Annals of the Deaf, 125*, 564–575.

Padden, C. (2006). Learning to fingerspell twice: Young signing children's acquisition of fingerspelling. In B. Schick, M. Marschark, & P. Spencer (Eds.), *Advances in the sign language development of deaf children* (pp. 189–201). New York: Oxford University Press.

Padden, C., & Gunsals, D. (2003). How the alphabet came to be used in a sign language. *Sign Language Studies, 4*, 1–33.

Padden, C., & Ramsey, C. (1998). Reading ability in signing deaf children. *Topics in Language Disorders, 18*, 30–46.

Padden, C., & Ramsey, C. (2000). American Sign Language and reading ability in deaf children. In C. Chamberlain, J. Morford, & R. Mayberry (Eds.), *Language acquisition by eye* (pp. 165–189). Mahwah, NJ: Lawrence Erlbaum.

Pagliaro, C. (1998). Mathematics preparation and professional development of deaf education teachers. *American Annals of the Deaf, 143*, 373–379.

Pagliaro, C., & Ansell, E. (2002). Story problems in the deaf education classroom: Frequency and mode of presentation. *Journal of Deaf Studies and Deaf Education, 7*, 107–119.

Pagliaro, C., & Kritzer, K. (2005). Discrete mathematics in deaf education: A survey of teachers' knowledge and use. *American Annals of the Deaf, 150,* 251–259.

Palmer, S. (2000). Assessing the benefits of phonics intervention on hearing-impaired children's word reading. *Deafness & Education International, 2,* 165–178.

Parasnis, I., Samar, V., & Berent, G. (2001, Winter). Evaluating ADHD in the deaf population: Challenges to validity. *NTID Research Bulletin, 6,* 1, 3–5.

Paul, P. (1996). Reading vocabulary knowledge and deafness. *Journal of Deaf Studies and Deaf Education, 1,* 5–15.

Paul, P. (1998). *Literacy and deafness: The development of reading, writing, and literate thought.* Boston: Allyn & Bacon.

Paul, P. (2001). *Language and deafness* (3rd ed.). San Diego, CA: Singular.

Paul, P. (2003). Processes and components of reading. In M. Marschark & P. Spencer (Eds.), *The Oxford handbook of deaf studies, language, and education* (pp. 97–109). New York: Oxford University Press.

Paul, P., & Gustafson, G. (1991). Hearing-impaired students' comprehension of high-frequency multi-meaning words. *Remedial and Special Education, 12,* 52–62.

Peng, S., Spencer, L., & Tomblin, J. (2004). Speech intelligibility of pediatric cochlear implant recipients with 7 years of device experience. *Journal of Speech, Language, and Hearing Research, 47,* 1227–1236.

Perfetti, C., & Sandak, R. (2000). Reading optimally builds on spoken language. Implications for deaf readers. *Journal of Deaf Studies and Deaf Education, 5,* 32–50.

Perier, O., Bochner-Wuidar, A., Everarts, B., Michiels, J., & Hage, C. (1986). The combination of cued speech and signed French to improve spoken language acquisition by young deaf children. In B. Tervoort (Ed.), *Signs of life: Proceedings of the Second European Congress on Sign Language Research* (pp. 194–199). Amsterdam. (Reprinted in *Cued Speech Journal, 4*(7), 1990.)

Perier, O., Charlier, B., Hage, C., & Alegria, J. (1988). Evaluation of the effects of prolonged Cued Speech practice upon the receptionof spoken language, In I. G. Taylor (Ed.). *The education of the deaf: Current perspectives* (Vol. 1). London: Croom Helm.

Peterson, C., & Siegal, M. (1995). Deafness, conversation, and theory of mind. *Journal of Child Psychology and Psychiatry, 36,* 459–474.

Peterson, C., Wellman, H., & Liu, D. (2005). Steps in theory-of-mind development for children with deafness or autism. *Child Development, 76,* 502–517.

Piaget, J. (1952). *The origins of intelligence in children.* New York: Basic Books.

Pipp-Siegel, S., Sedey, A., & Yoshinaga-Itano, C. (2002). Predictors of parental stress in mothers of young children with hearing loss. *Journal of Deaf Studies and Deaf Education, 7,* 1–17.

Pisoni, D. (2000). Cognitive factors and cochlear implants: Some thoughts on perception, learning, and memory in speech perception. *Ear & Hearing, 21,* 70–78.

Pisoni, D. B., Conway, C. M., Kronenberger, W., Henning, S., & Anaya, E. (2010). Executive function, cognitive control and sequence learning in deaf children with cochlear implants. In M. Marschark & P. E. Spencer (Eds.), *The Oxford handbook of deaf studies, language, and education, vol. 2* (pp. 439–457). New York: Oxford University Press.

Pisoni, D., Conway, C., Kronenberger, W., Horn, D., Karpicke, J., & Henning, S. (2008). Efficacy and effectiveness of cochlear implants in deaf children. In M. Marschark & P. Hauser (Eds.), *Deaf cognition. Foundations and outcomes* (pp. 52–101). New York: Oxford University Press.

Pollack, D. (1964). Acoupedics: A unisensory approach to auditory training. *Volta Review*, 66, 400–409.

Pollack, D., Goldberg, D., & Coleffe-Schenk, N. (1997). *Educational audiology for the limited-hearing infant and preschooler: An auditory-verbal program.* Springfield, IL: C. C. Thomas.

Power, D., & Hyde, M. (1997). Multisensory and unisensory approaches to communicating with deaf children. *European Journal of Psychology and Education, 12,* 449–464.

Power, D., & Hyde, M. (2002). The characteristics and extent of participation of deaf and hard-of-hearing students in regular classes in Australian schools. *Journal of Deaf Studies and Deaf Education, 7,* 302–311.

Power, D., & Hyde, M. (2003). Itinerant teachers of the deaf and hard of hearing and their students in Australia: Some state comparisons. *International Journal of Disability Development and Education, 4,* 385–401.

Power, D., Hyde, M., & Leigh, G. (2008). Learning English from Signed English: An impossible task?. *American Annals of the Deaf, 153,* 37–47.

Powers, A., Elliott, R., Patterson, D., Shaw, S., & Taylor, C. (1995). Family environment and deaf and hard-of-hearing students with mild additional disabilities. *Journal of Childhood Communication Disorders, 17,* 15–19.

Powers, S. (1996). Inclusion is an attitude not a place: Parts 1 and 2. *Journal of the British Association of Teachers of the Deaf, 20,* 30–41 and 65–69.

Powers, S. (1999). The educational attainments of deaf students in mainstream programs in England: Examination results and influencing factors. *American Annals of the Deaf, 144,* 261–269.

Preisler, G., & Ahlstrom, M (1997). Sign language for hard of hearing children: A hindrance or a benefit for their development?. *European Journal of Psychology of Education, 12,* 465–477.

Preisler, G., Tvingstedt, A., & Ahlstrom, M. (2002). A psychosocial follow-up study of deaf preschool children using cochlear implants. *Child Care, Health and Development, 28,* 403–418.

Prinz, P., & Strong, M. (1994). *A test of ASL.* Unpublished manuscript, San Francisco State University, California Research Institute.

Psychological Corporation. (2002). *Wechsler Individual Achievement Test 2nd Edition.* San Antonio, TX: Harcourt Assessment.

Puente, A., Alvarado, J., & Herrera, V. (2006). Fingerspelling and sign language as alternative codes for reading and writing words for Chilean deaf signers. *American Annals of the Deaf, 3,* 299–310.

Pyman, B., Blamey, P., Lacy, P., Clark, G., & Dowell, R. (2000). The development of speech perception in children using cochlear implants: Effects of etiologic factors and delayed milestones. *American Journal of Otology, 21,* 57–61.

Qi, S., & Mitchell, R. E. (2007, April 10). *Large-scaled academic achievement testing of deaf and hard-of-hearing students: Past, present, and future.* Paper presented at the annual meeting of the Research on the Education of Deaf Persons SIG of the American Education Research Association, Chicago.

Quigley, S., Steinkamp, M., Power, D., & Jones, B. (1978). *Test of Syntactic Abilities.* Beaverton, OR: Dormac.

Quittner, A., Leibach, P., & Marciel, K. (2004). The impact of cochlear implants on young deaf children. New methods to assess cognitive and behavioral development. *Archives of Otolaryngology Head and Neck Surgery, 130,* 547–554.

Quittner, A., Smith, L., Osberger, M., Mitchell, T., & Katz, D. (1994). The impact of audition on the development of visual attention. *Psychological Science, 5,* 347–353.

Ramsey, C. (1997). *Deaf children in public schools: Placement, context, and consequences.* Washington, DC: Gallaudet University Press.

Rhoades, E. (2001). Language progress with an auditory-verbal approach for young children with a hearing loss. *International Pediatrics, 16,* 1–7.

Rhoades, E. (2006). Research outcomes of Auditory-Verbal intervention: Is the approach justified?. *Deafness & Education International, 8,* 125–143.

Rhoades, E., & Chisholm, T. (2000). Global language progress with an auditory-verbal therapy approach for children who are deaf or hard of hearing. *Volta Review, 102,* 5–25.

Richardson, J., MacLeod-Gallinger, J., McKee, B., & Long, G. (2000). Approaches to studying in deaf and hearing students in higher education. *Journal of Deaf Studies and Deaf Education, 5,* 156–173.

Ries, P. W. (1994). Prevalence and characteristics of persons with hearing trouble: United States, 1990–91. *Vital and Health Statistics,* Series 10 (No. 188). Washington DC: Department of Health and Human Services, U. S. Centers for Disease Control and Prevention.

Roald, I. (2002). Norwegian deaf teachers' reflections on their science education: Implications for instruction. *Journal of Deaf Studies and Deaf Education, 7,* 57–73.

Roald, I., & Mikalsen, O. (2000). What are the earth and heavenly bodies like? A study of objectual conceptions among Norwegian deaf and hearing pupils. *International Journal of Science Education, 22,* 337–355.

Roberts, J., Jurgens, J., & Burchinal, M. (2005). The role of home literacy practices in preschool children's language and emergent literacy skills. *Journal of Speech, Language, and Hearing Research, 48,* 345–359.

Roberts, S., & Rickards, R. (1994a). A survey of graduates of an Australian integrated auditory/oral preschool. Part I: Amplification usage, communication practices, and speech intelligibility. *Volta Review, 96,* 185–205.

Roberts, S., & Rickards, R. (1994b). A survey of graduates of an Australian integraded auditory/oral preschool. Part II: Academic achievement, utilization of support services, and friendship patterns. *Volta Review, 96,* 207–236.

Robertson, L., & Flexer, C. (1993). Reading development: A parent survey of children with hearing-impairment who developed speech and language through the auditory-verbal method. *Volta Review, 95,* 253–261.

Rosenhall, U., Nordin, V., Sandstrom, M., Ahlsen, G., & Gillberg, C. (1999). Autism and hearing loss. *Journal of Autism and Developmental Disorders, 29,* 349–357.

Rottenberg, C. (2001). A deaf child learns to read. *American Annals of the Deaf, 146,* 270–275.

Rottenberg, C., & Searfoss, L. (1992). Becoming literate in a preschool class: Literacy development of hearing-impaired children. *Journal of Reading Behavior, 24,* 463–479.

Rubin, K., Fein, G., & Vandenberg, B. (1983). Play. In P. Mussen (Series Ed.) & E. Hetherington (Vol. Ed.), *Handbook of child psychology: Vol. 4. Socialization, personality, and social development* (pp. 694–774). New York: Wiley.

Ruiz, N. (1995). A young deaf child learns to write. Implications for literacy development. *Reading Teacher, 49,* 206–217.

Rutter, M. (2005). Aetiology of autism: Findings and questions. *Journal of Disability Research, 49,* 231–238.

Rydberg, E., Gellerstedt, L. C., Danermark, B. (2009). Toward an equal level of educational attainment between deaf and hearing people in Sweden?. *Journal of Deaf Studies and Deaf Education, 14,* 312–323.

Samar, V., Paranis, I., & Berent, G. (1998). Learning disabilities, attention deficit disorders, and deafness. In M. Marschark & M. D. Clark (Eds.), *Psychological perspectives on deafness* (Vol. 2, pp. 199–242). Mahwah, NJ: Lawrence Erlbaum.

Sartawi, A., Al-Hilawani, Y., & Easterbrooks, S. (1998). A pilot study of comprehension strategies of students who are deaf/hard of hearing in a non-English-speaking country. *Journal of Childhood Communication Disorders, 20,* 27–32.

Sass-Lehrer, M. (in press). Birth to three: Early intervention. In M. Marschark & P. Spencer (Eds.), *The Oxford handbook of deaf studies, language, and education, vol. 1, second edition.* New York: Oxford University Press.

Scarborough, H. (1990). Index of Productive Syntax. *Applied Psycholinguistics, 11*(1), 1–22.

Schick, B. (2003). The development of American Sign Language and manually coded English systems. In M. Marschark & P. Spencer (Eds.), *The Oxford handbook of deaf studies, language, and education* (pp. 219–231). New York: Oxford University Press.

Schick, B. (2006). Acquiring a visually motivated language: Evidence from diverse learners. In B. Schick, M. Marschark, & P. Spencer (Eds.), *Advances in the sign language development of deaf children* (pp. 102–134). New York: Oxford University Press.

Schick, B., de Villiers, J., de Villiers, P., & Hoffmeister, R. (2007). Language and theory of mind: A study of deaf children. *Child Development, 78,* 376–396.

Schick, B., & Moeller, M. P. (1992). What is learnable in manually coded English sign systems?. *Applied Psycholinguistics, 13,* 313–340.

Schirmer, B. (2003). Using verbal protocols to identify reading strategies of students who are deaf. *Journal of Deaf Studies and Deaf Education, 8,* 157–170.

Schirmer, B., Bailey, J., & Lockman, A. (2004). What verbal protocols reveal about the reading strategies of deaf students: A replication study. *American Annals of the Deaf, 149,* 5–16.

Schirmer, B., & Williams, C. (2003). Approaches to teaching reading. In M. Marschark & P. Spencer (Eds.), *Oxford handbook in deaf studies, language, and education* (pp. 110–122). New York: Oxford University Press.

Schleper, D. (1997). *Reading to deaf children: Learning from deaf adults.* Washington, DC: Gallaudet University Pre-College National Mission Programs.

Schorr, E., Fox, N., van Wassenhove, V., & Knudsen, E. (2005). Auditory-visual fusion in speech perception in children with cochlear implants. *Proceedings of the National Academy of Science, U.S.A., 102,* 18748–18750.

Schorr, E., Roth, F., & Fox, N. (2008). A comparison of the speech and language skills of children with cochlear implants and children with normal hearing. *Communication Disorders Quarterly, 29,* 195–210.

Seal, B., Nussbaum, D., Scott, S., Waddy-Smith, B., Clingempeel, K., & Belzner, K. (2005, November). *Evidence for sign-spoken language relationships in children with cochlear implants.* Paper presented at the American Speech, Language, and Hearing Society Annual Conference, San Diego, CA.

Semel, E., Wiig, E., & Secord, W. (1995). *Clinical Evaluation of Language Fundamentals-III.* San Antonio, TX: Psychological Corporation, Harcourt Brace & Co.

Senechal, M., LeFevre, J., Hudson, E., & Lawson, E. (1996). Knowledge of storybooks as a predictor of young children's vocabulary. *Journal of Educational Psychology, 88,* 520–536.

Serrano Pau, C. (1995). The deaf child and solving problems of arithmetic: The importance of comprehensive reading. *American Annals of the Deaf, 140,* 287–291.

Shallop, J. K. (2008, November 7). *Complex children and cochlear implantation.* Paper presented at the Cochlear Implants 2008 State of the Art Conference, Nottingham, UK.

Sherman, L. (1998). The promise of technology. *Northwest Education, 3,* 2–9.

Silvestre, N., Ramspott, A., & Pareto, I. (2006). Conversational skills in a semistructured interview and self-concept in deaf students. *Journal of Deaf Studies and Deaf Education, 12,* 38–54.

Simms, L., & Thumann, H. (2007). In search of a new, linguistically and culturally sensitive paradigm in deaf education. *American Annals of the Deaf, 152,* 302–311.

Singer, B., & Bashir, A. (2004). Developmental variation in writing composition skills. In C. Stone, E. Silliman, B. Ehren, & K. Apel (Eds.), *Handbook of language and literacy: Development and disorders* (pp. 559–582). New York: Guilford Press.

Singleton, J., & Morgan, D. (2006). Natural signed language acquisition within the social context. In B. Schick, M. Marschark, & P. Spencer (Eds.), *Advances in the sign language development of deaf children* (pp. 344–375). New York: Oxford University Press.

Singleton, J., Morgan, D., DeGello, E., Wiles, J., & Rivers, R. (2004). Vocabulary use by low, moderate, and high ASL-proficient writers compared to hearing ESL and monolingual speakers. *Journal of Deaf Studies and Deaf Education, 9,* 86–103.

Smith, M. (1998). *The art of itinerant teaching for teachers of the deaf and hard of hearing.* Hillsboro, OR: Butte Publications.

Smith, L., Quittner, A., Osberger, M., & Miyamoto, R. (1998). Audition and visual attention: The developmental trajectory in deaf and hearing populations. *Developmental Psychology, 34,* 840–850.

Snyder, L., & Yoshinaga-Itano, C. (1998). Specific play behaviors and the development of communication in children with hearing loss. *Volta Review, 100*, 165–185.

Spencer, L., Barker, B., & Tomblin, J. B. (2003). Exploring the language and literacy outcomes of pediatric cochlear implant users. *Ear & Hearing, 24*, 236–247.

Spencer, L., & Bass-Ringdahl, S. (2004). An evolution of communication modalities. In R. Miyamoto (Ed.), *International congress series* (pp. 352–355). Indianapolis: Elsevier.

Spencer, L. J., Gantz, B. J. & Knutson, J. F. (2004). Outcomes and achievement of students who grew up with access to cochlear implants. *Laryngoscope, 114*, 1576 –1581.

Spencer, L., & Oleson, J. (2008). Early listening and speaking skills predict later reading proficiency in pediatric cochlear implant users. *Ear & Hearing, 29*, 270–280.

Spencer, L., & Tomblin, J. B. (2006). Spoken language development with "Total Communication." In P. Spencer & M. Marschark (Eds.), *Advances in the spoken language development of deaf and hard-of-hearing children* (pp. 166–192). New York: Oxford University Press.

Spencer, L., Tye-Murray, N., & Tomblin, J. B. (1998). The production of English inflectional morphology, speech production and listening performance in children with cochlear implants. *Ear & Hearing, 19*, 310–318.

Spencer, P. (1993a). Communication behaviors of infants with hearing loss and their hearing mothers. *Journal of Speech and Hearing Research, 36*, 311–321.

Spencer, P. (1993b). The expressive communication of hearing mothers and deaf infants. *American Annals of the Deaf, 138*, 275–283.

Spencer, P. (1996). The association between language and symbolic play at two years: Evidence from deaf toddlers. *Child Development, 67*, 867–876.

Spencer, P. (2000a). Every opportunity: A case study of hearing parents and their deaf child. In P. Spencer, C. Erting, & M. Marschark (Eds.), *The deaf child in the family and at school* (pp. 111–132). Mahwah, NJ: Lawrence Erlbaum.

Spencer, P. (2000b). Looking without listening: Is audition a prerequisite for normal development of visual attention during infancy? *Journal of Deaf Studies and Deaf Education, 5*, 291–302.

Spencer, P. (2004). Individual differences in language performance after cochlear implantation at one to three years of age: Child, family, and linguistic factors. *Journal of Deaf Studies and Deaf Education, 9*, 395–412.

Spencer, P., Bodner-Johnson, B., & Gutfreund, M. (1992). Interacting with infants with a hearing loss: What can we learn from mothers who are deaf?. *Journal of Early Intervention, 16*, 64–78.

Spencer, P., & Delk, L. (1989). Hearing-impaired students' performance on tests of visual processing: Relationships with reading performance. *American Annals of the Deaf, 134*, 333–337.

Spencer, P., & Hafer, J. (1998). Play as "window" and "room": Assessing and supporting the cognitive and linguistic development of deaf infants and young children. In M. Marschark and D. Clark (Eds.), *Psychological perspectives on deafness* (Vol. 2, pp. 131–152). Mahwah, NJ: Lawrence Erlbaum.

Spencer, P., & Harris, M. (2006). Patterns and effects of language input to deaf infants and toddlers with deaf and hearing mothers. In B. Schick, M. Marschark, & P. Spencer (Eds.), *Advances in the sign language development of deaf children* (pp. 71–101). New York: Oxford University Press.

Spencer, P., Marschark, M., & Spencer, L. J. (in press). Cochlear implants: Advances, issues and implications. In M. Marschark & P. Spencer (Eds.), *The Oxford handbook of deaf studies, language, and education, vol. 1, second edition.* New York: Oxford University Press.

Spencer, P., & Marschark, M. (Eds.). (2006). *Advances in the spoken language development of deaf and hard-of-hearing children.* New York: Oxford University Press.

Spencer, P., & Meadow-Orlans, K. (1996). Play, language, and maternal responsiveness: A longitudinal study of deaf and hearing infants. *Child Development, 67,* 3176–3191.

Stacey, P., Fortnum, H., Barton, G., & Summerfield, A. (2007). National evaluation of support options for deaf and hearing-impaired children: Relevance to education services. *Deafness & Education International, 9,* 120–130.

Stanwick, R., & Watson, L. (2005). Literacy in the homes of young deaf children: Common and distinct features of spoken language and sign bilingual environments. *Journal of Early Childhood Literacy, 5,* 53–78.

Steinfeld, A. (1998). The benefit of real-time captioning in a mainstream classroom as measured by working memory. *Volta Review, 100,* 29–44.

Stewart, D., & Kluwin, T. (2001). *Teaching deaf and hard of hearing students. Content, strategies, and curriculum.* Boston: Allyn & Bacon.

Stillman, R. (1978). *The Callier Azusa Scale.* Dallas: University of Texas at Dallas.

Stillman, R., & Battle, C. (1986). Developmental assessment of communicative abilities in the deaf-blind. In D. Ellis (Ed.), *Sensory impairments in mentally handicapped people* (pp. 319–335). London: Croom Helm.

Stinson, M., & Antia, S. (1999). Considerations in educating deaf and hard-of-hearing students in inclusive settings. *Journal of Deaf Studies and Deaf Education, 4,* 163–175.

Stinson, M. S., Elliot, L. B., Kelly, R. R., & Liu, Y. (2009). Deaf and hard-of-hearing students' memory of lectures with speech-to-text and interpreting/note taking services. *Special Education, 43,* 45–51.

Stinson, M., & Foster, S. (2000). Socialization of deaf children and youths in school. In P. Spencer, C. Erting, & M. Marschark (Eds.), *The deaf child in the family and at school* (pp. 151–174). Mahwah, NJ: Lawrence Erlbaum.

Stinson, M., & Kluwin, T. (in press). Educational consequences of alternative school placements. In M. Marschark & P. Spencer (Eds.), *The Oxford handbook of deaf studies, language, and education, vol. 1, second edition.* New York: Oxford University Press.

Stinson, M., & Liu, (1999). Participation of deaf and hard-of-hearing students in classes with hearing students. *Journal of Deaf Studies and Deaf Education, 4,* 191–202.

Stinson, M. S., Stuckless, E. R., Henderson, J. B. & Miller, L. (1988). Perceptions of hearing impaired college students toward real-time speech-to-print: RTGD and other support services. *Volta Review, 90,* 336–338.

Stinson, M., Whitmire, K., & Kluwin, T. (1996). Self-perceptions of social relationships in hearing-impaired adolescents. *Journal of Educational Psychology, 88*, 132–143.

Stokoe, W. (1960/2005). Sign language structure: An outline of the visual communication system of the American deaf. *Studies in Linguistics, Occasional Papers* 8. Buffalo, NY: University of Buffalo, Department of Anthropology and Linguistics. (Reprinted in *Journal of Deaf Studies and Deaf Education,* 10, 3–37).

Strassman, B. (1997). Metacognition and reading in children who are deaf: A review of the research. *Journal of Deaf Studies and Deaf Education, 2,* 140–149.

Strong, M. (1988). A bilingual approach to the education of young deaf children: ASL and English. In M. Strong (Eds.), *Language learning and deafness* (pp. 113–132). New York: Cambridge University Press.

Strong, M., & Charlson, E. (1987). Simultaneous Communication: Are teachers attempting an impossible task?. *American Annals of the Deaf, 132,* 376–382.

Strong, M., & Prinz, P. (1997). A study of the relationship between American Sign Language and English literacy. *Journal of Deaf Studies and Deaf Education, 2,* 37–46.

Strong, M., & Prinz, P. (2000). Is American Sign Language skill related to English literacy? In C. Chamberlain, J. Morford, & R. Mayberry (Eds.), *Language acquisition by eye* (pp. 131–141). Mahwah, NJ: Lawrence Erlbaum.

Svartholm, K. (2008). The written Swedish of deaf children: A foundation for EFL. In C. Kellet Bidoli & E. Ochse (Eds.), *English in international deaf communication* (pp. 211–249). Bern: Peter Lang.

Svirsky, M., Robbins, A., Kirk, K., Pisoni, D., & Miyamoto, R. (2000). Language development in profoundly deaf children with cochlear implants. *Psychological Science, 11,* 153.

Svirsky, M., Teoh, S-W., & Neuburger, H. (2004). Development of language and speech perception in congenitally, profoundly deaf children as a function of age at cochlear implantation. *Audiology & Neuro-otology, 9,* 224–233.

Swanwick, R., & Tsverik, I. (2007). The role of sign language for deaf children with cochlear implants: Good practice in sign bilingual settings. *Deafness & Education International, 9,* 214–231.

Swanwick, R., & Watson, L. (2005). Literacy in the homes of young deaf children: Common and distinct features of spoken language and sign bilingual environments. *Journal of Early Childhood Literacy, 5,* 53–78.

Swanwick, R., & Watson, L. (2007). Parents sharing books with young deaf children in spoken English and in BSL: The common and diverse features of different language settings. *Journal of Deaf Studies and Deaf Education, 12,* 385–405.

Swisher, M. V. (1985). Signed input of hearing mothers to deaf children. *Language Learning, 34,* 99–125.

Swisher, M. V. (1993). Perceptual and cognitive aspects of recognition of signs in peripheral vision. In M. Marschark & M. D. Clark (Eds.), *Psychological perspectives on deafness* (pp. 209–227). Hillsdale, NJ: Erlbaum.

Swisher, M. V. (2000). Learning to converse: How deaf mothers support the development of attention and conversational skills in their young deaf children. In P. Spencer,

C. Erting, & M. Marschark (Eds.), *The deaf child in the family and at home* (pp. 21–40). Mahwah, NJ: Lawrence Erlbaum.

Swisher, M. V., & Thompson, M. (1985). Mothers learning simultaneous communication: The dimensions of the task. *American Annals of the Deaf, 130,* 212–217.

Talbot, K., & Haude, R. (1993). The relationship between sign language skill and spatial visualization ability: Mental rotation of three-dimensional objects. *Perceptual and Motor Skills, 77,* 1387–1391.

Teale, W., & Sulzby, E. (Eds.). (1986). *Emergent literacy: Writing and reading.* Norwood, NJ: Ablex.

Thompson, B., Diamond, K., McWilliam, R., Snyder, P., & Snyder, S. (2005). Evaluating the quality of evidence from correlational research for evidence-based practice. *Exceptional Children, 17,* 181–194.

Todman, J., & Cowdy, N. (1993). Processing of visual-action codes by deaf and hearing children: Coding orientation or capacity?. *Intelligence, 17,* 237–250.

Todman, J., & Seedhouse, E. (1994). Visual-action code processing by deaf and hearing children. *Language and Cognitive Processes, 9,* 129–141.

Tomblin, J. B., Spencer, L., Flock, S., Tyler, R., & Gantz, B. (1999). A comparison of language achievement in children with cochlear implants and children with hearing aids. *Journal of Speech, Language, and Hearing Research, 42,* 497–511.

Torres, S., Moreno-Torres, I., & Santano, R. (2006). Quantitative and qualitative evaluation of linguistic input support to a prelingually deaf child with cued speech: A case study. *Journal of Deaf Studies and Deaf Education, 11,* 438–448.

Toscano, R. M., McKee, B., & Lepoutre, D. (2002). Success with academic English: Reflections of deaf college students. *American Annals of the Deaf, 147,* 5–23.

Traxler, C. (2000). The Stanford Achievement Test, 9th Edition: National norming and performance standards for deaf and hard-of-hearing students. *Journal of Deaf Studies and Deaf Education, 5,* 337–248.

Trezek, B., & Wang, Y. (2006). Implications of utilizing a phonics-based reading curriculum with children who are deaf or hard of hearing. *Journal of Deaf Studies and Deaf Education, 11,* 202–213.

Trezek, B., Wang, Y., Woods, D., Gampp, T., & Paul, P. (2007). Using Visual Phonics to supplement beginning reading instruction for students who are deaf or hard of hearing. *Journal of Deaf Studies and Deaf Education, 12,* 373–384.

Tripodi, T. (1998). *A primer on single-subject design for clinical social workers.* Washington, DC: National Association of Social Workers.

United Nations General Assembly. (1959). Declaration of the Rights of the Child: General Assembly Resolution 1386(XIV) of November 20, 1959. www.unhchr.ch/html/menu3/b/25.htm. Retrieved September 15, 2008.

Vaccari, C., & Marschark, M. (1997). Communication between parents and deaf children: Implications for social-emotional development. *Journal of Child Psychology and Psychiatry, 38,* 793–802.

Valdez-Maenchaco, M., & Whitehurst, G. (1992). Accelerating language development through picture-book reading: A systematic extension to Mexican day care. *Developmental Psychology, 28,* 1106–1114.

Van den Tillaart, B., & Janssen, M. (2006). CONTACT. Sint-Michielsgestel, The Netherlands: Aapnootmuis Educainment.

Van der Lem, T., & Timmerman, D. (1990). Joint picture book reading in signs: An interaction process between parent and child. In S. Prillwitz & T. Vollhaber (Eds.), *Sign language research and application: Proceedings of the International Congress* (pp. 77–88). Amsterdam: Signum Press.

Van Dijk, J. (1999). *Development through relationships: Entering the social world.* Paper presented at Development Through Relationships: Fifth Annual World Conference on Deafblindness, Lisbon, Portugal.

Van Dijk, R., Nelson, C., Postma, A., & van Dijk, J. (2010). Assessment and intervention of deaf children with multiple disabilities. In M. Marschark and P. Spencer (Eds.), *The Oxford handbook of deaf studies, language, and education, vol.* 2 (pp. 172–192). New York: Oxford University Press.

Van Dijk, R., van Helvoort, M., Aan den Toorn, W., & Bos, H. (1998). *Niet zomaar een gebaar.* [Not just a sign]. Sint-Michielsgestel, The Netherlands: Publication Instituut voor Doven.

Van Gurp, S. (2001). Self-concept of deaf secondary school students in different educational settings. *Journal of Deaf Studies and Deaf Education, 6*, 54–69.

Van Uden, M. (1977). *A world of language for deaf children.* Amsterdam: Swets & Zeitlinger.

Vermeulen, L., & van Dijk, J. (1994). Social-emotional aspects in a sample of young persons with Usher's Syndrome Type 1. In A. Kooijman, P. Looijestijn, J. Welling, & J. van der Wildt (Eds.), *Low vision* (pp. 441–414). Amsterdam: IOS Press.

Vernon, M. (2005). Fifty years of research on the intelligence of deaf and hard-of-hearing children: A review of literature and discussion of implications. *Journal of Deaf Studies and Deaf Education, 10*, 225–231.

Vernon, M., & Rhodes, A. (2009). Deafness and Autistic Spectrum Disorder. *American Annals of the Deaf, 154*, 5–14.

Vieu, A., Mondain, M., Blanchard, K., Sillon, M., Reuillard-Artieres, R., Tobely, E., Uziel, S., & Piron, J. (1998). Influence of communication mode on speech intelligibility and syntactic structure of sentences in profoundly hearing impaired French children implanted between 5 and 9 years of age. *International Journal of Pediatric Otorhinolaryngology, 44*, 15–22.

Vohr, B., Singh, K., Bansal, N., Letourneau, K., & McDermott, C. (2001). Maternal worry about neonatal hearing screening. *Journal of Perinatology, 21*, 15–20.

Volkmar, F., Klin, A., Schultz, R., Rubin, E., & Bronen, R. (2000). Asperger's disorder. *American Journal of Psychiatry, 157*, 262–267.

Waddy-Smith, B., & Wilson, V. (2003). See that sound! Visual Phonics helps deaf and hard of hearing students develop reading skills. *Odyssey, 5*, 14–17.

Walker, L., Munro, J., & Rickards, F. (1998). Literal and inferential reading comprehension of students who are deaf or hard of hearing. *Volta Review, 100*, 105–120.

Wallis, D., Musselman, C., & MacKay, S. (2004). Hearing mothers and their deaf children: The relationship between early, ongoing mode match and subsequent mental health functioning in adolescents. *Journal of Deaf Studies and Deaf Education, 9*, 2–14.

Waltzman, S., Scalchunes, V., & Cohen, N. (2000). Performance of multiply handicapped children using cochlear implants. *American Journal of Otology, 21*, 329–335.

Watkins, S., Pittman, P., & Walden, B. (1998). The deaf mentor experimental project for young children who are deaf and their families. *American Annals of the Deaf, 143*, 29–35.

Watkins, S., Taylor, D., & Pittman, P. (2004). *SKI-HI Curriculum: Family-centered programming for infants and young children with hearing loss.* Logan: Utah State University, SKI-HI Institute, Department of Communicative Disorders/Deaf Education.

Watson, L. (1998). Oralism: Current policy and practice. In S. Gregory, et al. (Eds.), *Issues in deaf education* (pp. 69–76). London: David Fulton.

Watson, L., Archbold, S., & Nikolopoulos, T. (2006). Changing communication mode after implantation by age at implant. *Cochlear Implants International, 7*, 77–91.

Watson, L., Hardie, T., Archbold, S., & Wheeler, A. (2007). Parents' views on changing communication after cochlear implantation. *Journal of Deaf Studies and Deaf Education, 13*, 104–116.

Wauters, L., & Knoors, H. (2008). Social integration of deaf children in inclusive settings. *Journal of Deaf Studies and Deaf Education, 13*, 21–36.

Wauters, L., Tellings, A., van Bon, W., & Mak, W. (2008). Mode of acquisition as a factor in deaf children's reading comprehension. *Journal of Deaf Studies and Deaf Education, 13*, 175–192.

Waxman, R., & Spencer, P. (1997). What mothers do to support infant visual attention: Sensitivities to age and hearing status. *Journal of Deaf Studies and Deaf Education, 2*, 104–114.

Wellman, H., & Liu, D. (2004). Scaling of theory of mind tasks. *Child Development, 75*, 523–541.

Wessex Universal Hearing Screening Trial Group. (1998). Controlled trial of universal neonatal screening for early identification of permanent childhood hearing impairment. *Lancet, 352*, 1957–1964.

Whitehurst, G., Arnold, D., Epstein, J., Angell, A., Smith, M., & Fischel, J. (1994). A picture book reading intervention in day-care and home for children from low-income families. *Developmental Psychology, 30*, 679–689.

Whitehurst, G., Falco, F., Lonigan, C., Fischel, J., DeBaryshe, B., Valdez-Menchaca, M., & Caulfield, M. (1988). Accelerating language development through picture-book reading. *Developmental Psychology, 24*, 552–558.

Wilbur, R. (1977). An explanation of deaf children's difficulty with certain syntactic structures. *Volta Review, 79*, 85–92.

Wilbur, R. (2000). The use of ASL to support the development of English and literacy. *Journal of Deaf Studies and Deaf Education, 5*, 81–104.

Wilbur, R., & Petersen, L. (1998). Modality interactions of speech and signing in Simultaneous Communication. *Journal of Speech, Language, and Hearing Research, 41*, 200–212.

Wilkins, M., & Ertmer, D. (2002). Introducing young children who are deaf or heard of hearing to spoken language: Child's Voice, an oral school. *Language, Speech, and Hearing Services in Schools, 33*, 196–204.

Williams, C. (1994). The language and literacy worlds of three profoundly deaf preschool children. *Reading Research Quarterly, 29,* 125–155.

Williams, C. (1999). Preschool deaf children's use of signed language during writing events. *Journal of Literacy Research, 31,* 183–212.

Williams, C. (2004). Emergent literacy of deaf children. *Journal of Deaf Studies and Deaf Education, 9,* 352–365.

Wilson, M., Bettger, J., Niculae, I., & Klima, E. (1997). Modality of language shapes working memory: Evidence from digit span and spatial span in ASL signers. *Journal of Deaf Studies and Deaf Education, 2,* 152–162.

Winn, S. (2007). Preservice preparation of teachers of the deaf in the twenty-first century: A case study of Griffith University, Australia. *American Annals of the Deaf, 152,* 312–319.

Wood, D., Wood, H., Griffith, A., & Howarth, I. (1986). *Teaching and talking with deaf children.* New York: Wiley.

Wood, D., Wood, H., & Howarth, P. (1983). Mathematical abilities of deaf school-leavers. *British Journal of Developmental Psychology, 54,* 254–264.

Wood, H., Wood, D., & Kingsmill, M. (1991). Signed English in the classroom, II: Structural and pragmatic aspects of teachers' speech and sign. *First Language, 11,* 301–325.

Woodcock, R., & Mather, N. (1989, 1990). *Woodcock-Johnson Psycho-Educational Battery—Revised.* Allen, TX: DLM Teaching Resources.

Woolfe, T. (2001). The self-esteem and cohesion to family members of deaf children in relation to the hearing status of their parents and siblings. *Deafness and Education International, 3,* 80–95.

Woolsey, M., Satterfield, S., & Robertson, L. (2006). Visual phonics: An English code buster?. *American Annals of the Deaf, 151,* 434–440.

World Health Organization. (2001). *Guidelines for hearing aids and services for developing countries.* Geneva: WHO.

Wray D., Flexer C., & Vaccaro V. (1997). Classroom performance of children who are hearing impaired and who learned spoken communication through the A-V approach: An evaluation of treatment efficacy. *Volta Review, 99,* 107–119.

Yaden, D., Rowe, D., & MacGillivray, L. (1999). *Emergent literacy: A polyphony of perspectives.* Ann Arbor: University of Michigan, Center for the Improvement of Early Reading Achievement.

Yore, L. (2000). Enhancing science literacy for all students with embedded reading instruction and writing-to-learn activities. *Journal of Deaf Studies and Deaf Education, 5,* 105–122.

Yoshinaga-Itano, C. (2003). From screening to early identification and intervention: Discovering predictors to successful outcomes for children with significant hearing loss. *Journal of Deaf Studies and Deaf Education, 8,* 11–30.

Yoshinaga-Itano, C. (2006). Early identification, communication modality, and the development of speech and spoken language skills: Patterns and considerations. In P. Spencer & M. Marschark (Eds.), *Advances in the spoken language development of deaf and hard-of-hearing children* (pp. 298–327). New York: Oxford University Press.

Yoshinaga-Itano, C., Coulter, D., & Thomson, V. (2001). Developmental outcomes of children born in Colorado hospitals with universal newborn hearing screening programs. *Seminars in Neonatology, 6,* 521–529.

Yoshinaga-Itano, C., & deUzcategui, C. (2001). Early identification and social-emotional factors of children with hearing loss and children screened for hearing loss. In E. Kurtzer-White & D. Luterman (Eds.), *Early childhood deafness* (pp. 13–28). Baltimore, MD: York Press.

Yoshinaga-Itano, C., & Sedey, A. (2000). Speech development of deaf and hard-of-hearing children in early childhood: Interrelationships with language and hearing. *Volta Review, 100,* 181–212.

Yoshinaga-Itano, C., Sedey, A., Coulter, D., & Mehl, A. (1998a). Language of early- and later-identified children with hearing loss. *Pediatrics, 102,* 1161–1171.

Yoshinaga-Itano, C., Snyder, L., & Day, D. (1998b). The relationship of language and symbolic play in children with hearing loss. *Volta Review, 100,* 135–164.

Yoshinaga-Itano, C., Snyder, L., & Mayberry, R. (1996). How deaf and normally hearing students convey meaning within and between written sentences. *Volta Review, 98,* 9–38.

Young, A., & Tattersall, H. (2005). Parents of deaf children's evaluative accounts of the process and practice of universal newborn hearing screening. *Journal of Deaf Studies and Deaf Education, 10,* 134–145.

Young, A., & Tattersall, H. (2007). Universal newborn hearing screening and early identification of deafness: Parents' responses to knowing early and their expectations of child communication development. *Journal of Deaf Studies and Deaf Education, 12,* 209–220.

Zacher, D., Ben-Itzchak, E., Rabinovich, A., & Lahat, E. (2007). Change in core autism symptoms with intervention. *Research in Autistic Syndrome Disorders, 1,* 304–317.

Zandberg, S. (2005). *Education of children with hearing impairment: Targets and their realization.* Jerusalem: Israel Ministry of Education.

Zarfaty, Y., Nunes, T., & Bryant, P. (2004). The performance of young deaf children in spatial and temporal number tasks. *Journal of Deaf Studies and Deaf Education, 9,* 315–326.

Zevenbergen, A., & Whitehurst, G. (2003). Dialogic reading: A shared picture book reading intervention for preschoolers. In A. Van Kleeck, S. Stahl, & Bauer, E. (Eds.), *On reading books to children: Parents and children* (pp. 117–202). Mahwah, NJ: Lawrence Erlbaum.

Zimmerman, I., Steiner, V., & Evatt Pond, R. (1997). *Preschool Language Scales (PLS-3) (UK Adaptation).* London: Psychological Corporation.

Zwiercki, R., Stansberry, D., Porter, G., & Hayes, P. (1976). The incidence of neurological problems in a deaf school age population. *American Annals of the Deaf, 121,* 405–408.

INDEX

CPSIA information can be obtained at www.ICGtesting.com
Printed in the USA
BVOW06s1254140916

461750BV00009B/8/P